March

with two witness

Nicholas

New York
May 1995

JOURNAL FOR THE STUDY OF THE NEW TESTAMENT SUPPLEMENT SERIES
66

Executive Editor
David Hill

JSOT Press
Sheffield

PAUL, ANTIOCH
AND
JERUSALEM

A Study in Relationships and Authority in Earliest Christianity

Nicholas Taylor

Journal for the Study of the New Testament
Supplement Series 66

in memoriam

Commander
Patrick Hugh Bisset Taylor
OBE DL RN

19 February 1916–30 July 1989

Published by JSOT Press
JSOT Press is an imprint of
Sheffield Academic Press Ltd
The University of Sheffield
343 Fulwood Road
Sheffield S10 3BP
England

Typeset by Sheffield Academic Press
and
Printed on acid-free paper in Great Britain
by Billing & Sons Ltd
Worcester

British Library Cataloguing in Publication Data

Taylor, Nicholas
    Paul, Antioch and Jerusalem: a study in
    relationships and authority in earliest Christianity.
    —(Journal for the study of the New Testament.
    ISSN 0143-5708; 66)
    I. Title II. Series
    225.92

    ISBN 1-85075-331-8

CONTENTS

PREFACE

This book is a revised version of my 1990 Durham University PhD thesis. In it I have sought to explore and illuminate an issue that has long been of concern to New Testament scholars. The relationship of Paul, whom Christian tradition recognizes as the Apostle to the Gentiles, with the Jewish Christians of Jerusalem and their leaders Peter and James, can be understood only if the importance of the church of Antioch in early Christianity, and specifically in Paul's life, is recognized. This I have sought to illustrate, drawing on the insights of the social sciences to complement the historical-critical method. The image of Paul that results is of one who was forced to redefine his beliefs and rebuild his life not only after his 'Damascus Road' experience, but also on several occasions thereafter, the significance of which previous scholarship has not fully appreciated. One recent development in New Testament studies of which I have not taken full advantage in this work is rhetorical analysis. My subsequent paper (1991b) has sought to rectify this, and I am persuaded that its insights confirm my earlier conclusions.

I would like to express my thanks to my supervisor, Professor James Dunn, for his support and encouragement both during the years when my research was in progress, and subsequently while I have been working on the revisions. I would also like to thank my examiners, Dr Francis Watson and Dr A.J.M. Wedderburn, and Dr David Hill and Stephen Barganski of Sheffield Academic Press, for their comments and suggestions. The revised text, of course, remains my responsibility, and any errors in it are of my own making.

I owe a considerable debt of gratitude to my family for their support, both moral and material, during the years of my research; most particularly to my parents, without whom my years of study would not have been possible, and to my late uncle, who did so much to enable this work, but who died before its completion and to whose memory it is dedicated. Other family and friends, too numerous to mention, have been of immense encouragement and companionship over the years, and their anonymity here does not in the least diminish my appreciation of them.

The financial support of the Scarbrow Trustees and the Committee of University Principals and Vice Chancellors is hereby acknowledged. Any opinions expressed in this book are those of the author alone, and do not reflect the views of these bodies, or any of their officers.

ABBREVIATIONS

ANRW	*Aufstieg und Niedergang der römischen Welt*
ATR	*Anglican Theological Review*
BJRL	*Bulletin of the John Rylands University Library of Manchester*
BJSoc	*British Journal of Sociology*
BTB	*Biblical Theology Bulletin*
BZ	*Biblische Zeitschrift*
CBQ	*Catholic Biblical Quarterly*
ExpTim	*Expository Times*
HTR	*Harvard Theological Review*
Int	*Interpretation*
JAAR	*Journal of the American Academy of Religion*
JBL	*Journal of Biblical Literature*
JJS	*Journal of Jewish Studies*
JQR	*Jewish Quarterly Review*
JSNT	*Journal for the Study of the New Testament*
JSS	*Journal of Semitic Studies*
JSSR	*Journal for the Scientific Study of Religion*
JTS	*Journal of Theological Studies*
NovT	*Novum Testamentum*
NTD	Das Neue Testament Deutsch
NTS	*New Testament Studies*
RB	*Revue Biblique*
RevScR	*Revue des sciences religieuses*
RHPR	*Revue d'histoire et de philosophie religieuses*
RQ	*Restoration Quarterly*
RSRev	*Religious Studies Review*
SJT	*Scottish Journal of Theology*
SocAn	*Sociological Analysis*
SociolRev	*Sociological Review*
ST	*Studia Theologica*
TDNT	G. Kittel and G. Friedrich (eds.), *Theological Dictionary of the New Testament*
TynBul	*Tyndale Bulletin*
ZNW	*Zeitschrift für die neutestamentliche Wissenschaft*
ZTK	*Zeitschrift für Theologie und Kirche*

INTRODUCTION

1. *The Problem*

a. *The Beginning of the Modern Debate*
Paul's relationship with the church at Jerusalem, and with Peter and
James in particular, has been a crucial issue in New Testament
scholarship since the second quarter of the nineteenth century. The
seminal figure in the debate was F.C. Baur, the founder of the so-
called Tübingen School. Baur's portrayal of early Christianity was
influenced by the dialectic philosophy of his day, epitomized by the
writings of Hegel. Baur and his followers posited a somewhat hostile
coexistence between two fundamentally incompatible Christian gospels, in which Paul was true to the universalist teaching of Jesus, while
Peter, James, and the Jerusalem church reverted from Jesus' teaching
to Jewish particularism.[1] This dichotomy is closely identified with the
issue of the continuing relevance of the Mosaic Law in Christianity,
which is seen to be directly relevant to Paul's relationship with the
Jerusalem church. Irrespective of Baur's debatable direct or conscious
dependence on Hegel, he was nevertheless the product of the thought
world of his time, and the Tübingen school has been widely criticized
for its dependence on dialectic theory. It has been argued that, in their
reconstruction of early Christianity, they 'did not reach the true
solution because of [their] subjection to the "dialectic" of the
philosopher Hegel' (Sandmel 1958: 146).[2] Baur's reconstruction also
required the selective use and interpretation of the sources, both in his
reliance on the *Pseudo-Clementine Homilies* (1875: 85-89), and in his
effective dismissal of the testimony of Acts as 'intentionally deviating
from historical truth in the interest of the special tendency which it

1. Baur 1875: 59, 125-28; Baur 1878: 43, 61.
2. Cf. also Munck 1959: 69-87; Lüdemann 1983: 21-25; Kyrtatis 1987: 4;
Sumney 1990: 15-22.

represents', and uncritical acceptance of Paul as an 'eye-witness' (1875: 105).

b. *The Direction of this Study*
Baur and the Tübingen school have had a continuing influence in New Testament scholarship, and the issue of Paul's relationship with the Jerusalem church remains contentious. The identification of Paul and the Jerusalem church with particular positions regarding the Mosaic law, an issue of importance in its own right, has led to neglect of other factors in their relationship, which I hope to rectify. It is my contention that Paul's relationship with the Jerusalem church cannot be understood simply in terms of their respective understandings of the Mosaic law, which were neither monolithic in the case of the Jerusalem church nor inflexible in the case of Paul. Furthermore, the notion of a dichotomy between Paul and the leadership of the Jerusalem church has led to too individualistic, and too static, a conception of Paul and the movement within early Christianity with which he is associated. I shall be arguing that this dichotomy is largely the product of uncritical reading of Paul's statements about himself, particularly in Galatians, and is wholly inappropriate for understanding his relationship with the Jerusalem church. Paul's self-conception as reflected in his letters, and his accounts of and allusions to events, are to be understood in the context of the specific circumstances in and to which he wrote, and not as objective historical truth. Paul was isolated in the Church after his confrontation with Peter at Antioch, and consequently needed to legitimate his authority independently of any Christian community or authority figure. For the greater part of his ministry prior to the period during which his letters were written, Paul was a member and apostle of the church at Antioch. The importance of this association has been seriously underestimated in previous scholarship, and I hope to rectify this, both by demonstrating the significance of the association itself and by illuminating the degree to which Paul's apostolic self-conception, as reflected in his letters, was a response to the termination of this association. If the importance of the Antiochene church in Paul's Christian career is appreciated, then the notion of a dichotomy between him on the one hand, and Peter and the Jerusalem church on the other, becomes untenable. The relevant relationship during the earlier period of Paul's ministry was that between the churches of Jerusalem and Antioch, in which Paul was a

participant by virtue of his membership of the Antiochene church, and not as an individual apostle. This relationship, far from being one of hostile coexistence, was one of amicable κοινωνία, in which the diversity of Christian expression was contained within a greater, mutually respecting, unity.

The logical similarity between the Neo-Platonic dialectics associated with Hegel and Baur, and the Lutheran dichotomy between law and faith (a theological presupposition of much modern New Testament scholarship) may account for the tendency to view early Christianity in terms of conflict between two distinct forms of Christianity represented by Paul and his opponents in Jerusalem, and the apparent reluctance of scholarship to take seriously either the full range of diversity within early Christianity, or the conscious unity which embraced that diversity. The introduction to New Testament studies of sociological methods of analysis, which have been developed outside the realms of ecclesiastical polemic, would seem to provide an opportunity to reconsider the question of Paul's relationship with the Jerusalem church, with the benefit not merely of the fresh insights which can be gained through employment of such methods, but also of greater critical distance from the methodological presuppositions of Baur and his successors, and indeed of many of his critics. The work of B. Holmberg (1978) in particular has been a valuable contribution in this direction, and provides a basis for more rigorous scrutiny of the crucial issue of Paul's relationship with the Jerusalem church. Before proceeding with an account of Paul's relationship with the Jerusalem church, which takes into account the neglected factors mentioned above, a review of some of the major contributions of previous scholars to this debate would be appropriate.

c. *Review of Scholarship since Baur*

I shall begin this review with a number of Baur's earliest critics and their successors. Their work reveals a fundamental problem of paradigm. I shall therefore review also the major paradigms of early Christianity since W. Bauer. It will then be possible to consider previous contributions to the central issue of this study.

Baur's early critics, such as J.B. Lightfoot and A. von Harnack, while severe in attacking his method and interpretation of the sources, nevertheless reached conclusions not significantly different from his, in that they identify Paul's opponents as a Judaistic faction in the

Jerusalem church, rather than that community and its leadership as a whole.[1] This tendency has continued through the twentieth century, except where the history of religions school has posited a Gnostic background to Paul's opponents.[2] Even in this tradition, a certain rift between Paul and the Jerusalem church on the issue of the Mosaic law has been postulated (Schmithals 1971b, 1965a).

A significant number of more recent scholars, including H.J. Schoeps and G. Bornkamm, have emphasized the fundamental unity between Peter and James on the one hand, and Paul on the other, while not ignoring the differences between them on the crucial issue of the continuing significance of the Mosaic law, especially for Gentile Christians.[3] A position closer to Baur's has been advocated by E. Käsemann, C.K. Barrett and M. Hengel.[4] They affirm the existence of 'a planned and concerted anti-Pauline movement' (Barrett 1985: 22) emanating from the Jerusalem church, and which, to a greater or lesser extent, advocated the imposition of the Jewish law on Gentile Christians.

A major challenge to the notion of a dichotomy between Paul and the leadership of the Jerusalem church is that of J. Munck. He argues that Paul differed with Peter and James not in principle but in strategy, and that the Judaizers represent a Gentile Christian heresy against which Paul, Peter and James were united (1959: 93, 128, 131, 134, 232). Nevertheless, Munck retains a conception of Paul as unique among early Christian missionaries, including those preaching to the Gentiles (1959: 38-58). He retains also the idea of separation between Jewish and Gentile Christians, or at least of mission areas (1959: 119). While critical of Baur's use of sources (1959: 69ff.), Munck similarly discounts the evidence of Acts when it conflicts with that of Paul (1967: 86, 153, 154). These theological and methodological presuppositions weaken Munck's otherwise incisive challenge to the legacy of the Tübingen school, and mean that his conclusions are not as consistent or as radical as the evidence requires.

A fundamental problem with Baur, his successors, and some of his critics would seem to be one of paradigm. The scholars considered

1. Lightfoot 1890: 365ff.; Harnack 1908: 61, 62; cf. Baur 1875: 128.
2. Lütgert 1908; Bultmann 1947; Schmithals 1971a; Schmithals 1965b.
3. Schoeps 1961: 66-75; Bornkamm 1971: 28, 33.
4. Käsemann 1942: 36, 37; Barrett 1953: 1, 2, 17; Barrett 1982: 28-39; Barrett 1970; Barrett 1971: 246, 252, 253; Barrett 1985: 22; Hengel 1979: 86, 97.

above, while critical of Baur and the Tübingen school, nevertheless base their work on many of the same presuppositions. The identification of Paul with non-nomistic Christianity, and of the Jerusalem church with nomistic Christianity, while not totally incorrect, focuses too much on the person of Paul and tends to ignore the broader range of Christianity of which he was but one example, and in particular underestimates the importance of the Antioch church in the formation of the theological tendency Paul came to exemplify. These scholars operate within a framework too rigid and simplistic to accommodate the range of diversity in early Christianity, and the simultaneous processes of synthesis and diversification that accompany historical and theological developments. A more comprehensive and less rigid paradigm is therefore needed if the historical questions raised by Baur are to be pursued successfully. W. Bauer's overview of early Christianity in *Orthodoxy and Heresy in Earliest Christianity* (first published 1934), subsequently developed by H. Koester (partly in collaboration with J.M. Robinson) and also by J.D.G. Dunn and R.E. Brown, would seem to provide a more flexible framework for studying early Christianity, and in particular for pursuing questions such as that of Paul's relationship with the Jerusalem church, with which this study is concerned.

Koester's trajectory model examines the dissemination and development of Christianity in specific places. He associates the Judaistic tendency in Jerusalem with James, rather than with Peter (1982: 87), and identifies Paul's opponents in his various churches with diverse strands of Christianity, rather than as a single movement (1971: 144ff.; 1982: 127). Dunn's model (1977) is closer to Baur's, in that it divides the broad spectrum of early Christianity into two principal categories, Jewish and Hellenistic Christianity, not as rigid categories, but as general tendencies in a single, though diverse, spectrum. While Peter and James, and the Jerusalem church broadly represent Jewish Christianity, Paul represents Hellenistic Christianity. Others represent positions between and beyond these (1977: 306). Brown's paradigm is similar to Dunn's, but identifies the diverse tendencies in early Christianity specifically in terms of their position regarding the Mosaic law, particularly circumcision and the dietary laws, rather than simply as Jewish or Gentile (1983: 2). He places Peter and James in the second of four principal categories, and Paul in the third (1983: 3, 4), at the centre rather than the edge of the spectrum. The strength of Brown's paradigm is that it avoids a simplistic and potentially misleading classification of early Christian groups as Jewish or Gentile. However, by making attitudes to the Mosaic law the sole criterion for categorizing the various groups, Brown ignores other relevant criteria, which Dunn's paradigm is better able to accommodate. While Koester tends to emphasize historical events in his reconstruction of early Christianity, Dunn concentrates more on the development of ideas, and Brown on the specific issue of the Mosaic law. All three emphases are important, and the paradigms all provide potentially useful frameworks for studying early Christianity. Within the broader framework, however, we need to focus more closely on the specific issue of this thesis, Paul's relationship with the Jerusalem church.

A treatment of modern literature on the subject of this thesis can most appropriately begin with K. Holl's essay, 'Der Kirchenbegriff des Paulus in seinem Verhältnis zu dem der Urgemeinde' (1921). Like Baur, Holl posits a dialectic relationship between Paul and the Jerusalem church, but ecclesiology, and therefore authority, rather than attitudes to the Jewish law, is the basis of conflict (1921: 61-62). Holl sees James as the dominant figure in the Jerusalem church from the beginning (pp. 50, 54), while Peter led the missionary outreach of that community (p. 56). The Jerusalem church exercised some over-sight over other churches, the precise parameters of which are unclear (p. 58). The tension between Paul and the Jerusalem church did not lead the former to deny the apostolic validity of the 'Urapostel' (p. 62), or the latter actively to undermine Paul, even if they authorized some of the activities of those who were operating against Paul in Galatia and Corinth, and furnished them with commendatory letters (p. 57). This last point seems somewhat ambivalent, but it is an issue which has never really been resolved. Holl's article is important, at least partly because he raises or alludes to issues concerning relationships on which, with the benefit of contemporary sociological method, we may now be in a position to shed further light.

The traditional Catholic position on the structure of the early Church, and of Paul's place within that structure, is represented by W.L. Knox. He goes beyond Holl in portraying the early Church as a hierarchical organization ruled from Jerusalem. Knox argues that, on account of his prolonged absences from Jerusalem on missionary work, Peter delegated the leadership of that church to James (1925: 81, 169). Together with a body of presbyters, James led the Jerusalem church, while the twelve apostles were 'the rulers of the whole Christian society' (p. 180). The apostles, and by extension the Church as a whole, were under the influence of the Jerusalem church, but Knox nevertheless recognizes in Paul a degree of autonomy and authority that could prevail against the combined weight of Peter, James's representatives and Barnabas at Antioch (p. 193). However inconsistent with his main argument the last qualification may be, Knox raises a very important issue, that of the influence of the Jerusalem church beyond its own borders, which, with the benefit of sociological paradigms, we shall be able to consider further in the appropriate chapters of this book, and hopefully reach insights which can resolve this ambiguity.

O. Cullmann represents a position that is ecclesiologically oriented, but founded somewhat more securely on critical scholarship than that of Knox. He argues that Peter led the church in Jerusalem from its inception (1953: 33, 34), and that the local leadership devolved to James on Peter's departure (p. 37). Peter's missionary work was, more than Paul's, subordinate to the church in Jerusalem (p. 43), and he was therefore to a far greater degree subject to pressures emanating from Jerusalem (pp. 45, 50, 65). Peter's authority was illegitimately cited against Paul in Galatia and Corinth, when they were in reality in fundamental agreement (p. 54). A curious intrusion, which undermines Cullmann's assertion of Paul's independence, is his suggestion that Paul baptized only a few in Corinth because only the Twelve could confer the Holy Spirit, and Paul accordingly left the task to them (p. 53). The fundamentals of Cullmann's historical reconstruction represent little development from Harnack, but he is appreciative of the role of relations of dependence and authority in determining the course of events, and this provides a basis for further inquiry into the issue of Paul's relationship with the Jerusalem church and its leaders.

In contrast to the ecclesiological emphasis of Holl, Knox, and Cullmann, and the rabbinic formalism of B. Gerhardsson (1961, 1964), is the scholarly tradition which emphasizes the Holy Spirit rather than ecclesiastical structures as definitive for early Christian life. The work of R. Sohm (1892) was seminal in this regard, and the same line of thinking is apparent in the writings of E. Käsemann (1964: 63-94; 1969: 236-51) and, in a less extreme form, E. Schweizer (1959). However, the principal exposition of this point

of view is that of H.F. von Campenhausen (1969). These scholars tend
to concentrate on the internal life of individual congregations, but
the implications of their research also affect their perception of
the broader ecclesiastical community.[1] The preoccupation of
Campenhausen with such concepts as pneumatic inspiration (p. 58)
and freedom (p. 47), and his assertion that charismatic powers conveyed no authority on those who manifested them (p. 60), result in
naive and unrealistic conclusions, which require correction through
sociological analysis.

J.H. Schütz (1975) and B. Holmberg (1978) have provided the most
significant work that has sought to apply sociological insights to early
Christianity, specifically directed to the issue of authority. The
former, however, is concerned principally with Paul's self-expression,
and tends simply to paraphrase Paul's assertions using sociological
terminology, without making the necessary analysis of the communities and relationships behind the texts. This lack of sociological
analysis of context seriously undermines the usefulness of his work.

Holmberg's work is methodologically more sound, both in his use
of sociological analysis, and in integrating it with exegesis and historical criticism, and is accordingly a more substantial contribution to
discussion of the issues with which this study is concerned. Holmberg
is very conscious that Paul's career was not static and that due account
must be taken of developments in his life and thought. This applies
very much to his relationship with the Jerusalem church, and
Holmberg points to a significant factor in this: Paul's association with
the church at Antioch (p. 18). The Antioch church saw itself as subordinate to that at Jerusalem, and it was after Paul's break with that
community in the aftermath of his altercation with Peter, that he
claimed equality with Peter (pp. 18, 54-55, 64-65). Nevertheless, 'the
role of the Jerusalem apostolate as the highest doctrinal court of the
Church is part and parcel of Paul's salvation-historical conception of
his own apostolate' (p. 28). The Jerusalem church was able to assert a
degree of authority over other Christian congregations on account of
its proximity to the sacred, in terms of being at the source of the
Christian faith (p. 198). Paul was therefore dependent upon the
Jerusalem church for recognition of his apostolic claims (p. 54-55)
and unable to break with the Jerusalem church in the same way as he

1.   See particularly Campenhausen 1969: 31-34; Schweizer 1959: 97.

broke with the Antiochene (p. 204). His standing with the Jerusalem church affected his standing with other Christian communities, including those he himself had founded (p. 207). Holmberg's analysis of the development in Paul's relationship with the Jerusalem and Antiochene churches, while pointing to a very important issue, the dynamic nature of relationships, is historically questionable, largely because he does not follow through his own insights concerning the importance of the church at Antioch. In the final chapters of this book, I shall be arguing that Paul's break with the church at Antioch was temporary. Furthermore, while Holmberg is undoubtedly correct in describing a complete separation of Paul from the Jerusalem church as 'theologically and sociologically impossible' (p. 204) at the theoretical level, I shall seek to demonstrate that Paul had no effective relationship with the Jerusalem church between the Antioch incident and the delivery of the collection. While I concur in a great deal of Holmberg's analysis, I believe these aspects of his historical reconstruction to require substantial revision.

J.P. Sampley has portrayed Paul's relationship with Peter, James, John and Barnabas in terms of a legal, consensual *societas*, formed at the Jerusalem conference, and, by implication, ended by the Antioch incident (1980: 21-41).[1] This interpretation, however attractive, is problematic. Sampley recognizes that the conference concerned the churches represented as well as the named participants (p. 24), but nevertheless reconstructs the decision of the conference as though it were a contract entered by five people. In the relevant chapters of this book, I shall argue that the conference concerned the relationship between the churches of Jerusalem and Antioch, to which personal relations between their respective leaders and representatives were subordinate. However well Sampley may interpret Paul's anachronistic depiction of the Jerusalem conference in Gal. 2.1-10, this reconstruction does not reflect the historical relationship in terms of which the conference took place. The κοινωνία between the churches of Jerusalem and Antioch cannot simply be equated with a consensual *societas* between the leadership of those communities (cf. Sampley 1980: 29).[2]

1. For treatments of the Graeco-Roman legal background, see Schulz 1936: 150; Buckland 1939: 296; Nicholas 1962: 187.
2. Cf. also Jones 1956: 163; Judge 1960: 43.

The reconstruction of Paul's dealings with the Jerusalem church offered by J.D.G. Dunn (1982, 1983) grapples with the problems inherent in interpreting Paul's account of this relationship. Dunn brings out very clearly the tension within the text of Galatians 1–2 between Paul's assertions of his independence of the Jerusalem church, and his need to cite that community as being in unison with him on key issues. 'It was this attempt to hold on to Jerusalem's authority and yet at the same time to hold it at arm's length which explains the contortions of syntax in this section of Galatians' (1982: 469). Paul is not simply outlining the course of his relationship with the Jerusalem church, but in doing so he is refuting allegations made by his opponents in Galatia, to the effect that he is, or ought to be, subservient to the Jerusalem apostles, from whom he received his commission (1982: 471). Paul is forced to admit a degree of dependence upon the Jerusalem church, but emphasizes that this does not substantially affect his own apostolic work (1982: 471-72). When based at Antioch, Paul had willingly shared in the subordinate relationship of that community to the Jerusalem church (1983: 6-7). However, when Peter and Barnabas's view prevailed in the Antiochene church in the face of James's delegates, Paul repudiated that authority, and the Judaistic party spread its activities to churches that had been established under Antiochene auspices (1983: 39). Dunn's awareness of the tensions and ambiguities in the narrative of Galatians provides a basis upon which we can consider other tensions revealed in that text, particularly that between Paul's need to relate accurately the events of his past and his need to portray those events in the light of his situation at the time of writing.

The issue of the relevance of the Mosaic law for Christians has been crucial to modern understandings of Paul's relationship with the Jerusalem church. The work of F.B. Watson (1986) is significant for its historical reconstruction as well as for its method of interpretation. Watson identifies as a principal issue in the early Church whether it would remain a Jewish reform movement or become a non-Jewish sect (p. 49). This analysis is open to criticism as being a restatement of Baur's position using sociological concepts, and arguably using those concepts anachronistically, without avoiding the rigidity which is a major weakness of Baur's thesis (cf. Holmberg 1990: 105-106). The significance of Watson's thesis, however, lies in his argument that Paul's Christian career began as a missionary to Jews, and he became a missionary to Gentiles because he came to believe that Christian mission to Jews was futile (Watson 1986: 28-29, 53). This was a cause of tension with the Jerusalem church (pp. 53-56), and Watson opposes Holmberg's view that Paul remained bound to the Jerusalem church despite the events at Antioch (p. 192). As argued above, this is a major weakness in Holmberg's reconstruction, and Watson provides a useful corrective to this, as does P.J. Achtemeier (1987).

Achtemeier's work is dependent upon his particular reconstruction of the order of events related or alluded to in Paul's letters and in Acts. The issue of chronology is crucial to addressing the historical questions posed by Baur, with which this work is concerned. Especially since the work of J. Knox (1954), scholars have sought to bring the records of Acts into conformity with a chronology extrapolated from Paul's letters. Principal events, such as the Jerusalem conference, the Antioch incident, and the formulation of the Apostolic Decree, if arranged in an order other than that implied in Acts, can affect significantly our understanding of the relationship between Paul and the Jerusalem church. As well as Knox and Achtemeier, significant contributions in this direction have been made by A. Suhl (1975), R. Jewett (1979), G. Lüdemann (1984) and N. Hyldahl (1986). Their various hypotheses will be treated in a discussion of chronology below, rather than in this review.

To summarize, the nature of Paul's relationship with the Jerusalem church, first raised in modern New Testament studies by Baur, remains a matter of scholarly controversy. It is an issue closely related to that of the relevance of the Mosaic law for Christians, and especially for Gentile Christians. However, the diversity and complexity of early Christianity as a historical, social and religious phenomenon are more fully appreciated today than was the case with Baur. A dialectic model, albeit based on the crucial question of the Law, is inadequate for understanding early Christianity, which cannot be simplified into a struggle between two parties, one particularist and the other universalist. Greater awareness of diversity inevitably relativizes the importance of the parties previously regarded as definitive of early Christianity, but the relationship between Paul and the Jerusalem church, through the successive stages of Paul's ministry, nevertheless remains an important question. Paul may no longer be regarded as typical of early Christianity, and the question of how representative his life and thought were is therefore more, and not less, crucial. The question of Paul's role in the early Church, and specifically in relation to the Jerusalem church, is one that has not been adequately resolved through the historical-critical method, however valuable its contribution. The use of sociological analysis to illuminate the historical information has been shown to be fruitful in the work of Holmberg and others. The questions nevertheless remain primarily and essentially historical, and must be addressed as such.

As stated above, it is my contention that previous work on Paul's relationship with the Jerusalem church has seriously underestimated the importance of the church of Antioch, although in recent years Holmberg, Dunn, Meier and Achtemeier[1] have made significant advances in this direction. I shall argue that scholars have been too uncritical in accepting Paul's anachronistic interpretation of events in Gal. 1.11–2.14, in particular the notion that he was an apostle to the Gentiles, independent of any Christian community, from the moment of his conversion.[2] Far from having been the independent apostle to the Gentiles, equalling Peter in pre-eminence, from the moment of his conversion, or even from the Jerusalem conference, Paul's independence was the consequence of his alienation from the Antiochene church in the aftermath of his confrontation with Peter (cf. Schütz 1975: 105). The theological rationale for this independence, and the reinterpretation of past events in the light thereof, serve to compensate for his severance of his relationship with the Antiochene church. Until then, Paul's dyadic identity and self-understanding[3] had been derived from the Christian community in Antioch, of which he was a member, and in whose apostolate he was engaged.

Paul's break with the Antiochene church therefore required a complete reorientation. He lost not merely the base and structural support of his missionary work, but also the very basis of his human and Christian identity. Both his self-understanding and his missionary work came to be expressed in terms of a personalized notion of

---

1.   Holmberg 1978; Dunn 1982; Dunn 1983; Brown and Meier 1983; Achtemeier 1987.

2.   This view has been argued by, *inter alia*, Hahn 1965: 97; Georgi 1965: 94; most recently McLean 1991: 67.

3   The theory of dyadic identity, developed by C. Geertz (1976) and J.A. Pitt-Rivers (1977), was first applied in New Testament studies by B.J. Malina (1979, 1981: 53-60). See also Meeks (1983a: 78), Countryman (1988) and the discussion in section 3a below.

apostleship, derived directly from God. In the absence of a community in which he could be embedded dyadically, Paul derived his identity from his apostolic vocation, which he conceived as having come directly from God, and which he closely identified with his conversion experience. Galatians reflects a response to isolation through social, psychological and theological self-sufficiency, which belongs to a specific period in Paul's life, after the Antioch incident, and can be understood only if his previous identification with the church at Antioch is fully appreciated.

2. *Principles of Method*

A fundamental problem with previous scholarship identified in the discussion above has been that of method. The rigidity of Baur's paradigm, in terms of which Paul was seen as the dialectic opposite of the Jerusalem church, has strongly influenced successive generations of New Testament scholars towards an understanding of early Christianity that conflicts with the evidence when seen in terms of the more fluid and broader paradigms that have been proposed as alternatives. I have suggested that sociological paradigms can help illuminate the issues further. The influence of methodology in shaping our understanding of the data requires that particular attention be given to the methods employed in this study.

a. *The Historical-Critical Method and Cognitive Philosophy*
New Testament scholarship has long recognized the need to locate the early Christian writings in their historical context as a prerequisite to sound exegesis, and all the works cited above are essentially historical in their method. The process of historical research, however, is complicated by unavoidable issues of meaning, method and interpretation. It is necessary to be aware of the limitations, both to the acquisition of knowledge, and to objectivity in its interpretation, that are inherent in history, as in other sciences.

R. Bultmann's definition of history as 'a closed continuum of effects in which individual events are connected by the succession of cause and effect' (1961: 291) well illustrates the point that methodological presuppositions underlie any academic inquiry. Gager's statement that 'meaningful descriptions can never be devoid of assumptions, whether explicit or not, that verge on being theories in disguise' (1982: 259)

demonstrates the problem that facts cannot be assimilated and analysed
without reference to some interpretative framework, which can, if not
used with due caution, become prescriptive of the results of the
research. A further problem is that of perspective, and Thiselton
points out that 'the modern interpreter, no less than the text, stands in
a given historical context and tradition' (1980: 11). Even the questions
with which we approach the sources constitute presuppositions (cf.
Bultmann 1961: 294). It is therefore impossible to avoid presuppositions, at least not without depriving the academic exercise of any
meaning. A disciplined, and self-conscious, methodology is therefore
essential to any academic inquiry, whereby the methodological presuppositions are clearly defined, and the danger of prescriptive rather
than analytic reconstruction is controlled, and in which meaningful
investigation is possible.

The historical-critical method is of necessity primary in any study
of early Christianity. The reconstruction of past events and their
significance, and the interpretation of ancient texts, are complicated by
the sparsity of evidence, which seriously reduces the potential for
certainty. R.G. Collingwood argues that 'The past does not exist and
cannot be perceived; our knowledge of it is not derived from observation, and cannot be verified by experiment' (1930: 13). The conclusions of historical investigation can only be tentative and provisional,
so far as the evidence allows reconstruction of past events and situations. The assertion of Sumney, therefore, that historical reconstruction requires probability and not simply possibility and plausibility
(1990: 81), not only assumes that information can be elicited from the
sources with greater assurance than is possible, and that there are
sufficient data for certainty when there usually is not, but it also
ignores the relativity of the distinction between probability and
possibility. While it is true that possibility does not constitute proof,
neither does probability. Probability is determined by calculation on
the basis of such evidence as is available, and the likelihood established
on the basis of probability is unaffected by whether or not the calculation proves to be correct in a particular instance.[1] Probability is
based upon a category of events, of which the specific case is an
example, and is 'impervious to strict falsification' when projected into
a particular situation (Popper 1980: 146). Sumney employs a notion

1.   For treatment of this issue, see Popper 1980; cf. also Wittgenstein 1974.

of probability that is all but prescriptive, and methodologically somewhat non-descript. He does not recognize the degree of uncertainty with which all scientific scholars, including historians and New Testament critics, are obliged to work. Furthermore, the historical-critical method needs to recognize degrees of probability.[1]

Sumney also attacks the use of analogy in historical reconstruction, and in the methodologically parallel process of exegesis, which he argues should be undertaken without primary reference to verbal parallels (1990: 89-93). This curious argument raises the question as to how words can have meanings other than in the context of a particular language at a particular time. This principle is essential to semantics and lexicography, and analogy is likewise fundamental to historical method. The perils of anachronism and prescription in analogy need to be guarded against, but the process of conjecture on the basis of analogy is nonetheless essential to the historical-critical method, even though the results that can be obtained are inherently uncertain and speculative.[2]

Even where the historical facts can be established, their significance cannot be definitively understood (Bultmann 1961: 295), and knowledge of facts does not constitute understanding (Hengel 1979: 130). Comprehension of events and their significance requires arrangement of the facts in a conceptual framework. Chronological ordering of the events, and the extrapolation of hypothetical events and circumstances, and their interpretation on the basis of analogy involve the use of controls external to the sources but nevertheless essential to the analytic process (cf. Holmberg 1978: 3). The use of such conceptual tools is essential, and MacIntyre has correctly observed that 'perceivers without concepts are blind' (1985: 79; cf. Popper 1972: 186). Care, however, must be taken not to incorporate anachronistic and inappropriate categories, alien to the context, in the interpretation of the sources (Garnsey and Saller 1987: 109). Care must also be taken not to rationalize events into a simplistic system of cause and effect, which ignores the complexities of reality, inevitable though simplification is in historical analysis (Hengel 1979: 130).

The historical-critical method is essential to New Testament

---

1. For discussion, see Popper 1980: 112. For theological treatment, see Harvey 1967: 81. For New Testament application, see Hengel 1979: 132.
2. See further discussion in Collingwood 1946: 251; Hengel 1979: 129.

scholarship, however tentative and provisional its results, notwith-standing the attacks of some literary critics.[1] While it needs to be recognized that 'the *meaning* of a text is inseparable from the forms in which it is expressed' (Poland 1985: 2),[2] the historical quest neverthe-less remains a legitimate exercise, whose usefulness 'only clever but unscientific minds can deny' (Dilthey 1976: 204). Other methods of analysis, complementary to the historical-critical method, but equally limited in their scope and potential for certainty, can broaden our understanding of early Christianity. In our review of previous writings pertaining to the subject in question, particular attention was given to that work which sought to integrate sociological insights with historical analysis, as will be the approach of this study.

b. *The Historical-Critical Method and the Social Sciences*
The intention of scholars who apply sociological method to New Testament studies is not to supersede the historical-critical method, but to extend its scope. Sociology is 'a natural and inevitable concomi-tant of the historical-critical method' (Watson 1986: ix). 'Sociological explanation is necessarily historical' (Abrams 1982: 2).[3] The sociol-ogist 'does not need to work over the research of historians, but neither can he welcome passively and naively every bit of information that comes to his hand' (Durkheim 1938: 134). Sociological analysis does not entail the repudiation of all that historians have accom-plished, but at the same time it cannot be uncritical of the conclusions reached through historical analysis. Sociological study 'complements and improves the prevailing method of biblical interpretation through more rigorous attention to the social dimension of the biblical text and to the sociological dimension of the exegetical task' (Elliott 1979: 1). This methodological development is not unique to New Testament studies, and we can therefore benefit from the work of other historians who have sought to incorporate a sociological dimension in their research methodology, and also from that of social scientists who have sought to be historically aware.

The need for interdisciplinary approaches to scholarly issues is

1.   For discussion of this question, see Petersen 1978: 32.
2.   For fuller treatment of this issue, see Morgan 1988: 240.
3.   This point is emphasized strongly by Holmberg in his review of sociological approaches to New Testament studies (1990: 8-12).

widely accepted, and does not in itself require argument here. We do need to consider, however, problems relating to the application of such an interdisciplinary approach to the New Testament. A major problem with applying the methods of the social sciences to historical situations is that the research techniques have been developed for the purpose of data gathering through field work and other forms of direct observation. This is, of course, not possible with extinct societies, such as the Graeco-Roman world during the first century CE. When extinct societies, and earlier stages in the development of extant societies, are studied by sociologists and anthropologists, the only means of observation available to them are indirect, and inevitably incomplete. This is not, however, an insuperable obstacle to the use of the methods of the social sciences for our purposes. Such pioneers in the social sciences as M. Weber did considerable amounts of work on historical rather than contemporary societies, and they continue to provide the basis of their successors' work in a way which is not the case with other sciences. Whereas in other branches of knowledge a cumulative and generally linear development takes place, in the social sciences contemporary scholars, while not unaware of or uninfluenced by each other, tend to build their work directly on the models formulated by Durkheim, Marx, Weber or Malinowski (Merton 1967: 3-5). This is particularly useful for the more systematic application of the sociological methods to historical situations. Even though the seminal works may be crude and inadequate by contemporary standards, they remain a basis on which a methodology suitable for New Testament studies can be built. Later developments, concerned with methods of observation and analysis of selected data, which are not available to the New Testament scholar, need not obscure the fundamental principles propounded by the founders of the social sciences, which can continue to be developed and refined for the purpose of application to historical situations.

The incompleteness of the data is a problem shared with the historical-critical method, but the social sciences, being concerned with general tendencies rather than specific events, are better able to extrapolate a situation on the basis of incomplete data. 'In order to obtain results, a few facts suffice. As soon as one has proved that, in a certain number of cases, two "analogous" phenomena vary with one another, one is certain of being in the presence of a law' (Durkheim 1938: 133). Durkheim may give the impression of over-confidence and of willingness to be prescriptive without sufficient evidence (cf. Popper 1972: 2-5), and here caution must be exercised, as in the historical-critical method. Nevertheless, it remains a fundamental premise of the social sciences, as with history, that analogy and comparison are useful in reconstructing lacunae in our knowledge of the situation under discussion. The difference between the two approaches is that history is concerned with specific events, whereas the social sciences are concerned with general social norms. 'A sociological statement seeks to describe and explain interpersonal behavior with reference to those characteristics which transcend the personal' (Theissen 1982: 176). Such methods of extrapolation as analogy and, to a lesser extent, logical prediction, are more suited to the general reconstructions of the social sciences than they are to the specific reconstructions of history. When historians apply these techniques, they are extrapolating from a general norm to a specific event, with a degree of speculation and prescription corresponding to the lack of concrete evidence. The social sciences can be useful in describing social conditions and norms, but they cannot prescribe the response of any individual or group to those circumstances.[1] Both disciplines encounter the same methodological problems, a fact which increases their complementarity. As Burke has observed, 'The historical and the sociological approaches are both complementary and dependent on one another, and both necessarily involve the comparative method' (1980: 33). Therefore we can use sociological insights to assist in our reconstruction of historical circumstances and events, but sociology is 'not a substitute for historical evidence, but a way of interpreting the evidence' (Watson 1986: x).

More significant and more problematic than the incomplete state of the information is the dependence of the sociologist and anthropologist on documentary records and archaeological artefacts. While the methods of historical research were developed specifically for the analysis of such data, the latest research methods of the social sciences, as noted above, were developed in and for the study, by direct observation, of living social entities. Anthropology, however, is not

---

1. See Scroggs 1980: 167 for discussion of this problem in New Testament studies. For a more general treatment of the methodological principles, see MacIntyre 1985: 93-95.

unaccustomed to relating to historical situations. E.E. Evans-Pritchard explains how social anthropology studies

> social behaviour, generally in institutionalised forms, such as the family, kinship systems, political organization, legal procedures, religious cults, and the like, and the relations between such institutions; and it studies them either in contemporaneous societies or in historical societies for which there is adequate information of the kind to make such studies feasible (1951: 5).

The social scientist studying historical situations therefore requires historical competence, and de Sainte Croix cautions that:

> Sociologists not thoroughly trained as historians who have ventured outside their own familiar world into earlier periods of history have often made disastrous mistakes and have sometimes produced conclusions of little or no value, simply because of their inability to deal properly with historical evidence (1981: 85).

Sociological techniques of analysis cannot be applied to historical situations without reference to historical methods. This is widely recognized, and the methods have been adapted accordingly and can therefore be of use for our present purpose.

The same principle applies to historians who wish to extend the scope of their studies beyond their traditional parameters to include sociological and anthropological questions. C. Lévi-Strauss warns that, without training in the social sciences,

> all that the historian. . . can do. . . is to enlarge a specific experience to the dimensions of a more general one, which thereby becomes accessible *as experience* to. . . another epoch (1963: 17).

Both historical and social sciences need to be applied competently if satisfactory and reliable results are to be attained in social studies of extinct societies. The aim of both disciplinary traditions, in the words of Evans-Pritchard, is 'to translate one set of ideas into another, their own, so that they may become intelligible, and they employ similar means to that end' (1962: 58). The methods of history and of sociology and anthropology are fundamentally compatible, and there are many situations, such as that with which this study is concerned, where the one cannot be used without the other.

The historical-critical method is largely the product of the German Enlightenment, and has been applied to New Testament studies with a definite Protestant theological agenda, as was clear in the work of

Baur and others considered above, and the use of sociological paradigms can help rectify this tendency (cf. Gager 1975: 4), as is especially clear from the work of Holmberg (1978, 1980). This is not to say that the social sciences are inherently objective and neutral, but they were developed without reference to the theological agenda that has shaped modern critical New Testament scholarship, and they have been introduced to New Testament studies at a time when confessional dispositions are less dominant than has been the case in the past. They therefore present an opportunity for greater objectivity, as well as being designed to avoid the imposition of the cultural presuppositions of the scholar. B.J. Malina explains that:

> What we need in order to understand. . . the New Testament writings and the behavior of the people portrayed in them. . . are some adequate models that would enable us to understand cross-culturally, that would force us to keep our meanings and values out of their behavior, so that we might understand them on their own terms (1981: 18).

The social and historical sciences, therefore, share the same aims, and, to a substantial degree, methods and limitations. They are not only compatible, but interdependent and complementary. An interdisciplinary approach is essential to satisfactory results from research into areas where both can contribute. The New Testament, and the communities in which the texts were produced, can be more fully understood if the insights of the social sciences, as well as the historical, are used in the analysis of the records. We turn now to consider particular methodological paradigms relevant to this study.

3. *Relationships and Authority*

Relationships involve the exercise of, and assent or resistance to, authority. The questions posed in this book largely concern this issue of authority, and it is therefore necessary to clarify the concept of authority, and the related concept of power, before proceeding further. This is particularly important in a religious movement such as early Christianity where divine power is also involved. As K.O.L. Burridge has observed, religions 'are concerned with the systematic ordering of different kinds of power, particularly those seen as significantly beneficial or dangerous' (1980: 5). It is therefore important to take into account the power perceived and wielded within

the framework of a particular set of religious beliefs. Neither historical nor social sciences can verify or quantify the perceived manifestations of divine power that are integral to most religious systems, but
they must nevertheless take account of the assertions and beliefs of the
people concerned. This must include both the divine power attributed
to deities in whatever form, and the power wielded by dominant
individuals and groups within the religious system.

In this study we are not concerned so much with manifestations of
divine power, except in so far as such perceived manifestations form
the basis of the power wielded and the authority asserted by individuals and groups in the religious community. The concepts of
authority and power, and their interaction with each other, are a
matter of considerable controversy in the social sciences and therefore
require some consideration.

a. *Authority and Power*
Theories vary considerably as to what constitutes authority and
power, and how the two are related. C.K. Barrett's treatment of
δύναμις and ἐξουσία in the Gospels, where he describes the former
as kinetic energy and the latter as potential energy, ἐξουσία being the
authority antecedent to δύναμις (1966: 78, 79), however useful in
itself, cannot be used to equate the terms with contemporary technical
usage. The crucial issue in contemporary social scientific debate
appears to be whether authority is a form of power,[1] or whether the
two concepts are independent but overlapping, authority being charac-
terized by legitimacy and excluding coercive force, while power is the
capacity to use force to achieve the given objective,[2] or even whether
the two can be distinguished at all (Stowers 1985: 167).

It is neither possible nor appropriate to attempt to resolve the
scholarly questions about authority and power here. As with all social
scientific paradigms, those which include the concepts of authority
and power are question-specific, and not of universal application
(Malina 1982: 237; cf. Popper 1972: 186). Authority and power are
multifaceted concepts, exercised in social relationships and phenomena

1. This is argued by Lasswell and Kaplan 1952: 133; Wrong 1979: 24; and Sennett
1980: 20. It has been adopted in New Testament studies by Schütz 1975: 10-14.
2. This is argued by Arendt 1958: 82; Friedrich 1958: 35; and Jouvenal 1958:
161. This paradigm is preferred by Holmberg 1978: 131-36.

of varying complexity, and therefore elude comprehensive definition and typology (cf. Peabody 1968: 474). We therefore need to find a paradigm that is appropriate to the questions with which we are concerned, rather than one which seeks to account for all possible situations and eventualities. A paradigm of authority that emphasizes the relationships involved would be particularly appropriate for our purpose.

Several scholars have concerned themselves with relationships as the essential context and medium of authority and power. The influence of M. Weber on these scholars is clear, but they have all modified his paradigm, or aspects of it, for their own particular needs. R. Bierstedt asserts that authority is 'always a property of social organization' and exists only within defined parameters, in a status relationship in a formal structure (1954: 72-75). C.J. Friedrich argues that authority exists only in the context of communication and that it is essential to all human relationships and communities (1958: 37-38). The principal distinction between Bierstedt and Friedrich would seem to be that, whereas the former recognizes that authority can exist in latent form when it is not being exercised, the latter insists that it exists only when asserted. The potential for authority to be exercised does not, in Friedrich's definition, in itself constitute authority. There is clearly truth in both positions, in that authority, or latent or potential authority, is weakened through disuse, and entrenched and strengthened through successful assertion. However, the potential for authority can often be perceived, and authority therefore be effective, when it is not being asserted, and allowance must therefore be made for some degree of latency. While communication and the exercise of authority are undoubtedly essential to the perpetuation of the authority relationship, we need to take a position somewhat closer to Bierstedt's than to Friedrich's, and see authority as present and latent in the structures that form relationships.

J.M. Bocheński seeks to draw together the insights of those paradigms which consider authority a quality related to the competence and influence of the individual, and those which see authority as a matter of the relationship in society rather than the quality of the individual. He defines authority as 'Status in Beziehung', and notes that it is an ambiguous concept, in that it has aspects of quality (*Eigenschaft*) as well as of relationship (*Beziehung*) (1974: 17-20). This relationship is three-cornered, including not only the bearer of authority (*Träger*) and the subject, but also the context (*Gebiet*), the ideal sphere in which that relationship of authority is exercised (1974: 23-28). Bocheński's paradigm is comprehensive in its range, but not in its prescription of details. It therefore provides a helpful framework in which the various aspects of authority can be considered in given situations.

T. Parsons offers a definition of authority as 'an institutionalized complex of norms' (1954: 205),[1] which provides for social conventions and other intangible forces that influence human behaviour, as well as for authority that is perceived to be vested in a specific person or office. This is useful, since social norms can direct individual or group behaviour in a way that is similar to the prescriptive exercise of authority on the part of an individual in the context of a specific relationship. The relationships that form society are governed by social conventions in much the same way as those that define institutions are governed by specific rules and the exercise of formal authority. Society therefore exercises a degree of authority over its individual members in the form of norms which direct their behaviour, and this authority is present in every relationship which exists within that society. This intangible, but ubiquitous, authority needs to be taken into account as well as formal authority, when considering relationships, as in the case of the early Church.

For the purposes of this study it is possible to accept, with one qualification, Holmberg's definition of authority as a 'social relation of asymmetric power distribution considered legitimate by the participating actors' (Holmberg 1978: 3). While authority would always be regarded as legitimate by the party asserting it, and by those who willingly acquiesce in its exercise, this is not the case with those who resist authority. The relationship of authority can exist, and be effective, even if the subordinate party resists it precisely on the ground that it is illegitimate. On the macrocosmic level, society, as an abstract but nevertheless potent entity, exercises effective authority over its individual and corporate members, shaping every relationship, and pervading every context in which social and cultural norms are believed to be relevant, appropriate and prescriptive for human behaviour. On the microcosmic level, a specific party exercises authority within a defined structure, which embraces those aspects of the lives of its

1. Cf. Schulz 1936: 164, who defines authority as 'a rule-forming quality'.

members or subjects over which the institution claims jurisdiction.

Power is perhaps more easily quantifiable than authority, even though it takes many forms. The essential ingredient of power would seem to be force, or the capacity to use force to achieve a desired goal.[1] Another basis of power is control over resources (Weingrod 1977: 43). The scholarly controversy as to how authority relates to power[2] would seem attributable not only to problems of definition, and how the two concepts relate in terms of competence, influence, coercion and other similar terms, but also to the variety of situations in which the concepts are applied for the purpose of analysis. For the purposes of this study, therefore, 'power' will be used of the capacity to apply force or coercion, and to exercise effective control, as a means of achieving a desired objective or of determining the outcome of a specific process.

In the context of early Christianity, power can be discerned both in the capacity to exercise or to repudiate social constraints, however limited, and in the claim to, and perception of, supernatural inspiration, however quantified. Power derived from perceived supernatural inspiration cannot be distinguished from authority, except where the assertion of authority on the basis of such inspiration exceeds the capacity for enforcement. In such cases, the authority asserted is not matched by the power available for coercion where that authority is not recognized, or is actively defied. Where authority is based upon traditional criteria, in Weberian terms, it does not in itself constitute power, and can be enforced only through power derived from other sources. Where control over resources takes the form of custodianship over sacred objects or places, this can form the basis of power, but when custodianship is over intangible traditions, this is less monopolistic, although it can form the basis for the assertion of authority. Power and authority may or may not coincide, and there is no definitive basis for relating the two. We shall therefore use the terms independently, recognizing that in some situations power and authority coincide, and in others they do not, in which case either authority cannot be enforced or power is not legitimated.

1.	Etzioni 1961: 4; Lukes 1974: 13; Wrong 1979: 2; Sennet 1980: 18, 170. For a New Testament treatment, see Malina 1986: 82.

2.	The conflicting approaches to this issue in New Testament studies of Schütz (1975) and Holmberg (1978) were noted above.

b. *Social Relationships and the Individual*

Society consists of people, their relationships with one another, and the institutions, formal and informal, created by these relationships, and the relationships that the institutions in their turn make. To understand society and its component units, therefore, it is necessary to understand relationships. This applies as much to religious movements, including early Christianity.

The individual is the smallest, but not necessarily the basic, unit of society. In Graeco-Roman society, with which we are concerned, the individual was not the basic unit, but rather the household or family to which the individual belonged (Garnsey and Saller 1987: 126). Individuality was restricted for all but heads of households and those few who broke with the fundamental structure of society, and even these were psychologically dependent upon the regard of those about them. Human identity was dyadic, meaning that the individual derived his or her identity from the group to which he or she belonged.[1] The group was the basis and focus of identity, and care must therefore be taken to avoid reading anachronistic individualistic notions into accounts of events and life in the early Church.

A.R. Radcliffe-Brown defines social relationships as follows:

> A social relation exists between two or more individual organisms when there is some adjustment of their respective interests, by convergence of interest, or by a limitation of conflicts that might arise from divergence of interests (1952: 199).

A social relationship therefore exists only when the contact between people is such that the lives of the various parties are affected by that contact. An incidental meeting does not create a relationship, unless it results in some form of bond between the parties. It need not be assumed, however, that the processes necessary to the formation of a relationship must be conscious or deliberate, or even that any two individual parties are directly involved in the formation of a relationship between them.

Relationships operate in systems, which can appropriately be depicted as networks, where the relations between various people are interconnected in a single, complex whole. 'Human beings are

---

1. Dyadic theory was first applied in New Testament studies by Malina (1979: 127-28; 1981: 51-55). For more detailed treatments of the theory, see Geertz 1976: 225-37 and Pitt-Rivers 1977: 1-17.

connected by a complex network of social relations' (Radcliffe-Brown 1952: 190). Mitchell defines such networks as 'a specific set of linkages among a defined set of persons' (1969: 2). Understanding relationships in terms of such networks is useful, in that the interconnectedness of relationships is at all times clear, while it is nevertheless possible to focus attention on a specific relationship or set of relationships.

While society ought strictly to be considered as a single network, inclusive of all social relations within it, this is not a feasible analytic method. Such a network would be far too complex to be capable of reconstruction, and would not be useful or relevant for most analytic purposes. For our purpose, it is sufficient to reconstruct those relationships relevant to the issues under consideration, and to work with the network that results. One potential problem with network analysis is that its reconstructions have no temporal dimension. As the method was developed in the study of relatively static societies, and was concerned with positions in the social structure rather than with personalities, it needs to be adapted for application in contexts of more rapid development where the structures tend to be less clearly defined. A network depicts the relationships as they are at one particular point, and each stage in the development of a relationship therefore requires a separate reconstruction of the network.

Relationships take particular forms, and it is therefore necessary to define more closely what we mean when discussing a particular case. The importance of patronage, particularly in local churches, has been shown by Theissen, Meeks, Marshall and, in the broader Graeco-Roman context, by Saller.[1] While of fundamental importance in understanding the situations of churches such as those at Corinth and Rome, and possibly also Antioch and Jerusalem were the data adequate, patronage is less important for a study of relations between churches, and the leaders of different churches. While it may be important for understanding the relationship between a missionary church such as Jerusalem or Antioch and the churches established under its auspices, the information is not available, except in so far as Paul's relationship with his churches as reflected in his letters may be analogous to such relationships. Since we are not directly concerned with this aspect of the network of early Christian relationships, it is

1.   Theissen 1982: 69-143; Meeks 1983a; Marshall 1987; Saller 1982.

sufficient to note the possibility. For consideration of the relationships at issue in this thesis, the institution of consensual *societas* or κοινωνία requires consideration, as Sampley (1980) has shown.

As argued above, the precise nature of the κοινωνία Sampley posits is open to serious question. Sampley argues a relationship between individuals rather than churches, while in the appropriate sections of this book I shall argue the latter. Nevertheless, Sampley has indicated an important model for understanding relationships in early Christianity, and it merits serious consideration.

Consensual *societas* in Roman law was an informal contract (Nicholas 1962: 185), 'the union of two or more persons to promote a common purpose by joint means' (Kaser 1965: 187). The amalgamation of resources for the pursuit of a common interest does not constitute incorporation, and a consensual *societas* is not a legal person (Sampley 1980: 16). The terms of consensual *societas* in Roman law have been outlined by Buckland as follows (1939: 294-99). The consensual nature of the union meant that mutual acceptance between the partners (*socii*) was required. *Societas* could involve the total commitment of all partners in all matters (*societas omnium bonum*), or its scope could be narrowed to cooperation in a single venture. The partners could delegate the operation of the *societas* to one of their number or to another person. *Societas* was ended on the completion of its purpose, or the destruction of the means to that common goal, and on the death or withdrawal of one of the partners. The remaining partners could form a new *societas* to continue the purpose of the old.

The κοινωνία of the Greek world was a rather more broadly defined category of institutions than the Roman consensual *societas*, which tended to function specifically for commercial purposes. κοινωνία designates unincorporated voluntary associations (Judge 1960: 43), which were formed for a range of social purposes in the Graeco-Roman world.[1] These groups had elected office bearers and expressed their unity through common cultic observance (Jones 1956: 161; Judge 1960: 40).

It is against the background of the conventions reflected in these institutions, and not in terms of them, that the conduct of relationships in early Christianity must be considered. It was not necessary for the

---

1. For discussion of early Christian groups as voluntary associations, see Meeks 1983a: 84.

first Christians consciously to model themselves on the legal and social institutions of the world around them before they conducted their own business according to conventional procedures. These institutions reflect normative behaviour in specific categories of situation in the Graeco-Roman world, and can therefore illuminate the conventions which would have influenced early Christian conduct in analogous situations.

Relationships are not necessarily constantly amicable, and conflict can from time to time erupt within them. Occasions of conflict provide useful insights into the nature of the relationship involved.

> The value in studying points of conflict lies in their tendency to bring to the surface otherwise hidden or taken-for-granted values and assumptions (Barton 1986: 225).

The work of L.A. Coser is particularly informative in this regard. According to Coser, conflict serves to define the boundaries of a group, and some degree of antagonism is therefore essential to the creation of a group (1956: 35-36). Conflict serves therefore to identify, to clarify, and to focus attention on, those values and objectives which are the basis of coherence of the group. The usefulness of occasions of conflict in reconstructing relationships will become apparent when the records of controversy about Gentile Christian obligations in terms of the Mosaic law are considered in order to understand the underlying relationships.

In studying relationships and authority in early Christianity, we need to be constantly aware of the social factors which influence relationships, of the way people in Graeco-Roman society related to each other, and of the interdependence of relationships. The network paradigm pioneered by Radcliffe-Brown, and the legal institutions of the Graeco-Roman world which Judge, Sampley, and Meeks especially have brought to bear upon New Testament studies, enable us to understand more fully the biblical texts, and to reconstruct more competently the relationships relevant to this study. If we can establish the conventions in terms of which Paul related to the Jerusalem church and vice versa, then we are in a position to understand more clearly the relationship between them, and their respective expectations in terms of that relationship.

c. *Charisma and Religious Rebellion*

Religious developments are frequently the work of dissenting parties in an established religious movement, and the role of Paul in early Christianity, and particularly his conflict with the recognized authorities in Jerusalem, can be understood partly in such terms. M. Weber's typology of authority and his conception of the charismatic prophet are sufficiently well-known not to require detailed treatment here. It is the developments in Weber's theory by K.O.L. Burridge and B.R. Wilson that are particularly helpful for the present purpose.

Wilson identifies the concentration of authority in the hands of an elite as a principal catalyst for religious revolt (1982: 121), and Burridge understands millenarian movements specifically as struggles for religious power (1980: 143). In studying early Christianity, we need to consider the role of custodianship over sacred traditions, rather than cultic objects and office, as the means to monopoly of religious authority. If Paul was excluded from, and alienated by, the concentration of authority in the Jerusalem church and its leaders, understanding this could illuminate the causes and the conduct of conflict between him and the Jerusalem church.

Alienation does not constitute a total explanation of movements of religious protest, since not everybody who is alienated joins such movements when they arise, and not everybody who joins such movements necessarily shares the experience that gives rise to those movements (Zygmunt 1972: 457, 460). It is important therefore not to be reductionist in our analysis. Factors that may not be significant in giving rise to the religious movement may lead individuals and groups to join such movements. The phenomenology of the movement as a whole is not necessarily reflected in the experience and motives of the individual participants, who have different, even if analogous, reasons for joining.

Movements of religious dissent, especially millenarian movements, articulate the experience of the alienated group and at the same time provide a vision of imminent salvation from that condition of alienation, believing the movement to be instrumental in the realization of that vision. Religious alienation is ended through the creation of new channels of communication with the deity and the rejection, total or partial, of the existing religious institutions.

A charismatic prophet is central to most, but not all, millenarian movements (Wallis 1982: 2). The prophet is not necessarily the founder of the movement, but gives it coherence through articulation of the grievances of the people, and direction through leadership in the struggle, physical or spiritual, against the old order and in the establishment of the new. The prophet is perceived to be endowed with supernatural power, and may function as the new channel for communication with the deity, the new means of access to divine power. Manifestations of divine power, whether vested in a person or not, are, according to Burridge, essential to the rise of millenarian movements (1980: 143). Such power must be beyond the control of, and in opposition to, the established order. The expression of the existential state of the oppressed and alienated, with its implicit if not explicit rejection of the prevailing order, enables the less articulate to identify their own state, to externalise their emotions, and to participate in their own redemption. If a movement is successfully launched, it may overthrow the prevailing order and establish a new order, or destroy itself through failure to do so.

The millenarian prophet of Burridge is a development of Weber's charismatic prophet. He or she is a rebel outside and against the power structures of the prevailing order, which the movement seeks to replace. In the words of Wilson,

> Charisma operates to break the existing authority structure, to lift sanctions on previously proscribed behaviour, and to promise men new freedoms—but it is also the occasion on which new men make new claims to obedience (1975: 26).

Prophetic figures depend on the recognition of their divine inspiration by those whose alienation and aspirations they express, and their consequent loyalty and obedience. Charismatic authority can exist only where it is acknowledged and obeyed, and prophets without a following are powerless and effectively outcast, estranged from the groups against which they rebel, and without the basis for forming their own groups.

The charismatic prophet, while a rebel against the old order, is also the instigator of the new. This involves the establishment of a new bureaucracy, a new tradition of legitimation, in however embryonic a form. As Zygmunt notes, the survival of such movements depends upon their organizational development, both in terms of institutional structure and in terms of symbol systems (1972: 454). Rebel movements need, in Stark's terms, both a founder and a 'second'

(1969: 77). As well as an instigator, such movements need someone who can give coherence and order, in Weberian terms, someone who effects the routinization of charisma. The two can be combined in one person, and Stark sees both Peter and Paul in such a role (1969: 77).

Not all incipient rebel movements come to fruition. What Etzioni terms 'protest absorption' (1975: 219-21) can take place, whereby the activities and emotions of potential revolutionaries are redirected within the parameters of the prevailing order in such a way that the old order is reinforced, and the threat of open rebellion removed. The appointment of rebel or potential rebel leaders to positions of responsibility within the existing structure serves to discipline and control their leadership, and possibly also to divert their energy and attention from the issues that could give rise to rebellion. Such cooption into the system can also satisfy the personal aspirations of the potential rebel leader, and, even if it does not, such appointment would almost always separate the leader from any dissident following, with considerable cost to his or her credibility. It can happen that charismatic groups as a whole are coopted into the prevailing system before they break away altogether. In such circumstances, in return for a degree of recognition, they would normally be expected to restrict their activities within defined limits, and to regularize and formalize their conduct and management of resources (Etzioni 1975: 221).

A number of tendencies in emergent movements of religious protest have been identified which are potentially useful for understanding Paul's relationship with the Jerusalem church. Paul's principal act of rebellion against the Jerusalem church took place in his confrontation with Peter at Antioch. This incident will be studied in detail, and Wilson and Burridge, building on Weber, have provided some useful insights in their study of analogous phenomena through which we can seek to illuminate that stage in Paul's relationship with the Jerusalem church.

d. *Cognitive Dissonance*
The cognitive dissonance theory, pioneered by L. Festinger (1956, 1957), has been usefully applied to a number of issues in New Testament studies (cf. Gager 1975). Cognitive dissonance is that state where two or more incompatible but subjectively irrefutable data are contained within a single body of knowledge. Dissonance is reduced in

various ways,[1] of which the most important for the purposes of this study are the redefinition of one item in terms of the other, and the inclusion of further data within the system. The aim of dissonance reduction is to preserve inviolate, as far as possible, the most significant or preferred item of dissonant knowledge, and to accommodate the other(s) to it.

For the purposes of this study, it is specifically post-decision dissonance (Festinger 1964) with which we are concerned. The recent work of A.F. Segal (1990) has considered in some detail Paul's conversion and subsequent developments in his life in the light of cognitive dissonance theory, but the opportunities for fuller consideration of post-conversion dissonance have not yet been fully explored. The cognitive dissonance theory is, however, undoubtedly illuminating of the period immediately following Paul's conversion, and enables a fuller appreciation of the transformation in his life occasioned by joining the Antioch church, which in turn informs our understanding of Paul's departure from Antioch.

We have considered a number of sociological paradigms which could potentially be useful in addressing the issues with which this work is concerned. These paradigms, however illuminating, do not supplant the historical-critical method, which is, and must remain, the primary framework within which essentially historical questions are addressed. Nevertheless, sociological insights can be instructive, and will be employed where relevant in this book.

4. *The Primary Sources*

We have considered the methodological paradigms that will be applied in addressing the questions with which we are concerned. We need now to consider the sources from which the data will be extracted and to locate them in their appropriate historical context. The principal primary sources for this work are of course the New Testament texts, and in particular the letters of Paul and Acts, and it is to these that attention must now be given. Of the Pauline letters, those of concern are 1 Thessalonians, Galatians, 1 Corinthians, 2 Corinthians, Romans, and possibly Philippians.

---

1. This is discussed by Festinger in some detail, and summarized in 1956: 264-65.

a. *The Letters of Paul*

1 Thessalonians, although disputed by Baur (1876: 96), is almost universally recognized as authentically Pauline in recent scholarship, and the overwhelming majority of scholars accept its integrity. The letter is dated to c. 50 CE, within months of Paul's mission to Thessalonica, and was almost certainly written from Corinth.[1] It is a document of the period immediately subsequent to the incident at Antioch and Paul's separation from the church there.

Paul's authorship of Galatians is undisputed, but the date and destination of the letter are uncertain. Recent scholarship has tended to link these two issues, and to base its arguments on the chronology of Acts 16 and 18 and the question as to whether Galatia denotes the Roman province or the region, somewhat inappropriately referred to as south and north Galatia respectively. It would seem methodologically questionable, however, to rely on the undoubtedly incomplete itineraries of Acts to argue for date or destination (cf. Betz 1979: 4). The letter was addressed to a specific group of Christian communities in an area that was not necessarily coterminous with the boundaries of Galatia, by either definition, but whom Paul could address collectively as Galatians (Gal. 1.2; 3.1). I do not intend, therefore, to argue for either north or south Galatian hypothesis, but to concern myself only with the date of the letter. Accepting the identification of the conferences of Gal. 2.1-10 and Acts 15.5-29, I would argue for a date not very long after the Antioch incident, and prior to Paul's return to Antioch (Acts 18.22). The years 50–53 CE would therefore seem most likely. An early date is favoured by Burton, Richardson, Dunn and Longenecker.[2] Other than assumptions about the chronology of Acts and the question of province or region, the principal argument against an early date is based on the expression τὸ πρότερον in Gal. 4.13, which most scholars read as implying that Paul had visited the Galatian churches a second time, subsequent to his mission.[3] Barrett asserts that this is not necessarily the case (1985: 109), and

1.   Best 1972: 11; Kümmel 1975: 257; Robinson 1976: 53; Jewett 1986: 60.

2.   Burton 1921: lii; Richardson 1969: 71; Dunn 1990: 259; Longenecker 1990: lxxxiii.

3.   Lightfoot 1890: 22, 175; Burton 1921: xlv; Lagrange 1925: 113; Marxsen 1968: 45; Schlier 1971: 210; Kümmel 1975: 303; Oepke 1973: 26, 142; Mussner 1974: 307; Beker 1983: 42; Suhl 1987: 3079.

Blass–Debrunner–Funk argue that πρότερος does not mean 'the first of two', a meaning taken over by πρῶτος, but 'earlier' (1961: 34). Bauer is more equivocal (1957: 729), but it is nonetheless clear that the expression τὸ πρότερον does not in itself require the implication of two previous visits by Paul to Galatia. The question is one of chronology and not one of grammar. Betz argues that τὸ πρότερον is to be understood to mean 'originally' (1979: 220), and Longenecker similarly draws attention to the contrast between πρότερον and νῦν, and asserts that this excludes the possibility of an intervening visit (1990: 190). A further consideration is Gal. 1.6, where οὕτως ταχέως would seem to imply that Galatians was written not long after Paul's mission and the foundation of those churches (Burton 1921: xlv; Watson 1986: 59). While Betz is undoubtedly correct in pointing out the rhetorical aspect of Paul's statement (1979: 47), it is most unlikely that this deprives οὕτως ταχέως of all literal meaning. While a substantial number of scholars prefer a later date for Galatians,[1] the fact that Paul is content to portray the episode at Antioch as unresolved, and to give the impression of continuing hostility between himself and Peter, must favour an early date (cf. Dunn 1983: 39).

Paul's authorship of 1 Corinthians is undisputed in recent scholarship (Barrett 1968: 12; Kümmel 1975: 275), but its integrity is a matter of debate.[2] However, I would follow the substantial body within New Testament scholarship who accept the integrity of the letter,[3] even if allowing for a number of later insertions into the text.[4] Achtemeier places the letter prior to the Jerusalem conference (1987: 90), but the overwhelming majority of scholars date it later, including Lüdemann, who nonetheless dates the letter early (1984: 263). There

1. Kümmel 1975: 304; Mussner 1974: 11; Robinson 1976: 56; Roetzel 1982: 63.

2. Cf. Héring 1962: xiv; Schmithals 1973; Suhl 1975: 203-12; Jewett 1978; Sellin 1987: 2979.

3. Marxsen 1968: 76; Barrett 1968: 15-17; Kümmel 1975: 278; Lang 1986: 7.

4. For discussion of the place of 1 Cor. 9 in the canonical letter, see Conzelmann 1969: 151-53. In his judgment the balance of probability favours the integrity of the letter at this point. The scholarly trend which seeks to excise texts from Paul's letters offensive to contemporary political and religious thinking, such as his treatment of women, would seem to be special pleading. Cf. Roetzel 1982; Munro 1983.

can be little doubt that Paul's mission to Corinth took place after the incident at Antioch, since he was no longer working with Barnabas (2 Cor. 1.19). That 1 Corinthians post-dates Galatians has been argued plausibly by Watson, Achtemeier and Wedderburn,[1] all of whom note that the collection had become a matter of practical implementation in 1 Cor. 16.1-4. This would indicate, for reasons that will be argued fully below, that 1 Corinthians was written shortly after Paul's visit to Antioch in Acts 18.22. If the collection was intended for delivery in the sabbatical year 55 CE, then early 54 CE would be the most probable date. This is the date favoured by Barrett and Hyldahl, while Kümmel suggests 54 or 55 CE and Robinson 55.[2]

2 Corinthians is the object of rather more varied, and more complex, scholarly dispute than 1 Corinthians. With the exception of 2 Cor. 6.14–7.1, Paul's authorship is not disputed, and the question of dating is not seriously affected by the question of composition, as the component letters would all be dated within the period two years subsequent to 1 Corinthians. Here it is possible to discuss the question only so far as it affects the chronological reconstruction on which this study is based. A position close to that of Bornkamm (1961; cf. Koester 1982: 53-54), which recognizes the tensions in the text, but which also takes into account the arguments for the integrity of 2 Corinthians 1–9 (Watson 1984; Lang 1986), would seem most appropriate. I would follow Watson and Lang, and a number of earlier scholars[3] in arguing the priority of 2 Corinthians 10–13. 2 Corinthians 1–9 is more problematic, and certainty as to its integrity or redaction is not possible. I would suggest, contrary to the consensus among proponents of the four and five letter hypotheses, that all components of 2 Corinthians 1–9 post-date 2 Corinthians 10–13, 2 Cor. 2.14–6.13, 7.2-4 being its immediate sequel, followed by 2 Cor. 1.1–2.13, 7.5–8.24, and finally 2 Cor. 9.1-15. These would date between Paul's second and third visits to Corinth. If 1 Corinthians was written about Passover 54 CE, then 2 Corinthians 10–13 would have been written from Macedonia a few months later, 2 Cor. 2.14–6.13, 7.2-4

1. Watson 1986: 59; Achtemeier 1987: 90; Wedderburn 1988: 30. For the contrary view, see Suhl 1975: 222.
2. Barrett 1968: 5; Hyldahl 1986: 122; Kümmel 1975: 229; Robinson 1976: 54.
3. Lake 1911: 156-62; Plummer 1915: xxiii-xxxi; Héring 1967: xiv; also Roetzel 1982: 61-63, and Talbert 1987: xix.

would have been written, from Ephesus some months later, 2 Cor.
1.1–2.13, 7.5–8.24 from Macedonia early in the summer of 55 CE,
and 2 Corinthians 9 shortly thereafter. This hypothesis will be tested
more fully in the chronological section below, and in the discussion of
the crisis in Corinth in Chapter 8.[1]

That Romans was written by Paul is not doubted, and the overwhelming majority of scholars accept the integrity of Romans 1–15.[2]
It is Romans 16 that is most seriously disputed. Marxsen, Koester and
Roetzel argue that Romans 16 was originally addressed to the church
at Ephesus,[3] possibly as part of a covering letter for a copy of
Romans, but the majority of scholars argue that at least Rom. 16.1-23
were included in the original letter to Rome.[4] Most scholars accept the
traditional view that Romans was written during Paul's third visit to
Corinth, while Suhl argues that it was written from Thessalonica, just
before this visit (1975: 276). Scholars differ as to the precise date of
the letter, locating it between the winter of 51–52 CE (Lüdemann
1984: 263) and 57–58 CE (Wedderburn 1988: 63). The edict of
Claudius would have lapsed with the emperor's death in 54 CE, and
allowed those Jews who had been expelled to return to Rome. If this
includes any mentioned in Romans 16, Paul could not have envisaged
an imminent visit to Rome before 55 CE (cf. Wedderburn 1988: 14-
15). The winter of 55–56 CE would therefore seem the earliest possible date for Romans. This would coincide with our estimate of the
dating of Paul's last letters to Corinth earlier in 55 CE, and his visit to
Corinth later that year, and also with the projected date of delivery
for the collection.[5] This date is favoured by Kümmel, Cranfield and
Koester.[6] The crisis over taxation in 58 CE, however attractive
in retrospect, is not a necessary explanation for Rom. 13.1-7,[7]

---

1. For more detailed discussion of the problem of 2 Cor., see Taylor 1991a.
2. For the contrary position, see Schmithals 1975.
3. Marxsen 1968: 108; Koester 1982: 573; Roetzel 1982: 63.
4. Michel 1955: 471; Barrett 1957: 13; Schmidt 1966: 7; Kümmel 1975: 316;
Käsemann 1974: 409; Cranfield 1975: 11; Dunn 1988: 884.
5. See discussion below and in Chapters 4, 7, 8.
6. Kümmel 1975: 311; Cranfield 1975: 14; Koester 1982: 573. This date is also
within the period favoured by Dunn 1988: xliii; Robinson 1976: 55; and Jewett 1979:
165.
7. This is argued by Friedrich *et al.* 1976, and supported by Wedderburn 1988:
62-63.

and does not require a later date for the letter.

Philippians is of relevance to this study only if the hypothesis of Paul's imprisonment at Ephesus is accepted, and the letter dated to that period. If Philippians is dated to Paul's Roman[1] or Caesarean[2] imprisonments, then it post-dates the period under consideration. The Ephesian hypothesis, however, is widely supported.[3] It is not feasible to discuss the merits of the various hypotheses here, but, if Philippians was written from Ephesus, it would be contemporary with the Corinthian correspondence. In the absence of any explicit reference to the Jerusalem church and its leadership in Philippians,[4] the degree of uncertainty inherent in the use of the letter is multiplied. It will therefore be treated in an Excursus at the end of Part III rather than in Chapter 8, and it will be noted that any allusions to Paul's relationship with the Jerusalem church may reflect his period of independent mission, or his subsequent imprisonment.

b. *Acts*

The use of Acts as a historical source, particularly for the study of Paul, is an issue over which scholars are divided, and the problems cannot be resolved simply by addressing the questions of date and authorship. The traditional ascription of authorship to Luke or another, unnamed, companion of Paul is supported by Dibelius, Williams and Munck, the latter two dating the work to the late and early sixties CE respectively.[5] 'Lukan' authorship is rejected by Marxsen, Kümmel, Vielhauer and Schneider.[6] This position does not necessarily imply denial that the author used older traditions including eye-witness accounts,[7] but it does imply a later date, probably between

1. Lightfoot 1868: 1-28; Vincent 1897: xxii; Plummer 1919: xiii; Beare 1959: 23; cf. Knox 1954: 87; Wedderburn 1988: 22.
2. Robinson 1976: 60-61; Hawthorne 1983: xliii; cf. Kümmel 1975: 332.
3. Marxsen 1968: 65; Collange 1979: 17-19; Vielhauer 1975a: 169; Watson 1986: 73; Watson 1987: 126; cf. Knox 1954: 87; Gnilka 1976: 24-25.
4. Georgi 1986: 341; Holmberg 1978: 48; Watson 1986: 80.
5. Dibelius 1956: 104; Williams 1964: 7, 15; Munck 1967: xxix, liv. Robinson 1976: 91 follows Munck.
6. Marxsen 1968: 151; Kümmel 1975: 181; Vielhauer 1975a: 391; Schneider 1980: 111.
7. Marxsen 1968: 147-51; Haenchen 1971: 87, 186; Kümmel 1975: 178, 184; cf. Lüdemann 1984; Lüdemann 1989.

80 and 90 CE or slightly later.[1] While the author's relationship with Paul cannot be ascertained (cf. Lüdemann 1988: 112), a date between 80 and 90 CE seems to enjoy a degree of scholarly consensus, from which there seems no good reason to deviate.

The relative reliability of Acts and the historical information contained in Paul's letters, is one of the more contentious issues in contemporary New Testament scholarship. While some scholars such as Hengel (1979) assert the essential reliability of Acts, others tend more towards what Gager terms 'a hyper-Cartesian decision to doubt everything simultaneously' (1986: 91). The position represented by Lüdemann (1984, 1989) expresses a degree of confidence in the traditions contained in Acts, but virtually none in their arrangement, and re-edits the sources accordingly. The majority of scholars assume an intermediate position between these, and Dibelius writes:

> We cannot believe that every detail of popular tradition [contained in Acts]. . . is authentic, but neither should we discredit it as a matter of course (1956: 105; cf. Marxsen 1968: 149).

Holmberg has noted an increasing regard for Acts as a reliable historical record in recent scholarship (1990: 65), but this does not diminish the need for the utmost critical rigour in analysing its accounts. Such rigour, however, is abused if it becomes licence for wilful reordering of the material, or for uncritical acceptance of Paul's evidence against Acts.

Betz argues that:

> Paul's own account in Galatians 2 is that of a first-hand witness and it must have priority in case of doubt, but the circumstance and function of the defence in his letter to the Galatians have coloured his account (1979: 81).

While Betz recognizes the subjective nature of Paul's account, and his polemical purpose, in the specific case of Paul's dealings with the Jerusalem church he nevertheless assumes that Paul's account is more accurate than Acts. This may be a valid conclusion, but it cannot be a premise for critical investigation. Linton has shown that:

1.   Kümmel 1975: 186; Vielhauer 1975a: 407; Schneider 1980: 121; cf. Conzelmann 1987: xxxiii; Haenchen 1951; Marxsen 1968: 151.

there exist perhaps certain affinities between an early representation of St Paul's person and activity, an account contested by the Apostle himself, and the later literary image drawn in Acts (1949: 80).

The traditions preserved in Acts incorporate perceptions of and assertions about Paul at least as old as his response to them in Galatians. No *a priori* judgment between the discrepant accounts can therefore be presupposed, and each must be critically examined. Hurd suggests that Paul's accounts should be examined first, in order that they should not be, however subconsciously, subsumed into the more comprehensive historical scheme of Acts (1967: 233). Such an approach implies no judgment on either source, but enables their independent scrutiny before they are compared. This would seem methodologically more sound than *a priori* exclusion of everything in Acts that does not conform to Paul's more limited and sporadic allusions, or the uncritical synthesis and coalescence of divergent traditions.

5. *Chronological Questions*

Recent work on the chronology of Paul's life, including the work of J. Knox (1954), A. Suhl (1975), R. Jewett (1979), G. Lüdemann (1984) and P.J. Achtemeier (1987), has attempted to reconstruct Paul's career on the basis of the evidence contained in his own writings, and evaluating Acts on that basis. This approach can realize a relative chronology of Paul's life, particularly for the period up to the writing of Galatians, without reference to Acts, but it is the latter that provides two principal bases for absolute dating, in its references to the edict of Claudius expelling the Jewish population of Rome (Acts 18.2), and the proconsulship of Gallio in Achaia (Acts 18.12). Acts therefore cannot be ignored, but we can conveniently begin by considering the single externally datable episode alluded to by Paul.

In 2 Cor. 11.32-33, Paul mentions having fled Damascus during the rule of King Aretas. This event can be dated between the years 37 and 40 CE.[1] Paul mentions having been in the vicinity of Damascus around the time of his conversion, and for up to three years subsequently (Gal. 1.17-18; cf. Acts 9.19-25), apparently until his visit to Jerusalem to meet Peter (Gal. 1.18). There can be little doubt that Acts 9.25 and 2 Cor. 11.32-33 refer to the same incident (cf. Knox 1954: 77). Paul's

---

1. Ogg 1968: 16-22; Murphy-O'Connor 1983: 129.

conversion can therefore be dated to c. 35 CE. Precisely how Paul's second journey to Jerusalem relates to this is problematic. While there is no reason to doubt that Acts 9.26-30 records the journey following Paul's flight from Damascus (c. 38 CE), the interval between the two visits poses a difficulty. If the fourteen years of Gal. 2.1 date from the previous visit, a view towards which the majority of scholars incline,[1] then the later visit would not have taken place before c. 51 or 52 CE. A substantial minority of scholars, however, date the fourteen years from Paul's conversion or his return to Damascus from Arabia,[2] in which case the conference would have taken place in c. 48 or 49 CE. This is a question to which we must return after considering Paul's mission to Corinth.

Paul's second visit to Jerusalem after his conversion is recorded in Acts 11.27-30, and Acts 12.25 may represent the termination of the same visit. A minority of scholars accept the authenticity of this account.[3] Fitzmyer and Robinson accept that this visit took place, but do not regard it as that related in Gal. 2.1-10, and Hahn argues that it took place some years after the conference.[4] Koester dismisses Acts 11.27-30 as legendary (1982: 102), while Catchpole regards it as a doublet of Acts 15 (1977: 434-37). It would seem more likely, however, that this text is a misplaced account of Paul's final visit to Jerusalem for the delivery of the collection (cf. Rom. 15.25-28), as Dibelius, Schneider and Achtemeier argue.[5] In this case, Luke conflates the delivery of the collection from Antioch, which had been undertaken at the Jerusalem conference with Paul's collection and final visit to Jerusalem. The difference between this position and that of Hahn may be less than would at first appear, and this is a question to which we shall return.

The nature of the business conducted according to Gal. 2.1-10 is more compatible with the visit of Acts 15, and the overwhelming

---

1.   Lightfoot 1890: 102; Burton 1921: 68; Knox 1954: 78-79; Betz 1979: 83; Lüdemann 1984: 172.

2.   Georgi 1965: 13; Fitzmyer 1968: 219; Suhl 1975: 46-47; Hyldahl 1986: 121-22; Longenecker 1990: 45.

3.   Geyser 1953: 126-28; Sanders 1955: 136; Williams 1964: 30; Bauckham 1979: 61; Bruce 1982a: 108; Longenecker 1990: lxxxiii.

4.   Fitzmyer 1968: 219; Robinson 1976: 40; Hahn 1965: 82.

5.   Dibelius 1956: 106; Schneider 1980: 113; Achtemeier 1987: 46.

majority of scholars identify this visit with that which Paul recounts.[1] The major problem with identifying the conferences of Gal. 2.1-10 and Acts 15 is that the so-called Apostolic Decree is incompatible with Paul's account. It is probable that the association of the Apostolic Decree with the Jerusalem conference is anachronistic, and that it was in fact a later formulation; a view which enjoys wide scholarly support.[2]

Achtemeier identifies the visit of Paul to Jerusalem in Galatians 2 neither with that of Acts 11.27-30 nor with that of Acts 15, but rather with the meeting of Acts 11.1-18. He argues that Paul is omitted from this account by Luke in order that the beginnings of the Gentile mission be associated with Peter and be regarded as uncontroversial (1987: 48). The meeting of Acts 15 was held subsequently, and Peter, Paul and Barnabas were not present (1987: 14-19). The credibility of this view rests on the assumptions that Christian mission to the Gentiles was controversial at the time Acts was written and that Peter was erroneously associated with it (cf. Hahn 1965: 48-54). We need not doubt that Acts 15 represents as a single meeting a process that was of longer duration, as the authors cited previously also argue, but there seems no justification in Achtemeier's considerable violence to the text of Acts.

A number of recent scholars have identified the conference of Gal. 2.1-10 with the obscure and doubtful reference in Acts 18.22.[3] Not only is it questionable whether the text alludes to a visit by Paul to Jerusalem at all (Haenchen 1971: 480; Conzelmann 1987: 156), but this identification defies the correlations between Acts 15 and Gal. 2.1-10, which is an unjustified disregard for the evidence that has led the majority of scholars to identify those two accounts. That Acts 15, as well as representing the conference of Gal. 2.1-10, is also correctly positioned chronologically, I shall argue after considering the date of Paul's mission to Corinth. First, however, we must consider the chronological relationship of the conference and the Antioch incident.

1. Lightfoot 1890: 122; Burton 1921: 117; Conzelmann 1987: 121; Haenchen 1971: 64; Parker 1967: 181; Mussner 1974: 131; Holmberg 1978: 18; Dunn 1982; Brown and Meier 1983: 37-38.

2. Dibelius 1956: 96-107; Nickle 1966: 58; Catchpole 1977: 434-37; Hengel 1979: 115-17; Schneider 1980: 113; Schneider 1982: 191; Dunn 1983: 38.

3. Knox 1954: 68-69; Jewett 1979: 78-81; Lüdemann 1984: 149; Hyldahl 1986: 82.

Munck and Lüdemann argue that the incident at Antioch preceded the conference at Jerusalem,[1] as of course do those scholars who identify Paul's visit to Jerusalem in Gal. 2.1-10 with that of Acts 11.27-30 (cf. Longenecker 1990: lxxxiii). Lüdemann's argument is that the circumstances reflected in Gal. 2.11-14 would have been conceivable only before the Jerusalem conference had resolved the issues (1984: 75). Dunn, however, has argued that the Apostolic Decree represents a later compromise, subsequent to the incident at Antioch (1983: 38), and this view represents a degree of scholarly consensus (cf. Hahn 1965: 83). Furthermore, if the incident had taken place before the Jerusalem conference, Paul would surely have retained chronological order in order to demonstrate his vindication at Jerusalem, rather than tacitly admit defeat at Antioch, and leave the impression of unresolved conflict between himself and Peter. That Paul relates the conference and Antioch incident in chronological order, is affirmed by a significant majority of scholars,[2] and there would therefore seem to be no justification in doubting Paul's accuracy on this point.

We turn now to the dating of Paul's mission to Corinth. Lüdemann argues that the text of Acts 18.1-17 is a conflation of two traditions, concerning two visits by Paul to Corinth. His principal items of evidence are the names of two ἀρχισυνάγωγοι, and the alleged incompatibility of the edict of Claudius with the proconsulship of Gallio. The first ἀρχισυνάγωγος, Crispus, was converted during Paul's mission (Acts 18.8; cf. 1 Cor. 1.14), and would almost certainly have forfeited his office in the synagogue as a consequence, particularly if the rupture with the synagogue reported in Acts 18.7 had taken place. Despite Lüdemann's objection (1984: 159), subsequently moderated (1989: 204), there seems no reason to doubt that this could have accounted for Sosthenes' assuming the office of ἀρχισυνάγωγος (Acts 18.17). Furthermore, as Lüdemann regards the episode in Acts 18.12-17 as unhistorical (1984: 160), the methodological legitimacy of his use of it to support his conflation theory, and to date Paul's second visit to Corinth (1984: 172), would seem questionable. Furthermore, even if Γαλλίωνος δέ does imply the beginning of a different source to that for Acts 18.1-11, it does not follow that two sources require

1. Munck 1959: 94-107; Lüdemann 1984: 75.
2. Knox 1954: 59; Conzelmann 1987: 115; Fitzmyer 1968: 219; Ogg 1968: 92; Suhl 1975: 18; Jewett 1979: 83; Hyldahl 1986: 53; and others.

two different visits to Corinth. Murphy-O'Connor calculates that the proconsulship of Gallio occurred between 49 and 52 CE (1983: 142-46), and probably commenced in July 51 CE (1983: 149). The edict of Claudius presents a more complex problem. Dio Cassius (*Hist*. 6.6) mentions Jewish rioting in Rome in 41 CE, which resulted in the prohibition of meetings, but not the expulsion of the Jewish population of Rome. Lüdemann identifies this as the edict mentioned in Acts 18.2, and argues that Aquila and Priscilla must have arrived in Corinth shortly thereafter, and that Paul first reached Corinth in 41 CE, or soon thereafter (1984: 7, 250, 262; 1988: 115, 116). Murphy-O'Connor also identifies this as the edict in question, but points out that Aquila and Priscilla did not necessarily go directly to Corinth from Rome (1983: 136). He argues that the earliest possible date for Paul's arrival in Corinth is 45 CE, and the more likely date 49 CE (1983: 139-40). This is the date that would be suggested by Orosius (*Hist*. 7.6.15, 16) for the edict of Claudius mentioned by Suetonius (*Claudius* 25), in terms of which Jews were expelled from Rome. This dating is problematic in that Tacitus makes no mention of such an edict in his extant *Annales* for that year, and, more significantly, Orosius's citation of Josephus is not from any of his extant writings and may be spurious. Nevertheless, there can be little doubt that this is the edict mentioned in Acts 18.2, even if the dating is less certain. A substantial body of scholarly opinion accepts the date given by Orosius, 49 CE, and accordingly dates Paul's mission to Corinth shortly thereafter.[1] We can therefore estimate that Paul arrived in Corinth in c. 50 CE. We need to consider now whether this was before or after the Jerusalem conference.

Paul was accompanied on his mission to Corinth by Silvanus and Timothy (2 Cor. 1.19; cf. Acts 18.5). This indicates that the mission took place after the incident at Antioch, which ended Paul's association with the church there and with Barnabas, in which case the entire period in Paul's life covered in Gal. 1.11–2.14 can be dated prior to his mission to Corinth.[2] This is disputed by a number of recent

1. Suhl 1975: 339-40; Jewett 1979: 38-41; Hyldahl 1986: 121; Watson 1986: 92. Cf. Wedderburn 1988: 14.
2. Lake 1937: 250; Caird 1955: 211; Filson 1964: 398; Conzelmann 1973: 182; Hengel 1979: 137; Watson 1986: 57.

scholars.[1] Calculations of dates may reach either conclusion, but such evidence as is supplied by Paul (2 Cor. 1.19) confirms the testimony of Acts, and there is insufficient ground for disputing it. The lack of reference to the Apostolic Decree in Paul's dealing with the question of idol meat (cf. Hurd 1965) is quite adequately accounted for by Dibelius (1956: 96-101) and Dunn (1983: 38).[2]

It seems most likely, therefore, that the Jerusalem conference took place before Paul's mission to Corinth, in c. 48 or 49 CE. It was followed, probably within months, by Paul's confrontation with Peter at Antioch, which lost him the support of that community and his association with Barnabas. He thereupon embarked on his independent missionary career, during the course of which he established the church at Corinth, probably in 51 CE. Meanwhile the crisis in Antioch was resolved through the promulgation of the Apostolic Decree. We turn now to the chronology of Paul's work subsequent to his mission to Corinth.

According to Acts 18.22, Paul, shortly after his mission to Corinth and a brief visit to Ephesus, visited Caesarea and Antioch. It is, however, debated whether τὴν ἐκκλησίαν alludes to a visit to Jerusalem at this point. Haenchen, Conzelmann and Roloff argue that this is how Luke understood his source, but that the historicity of such a visit is doubtful.[3] Georgi and Ogg concur that no such visit took place.[4] Haenchen argues further that Paul's landing at Caesarea was caused by unfavourable seasonal winds, and was unanticipated, and that Antioch was the sole destination of the journey (1971: 547-48). Filson, however, argues that the 'immense importance of Jerusalem' argues in favour of a visit, and that it was not recorded because of its personal nature and Paul's less than cordial relationship with the church there (1964: 246; cf. Longenecker 1990: xxiv). It could equally be argued that the importance of Jerusalem required that any visit be recorded in full rather than alluded to ambiguously. Munck too argues that Jerusalem was the destination of Paul's journey (1967: 181), as does

1.   Knox 1954: 85; Jewett 1979: 78-85; Lüdemann 1984: 149, 172, 262-65; Hyldahl 1986: 121, 122; Achtemeier 1987: 90.
2.   Cf. Wilson 1983: 94-99; Countryman 1988: 70-77. These scholars argue that the Apostolic Decree was specifically directed against Christian participation in pagan cults.
3.   Haenchen 1971: 544; Conzelmann 1987: 156; Roloff 1981: 276-77.
4.   Georgi, 1965: 37; Ogg 1968: 128-29.

Williams (1964: 214), and of course those scholars cited above who locate the Jerusalem conference at this point. Schneider argues that this was only a brief visit to convey Paul's greetings (1982: 254). If this is so, it entailed a very substantial extension to Paul's journey, in which case the importance of the undertaking must have been considerable, so as to require fuller treatment. That Paul visited Jerusalem in c. 52 CE is therefore most unlikely, and it is more likely that his eastward journey was to Antioch only, and this visit we must now consider.

Haenchen argues that Paul returned to Antioch after his mission to Greece in order to strengthen his ties with the church there (1971: 548). Given the circumstances in which Paul had departed from Antioch, Conzelmann is perhaps somewhat more precise in arguing that it was to re-establish contact with the Antiochene church that Paul made his return (1973: 90). The visit was therefore possibly of comparable significance to the episode that had resulted in Paul's departure, and it would stand to reason therefore that the details of the visit would not be recorded in Acts. Georgi correctly points out that Paul's previous association with the Antiochene church was not restored, for Paul continued his independent work, but at the same time he demonstrated his membership of and commitment to the broader ecclesiastical community (1965: 37). Ogg suggests that Paul retired to Antioch in ill health (1968: 131-32), which need not be incompatible with the ecclesial agenda to which Conzelmann and Georgi have drawn attention. A particular aspect of Paul's business with the Antiochene church may well have been the arrangement of the collection, which occupied Paul's last years of freedom, as Suhl suggests (1975: 135-36).[1] The delivery would have been scheduled for 55 CE (Suhl 1975: 135; cf. Jeremias 1928).

The period after Paul's visit to Antioch has already been discussed in connection with the chronology of 2 Corinthians and can therefore be dealt with fairly briefly here. In 1 Cor. 16.3-6 Paul indicates his intention to visit the Corinthian church towards the end of the following travelling season, which we have estimated to be that of 54 CE. Paul would possibly travel to Jerusalem that autumn, or winter in Corinth and sail for Jerusalem, or proceed to work elsewhere, at the beginning of the 55 CE travelling season. That Paul's plans for 54 CE

1. Cf. Williams 1964: 213; Watson 1986: 175.

were frustrated, is clear from 2 Corinthians. It is not possible or
necessary to discuss the various hypotheses here, but it is apparent
from 2 Cor. 1.23–2.1 that Paul's plans were altered. It would seem
most likely that Paul learned, possibly from Timothy (1 Cor. 16.10),
of the crisis in Corinth precipitated by rivals infiltrating the church,
and accordingly visited Corinth at the beginning of the 54 CE travelling season, when he was not expected by the church. The visit proved
disastrous, and Paul withdrew from Corinth, and proceeded with
the work he had planned in Macedonia, from where he wrote
2 Corinthians 10–13, at which time he may still have intended to
return to Corinth that autumn (2 Cor. 13.1). The Corinthian church
fully expected Paul to return as originally envisaged, but instead he
returned to Ephesus (2 Cor. 1.23; 2.1),[1] from where he sent Titus to
Corinth with 2 Cor. 2.14–6.13, 7.2-4. It is possible that Paul was
imprisoned in Ephesus at this time, and that he wrote Philippians or
substantial parts of it during his incarceration. The crisis in Corinth
meant that Paul was unable to take or send the collection to Antioch *en
route* for Jerusalem as planned (1 Cor. 16.3-4). Early in 55 CE, Paul
crossed to Macedonia, where he met Titus (2 Cor. 2.13; 7.5-7), who
reported a satisfactory resolution to the crisis in Corinth. Paul accordingly sent Titus back to Corinth to complete the collection there,
having previously despatched 2 Cor. 1.1–2.13; 7.5–8.24. Shortly
thereafter, when he was ready to leave Macedonia for Achaia, Paul
sent 2 Corinthians 9 to Corinth, and perhaps to other churches in the
region, announcing his own impending arrival. Paul probably spent
the winter of 55–56 CE in Corinth, from where he wrote Romans,
before proceeding to Jerusalem with the collection in the spring of 56
CE.[2] This was over a year behind schedule, and Paul was anxious
about his reception (Rom. 15.31). His arrest in Jerusalem in 56 CE or
shortly thereafter[3] effectively ended Paul's missionary work, so far as

    1. Cf. Barrett 1973: 85; Bultmann 1985: 45; Furnish 1984: 140; Martin 1986:
30.
    2. For more detailed treatment, see Taylor 1991a. For other reconstructions, cf.
Knox 1954: 86; Bornkamm 1961; Hahn 1965: 93; Marxsen 1968: 79-81; Georgi
1986: 15-17; Georgi 1965: 95; Barrett 1973: 8-12; Suhl 1975: 224-56; Jewett 1978;
Jewett 1979: 100-104; Furnish 1984: 26-35; Watson 1984; Sellin 1987: 2994-95.
    3. Arguments based upon the Acts records of Paul's encounter with Felix (Acts
24), and which date the latter's recall to 60 CE, such as Schürer (1973: 165-66),
cannot legitimately require a later date for Paul's arrival in Jerusalem. The date of

it is recorded. It is with this termination of Paul's freedom that this study ends.

It has not been possible to discuss fully all the chronological reconstructions of Paul's life. We have, however, identified a number of nodal events, in terms of which his career, and his relationships with the Jerusalem and Antioch churches, is to be understood. It is within this chronological framework that the development of Paul's relationships with the Jerusalem and Antioch churches, and their leaders, will now be considered.

Felix's recall is uncertain, and Schürer acknowledges that it may have been as early as 58 CE. Furthermore, Paul was not necessarily arrested immediately upon his arrival in Jerusalem. The date calculated here for Paul's arrival is therefore entirely plausible, and the contrary argument leans too heavily upon conjecture derived from Acts.

Part I

PAUL'S CONVERSION AND THE BEGINNINGS
OF HIS CHRISTIAN CAREER

Paul's Christian career can be divided into a number of distinct
phases, between certain watershed events, which influenced changes
and developments in his relationships. These events cannot be assumed
to have been the sole causes or occasions of fluctuation in Paul's
relationships, but are nevertheless important indicators of reorientation in Paul's life, which in turn would have influenced, and perhaps
even have determined, his relationships. In this study, we are
concerned with the period in Paul's life between his conversion (c. 35
CE) and his arrest in Jerusalem, which effectively ended his missionary career (c. 56 CE). We need to be constantly aware that we are
dealing with dynamic relationships involving living people and communities, and not with any static network of relationships. We need
therefore to focus our attention separately on the successive phases in
Paul's Christian career, and in Part I we shall be paying particular
attention to that period in Paul's life between his conversion and his
joining the church of Antioch.

Chapter 1

PAUL'S CONVERSION AND ASSOCIATION
WITH THE CHURCH OF DAMASCUS

The period following Paul's conversion is very sparsely documented.
We know from Gal. 1.18 and 2.1 that the period in Paul's life concluding with the Jerusalem conference lasted for more than a decade,
and possibly for substantially longer. Galatians, as argued in the Introduction, was written during a very different, later, phase in Paul's
life, and his perceptions of his own past are shaped by subsequent
events and their effect on his vocational consciousness. This is a factor
of which previous scholarship has not been sufficiently aware. In
particular, Paul's portrayal of the course of his life as predetermined
(Gal. 1.15-16) has led to assumptions about the events surrounding
and following his conversion, and meant that a number of factors
pertaining to that event have been overlooked, and the diversity of
possible responses to his experience available to Paul has not been
recognized. In order to recognize that there was no inevitability in
the direction of his subsequent career, and to appreciate more fully
the significance of the church of Antioch in Paul's Christian life, it is
necessary that these issues be explored in this chapter.

Other than the very brief allusions in Gal. 1.16-17, our only information on the beginnings of Paul's Christian career is the account in
Acts 9.3-19, and repeated with variations in 22.3-21 and 26.9-23.
Such allusions as there may be in 1 Cor. 15.8, 2 Cor. 4.1-2 and
Phil. 3.3-11, while reflecting Paul's 'highly retrospective' (Gager
1981: 699) meditations on his conversion related for particular
rhetorical purposes, contain no historical information that could be of
use in our present purpose. Acts dates from even later than Galatians,
and, even if less personalized than Paul's first-hand account, the
problem of anachronism is somewhat greater. In this chapter, therefore, we are dependent upon accounts that have been reinterpreted to

serve later polemical and ecclesiological purposes. We must nevertheless seek to discern the historical reality behind the theological and
legendary elaborations in the texts.

1. *The Circumstances of Paul's Conversion*

Any discussion of Paul's conversion is complicated by considerations
determined by the subsequent history of the Christian church. Paul's
importance in the theology of the Protestant reformation has served to
entrench the historical naivety of previous generations. Uncritical
acceptance of the dramatic accounts of Paul's conversion, and more
especially of his own assertions that he was uniquely set apart for the
mission to the Gentiles, and became *the* apostle to the Gentiles from
the moment of his conversion (Gal. 1.15; Rom. 1.5), still prevails in
New Testament scholarship.[1] Paul's identification of God's purpose in
the revelation of Christ to him as that he should proclaim the gospel to
the Gentiles (Gal. 1.16) has led a number of scholars to question the
applicability of the concept of conversion to this event. Munck has
drawn attention to analogies between Paul's account of events and the
vocational experiences of the Old Testament prophets (1959: 11-35).
Stendahl has taken this argument further, and asserts that Paul's
experience was not a conversion, but a vocation to apostleship (1976:
7).[2] Conversion implies a change of religion, and therefore is not
applicable to Paul (1976: 11). This last assertion is in itself question-
begging, in that it raises the question of how and when Christianity
separated from Judaism, to which there is no simple answer. It is clear
that 'Paul did not leave Judaism entirely in becoming a follower of
Jesus' (Segal 1986: 103). Nevertheless, 'as a result of his experience at
Damascus...what he had formerly regarded as blasphemous he now
recognized to be God's will' (Walter 1989: 77). To define conversion
simply in terms of a radical change in religion is to impose narrow,
and somewhat anachronistic, constraints upon the concepts both of
religion and of conversion, as Straus has demonstrated (1979: 163).
Thouless has shown that conversion can take the form of reorientation

1.   Hahn 1965: 97; Georgi 1965: 22; Bornkamm 1971: 26-27; Dietzfelbinger
1985: 60; McLean 1991: 67.
2.   Cf. Betz 1979: 64-69; Kim 1981: 55-66; Fredriksen 1986: 16; Dunn
1987: 90.

from a conventional religiosity to a more intense or mystical form of the same religion (1971: 104-20),[1] and this may reflect the experience of all Jews who became Christians during this period. There can be no doubt that Paul's experience involved radical reorientation, or transformation as Gaventa prefers to call it (1986a: 40), with profound implications both for his beliefs and his subsequent career, and that it ultimately brought him into a different religious community (cf. Segal 1990: 300). The social aspect of religious conversion is of crucial importance, as Straus has shown (1979: 163). Sandmel's notion of 'conversion within Judaism' (1958: 63) is somewhat more satisfactory than Stendahl's denial that Paul experienced conversion, and it must be acknowledged that 'Paul was indeed a convert in the modern sociological definition of the word' (Segal 1986: 103; cf. James 1902: 12-14). It is with Paul's conversion that we are at present concerned. The close association, if not identification, of conversion and vocation in the records, it will be argued below, reflects Paul and Luke's subsequent perceptions in the light of later Christian experience.[2]

Both Paul (Gal. 1.12, 16) and Luke (Acts 9.3-8; 22.6-11; 26.13-18) are unequivocal in according the Jerusalem church and its leadership no part in Paul's conversion. This event, with its vocational overtones, anachronistic or otherwise, took place in the context of a revelatory experience,[3] and has become 'the verbal and imaginative pattern which ever since has typified sudden and complete conversion' (Krailsheimer 1980: 12). The medical particulars of this experience are incidental to its phenomenological significance for Paul's life, and the course of Christian history,[4] and need not concern us here. According to the Acts accounts Paul's conversion took place when he was on his way to Damascus in the course of his persecuting activities (9.3; 22.6; 26.12). That the event took place in or near Damascus, would seem to be confirmed by ὑπέστρεψα in Gal. 1.17 (cf. Lüdemann 1989: 114), but this does not confirm the detail of Luke's account.

1. Cf. Snow and Machalek 1983; Gaventa 1986a: 40; Segal 1986: 103; Taylor 1991b.
2. Cf. Lohfink 1976: 89; Segal 1990: 8.
3. Stuhlmacher 1968: 76-79; Bowker 1971: 159, 167-69; Rowland 1982: 375; J.J. Collins 1984: 208; Dunn 1990: 90.
4. For medical and psychological treatments, see James 1902: 14; Sargant 1957: 106; Callan 1986.

The fundamental distinction between the accounts of Luke and Paul, so far as this study is concerned, is not so much the discrepancy between visual (Gal. 1.16)[1] and auditory (Acts 9.4-6; 22.8-10; 26.14-18) aspects of the revelation, since these are stylized.[2] What is significant is that Luke recounts how Paul was directed in his audition to await further instructions once he had reached Damascus (Acts 9.6; 22.10). These directions, the vocational aspect of Paul's conversion experience, came to Paul through the mediation of Ananias (Acts 22.14-15; cf. 9.17). Paul is unambiguous, even if anachronistically so, that neither his conversion nor his vocation to apostleship was the result of human action (Gal. 1.2, 11-12).[3] Acts 26.15-18 may indicate that Luke saw no contradiction between direct revelation and human mediation,[4] but the vehemence of Paul's assertion is not to be ignored. We need not suppose that Paul received in his conversion experience every aspect of the Christian doctrine to which he gave his assent and which he was to preach,[5] but we nevertheless need to recognize that Gal. 1.15-16 excludes all human communication (Burton 1921: 55). The meaning of his conversion experience was contained in the revelation itself and required neither the confirmation nor the interpretation of any human authority (Dunn 1982: 463; cf. Bowker 1971: 172).

The question of the role of Ananias is crucial, especially in the light of the vehemence of Paul's assertions that would seem to exclude him from the story as it is related in Acts. Wilson has argued convincingly that Ananias is not a Lukan invention, as he could have attributed his role to a more eminent personage, had he so wished (1973: 164; cf. Lohfink 1976: 86). Luke does not, however, describe Ananias as a leader in the Damascene church, although he enjoys the respect of the Jewish community (Acts 22.12). Furthermore, if Luke had found it necessary to create a character for his story, he would not have given

1. Cf. 1 Cor. 9.1; 15.8. These visions are cited in the context of Paul's apostolic vocation rather than of his conversion, and may therefore not allude to the same experience. See Chapter 2 for further discussion.

2. Rowland 1982: 375; Gaventa 1986a: 90. Cf. Beckford 1978 for sociological treatment of this question.

3. See Burton 1921: 37-38 for discussion of the precise meaning of κατὰ ἄνθρωπον.

4. Cf. Klein 1961: 146; Lohfink 1976: 86-87; Gaventa 1986a: 42-92.

5. Gerhardsson 1961: 273; Fuller 1971: 27-29.

him the same name as the villain of the Acts 5.1-11 pericope, especially so soon in the narrative after that event, and thus have invited
unfavourable associations in the minds of his readers. We must therefore conclude that Ananias was a historical character who played a
role in Paul's life about the time of his conversion or shortly
thereafter.

Paul provides no detail at all in his allusion to his conversion experience in Gal. 1.16, other than that it took the form of a christophanic
vision. The omission of Ananias is therefore not necessarily any more
significant than that of any other details of the occurrence. Wilson
may, however, be correct in arguing that Paul was anxious not to
encourage a distorted version of Ananias's role currently circulating
(1973: 162). If that were the case, then οὐ προσανεθέμην σαρκὶ καὶ
αἵματι (Gal. 1.16) may refer specifically to Ananias. Any mention of
Ananias in Gal. 1.11–2.14 could have undermined Paul's claim to
have received both the gospel he preached and his apostolic vocation
without human mediation. Any subtlety of distinction between
Ananias's having been the interpreter of Paul's conversion and his
having been the mediator thereof would also have weakened the
argument. The possibility, however, needs to be considered that Paul's
encounter with Ananias was not the immediate sequel to his
conversion, and therefore not relevant to Gal. 1.16.

It is quite probable that Ananias was instrumental in Paul's being
received into the church at Damascus, despite his past record of persecution, as Luke indicates (Acts 22.12-16; cf 9.17-19).[1] There can be
little doubt that Paul was baptized at some stage,[2] and Dunn argues
that his conversion would not have been complete without initiation
(1970: 78). This assumes, however, that, at the time of his conversion,
Paul already knew baptism to be an essential Christian initiation rite
(cf. Segal, 1990: 27). The assumption that Paul sought baptism
immediately after his conversion contradicts both his own account and
that of Luke. According to the Lukan account, Paul did not undergo
baptism until directed to do so by Ananias (Acts 22.16), and Paul
states quite unambiguously οὐ προσανεθέμην σαρκὶ καὶ αἵματι
(Gal. 1.16). The question therefore remains whether Paul's reception

1. Dunn 1970: 73-78; Hengel 1979: 84.
2. Rom. 6.3; 1 Cor. 12.13. The first person form clearly implies that Paul himself had undergone Christian baptism.

into the church at Damascus was the immediate sequel to his conversion. We cannot assume that the extended conversion–initiation–vocation experience which Luke recounts accurately records a single episode in Paul's life (cf. Dunn 1970: 73-78; Gaventa 1986a: 23). The stylized portrayals of Acts (Gaventa 1986a: 42-92) may reflect accurately what was regarded as the normative conversion–initiation experience in the early Christian communities with which Luke and/or his source were familiar, albeit embellished with distinctive vocational aspects and reflecting anachronistic perceptions of Paul's importance in the early Church (cf. Lohfink 1976: 87). Paul's own testimony, however, does not justify the assumption that what became normative in fact had applied in his own extraordinary case. The conceptual unity of the early Christian conversion–initiation experience[1] does not, and cannot, imply that every such episode followed a uniform pattern. We must therefore consider Paul's specific experience in its own right, and according to his own testimony, without presupposing any paradigm regarded as normative in later Christian communities. The chronological order which Gal. 1.16-17 seems to suggest by εὐθέως...ἀπῆλθον εἰς ᾿Αραβίαν καὶ πάλιν ὑπέστρεψα εἰς Δαμασκόν is that Paul went to Arabia before making contact with the church at Damascus (cf. Hengel 1979: 84). This is a question to which we shall return when we have considered the period Paul spent in Arabia.

To recapitulate, therefore, the records of Paul's conversion consistently indicate an apocalyptic vision or audition, and not the evangelistic activity of the primitive Church, as the medium by which he received the gospel. Paul closely associates his apostolic vocation with this revelatory experience, while Luke attributes to Ananias the mediation of Paul's apostolic vocation.

2. *Arabia and Damascus*

We are not concerned so much with the geographical location of 'Arabia'[2] as with what Paul did there. There are two principal views of this question in contemporary scholarship. The first is that Paul withdrew into the wilderness for the purpose of contemplative

---

1. Rom. 6.3-11; 1 Cor. 6.11; 12.13; 2 Cor. 4.2-6.
2. See discussion in Lightfoot 1890: 88-89; Burton 1921: 57-58; Betz 1979: 74.

preparation for his subsequent work. The second view is that he began his missionary work in Arabia. A third possibility, not seriously considered in previous scholarship, is that Paul intended eremitic life in Arabia as a means to maintaining ritual purity in anticipation of the eschaton, or for some other purpose. Paul does not mention in Gal. 1.17 what he did in Arabia, or how long he stayed there, even though explicit evidence could have strengthened his argument. As Luke makes no mention of this episode at all, the sequence of events in Acts must be considered later.

Burton argues that Paul's time in Arabia was 'not a missionary enterprise but a withdrawal from contact with men'. He regards the former possibility as psychologically improbable, an issue to which we shall need to return subsequently. Rather, he argues that Paul undertook a period of prolonged contemplation of the implications of his conversion experience (1921: 55-57). This view is shared by Gerhardsson, who suggests that Paul's purpose was to rid himself of an old body of knowledge in order to prepare himself for a new task, which would involve taking on a new body of knowledge (1961: 289). While the texts Gerhardsson cites in support of his thesis (*b. 'Abod. Zar.* 19ab; *b. B. Meṣ.* 85a) are very late, the practice of solitary retreat into the wilderness is attributed to Elijah (1 Kgs 19.4-18), and therefore cannot have been unknown in Israel since before the Exile. Furthermore, the Synoptic Gospels depict Jesus in the wilderness between receiving baptism from John and the commencement of his public ministry (Mt. 4.1-11; Mk 1.12-13; Lk. 4.1-13). While we may wish to question the historicity of Matthew and Luke's portrayal of this episode in Jesus' life, we have no reason to doubt that such a retreat took place, and still less that it was a known religious practice of the time.

A larger number of scholars[1] assert that Paul went to Arabia for the purpose of mission. This view is all but a necessary corollary to that which perceives Paul as the apostle to the Gentiles from the moment of his conversion. The evidence for or against such a mission is minimal, and defies certainty. The fact that there is no record of any churches founded by Paul anywhere that might be described as 'Arabia' cannot be taken as conclusive evidence against a mission

---

1. Stuhlmacher 1968: 84; Bornkamm 1971: 27; Betz 1979: 74; Bruce 1982a: 96; Lyons 1985: 159.

there. Burton's objection that such activity on Paul's part so soon after his conversion is psychologically improbable is not to be lightly dismissed, but is at the same time too deterministic simply to be accepted without question. Psychological probability is a hazardous criterion on which to base speculation about historical events, as there is seldom, if ever, only one way in which human beings can respond to any particular experience. While the option of withdrawal, for a variety of purposes and durations, would certainly have been one which Paul could have considered, it would not have been the only one, and Gager has noted the resort to evangelism as a means of resolving cognitive dissonance after religious conversion (1981: 702).[1] Withdrawal, furthermore, would not necessarily have been for the purpose of preparation for subsequent evangelistic activity, which raises a third possibility.

An option which would have been available to Paul, but which has not been seriously considered in modern New Testament scholarship, is that of permanent withdrawal from society, either as a hermit or as a member of a community that had separated itself from the surrounding society. Were it not for the assumption that Paul became an apostle immediately upon his conversion, this possibility may well have enjoyed serious consideration. Both individual and communal withdrawal are attested in the Judaism of the period. The hermits Bannus (Josephus, *Life* 2) and John the Baptist (Mt. 3.1-4; Mk 1.2-8; Lk. 3.2-6; Josephus, *Ant.* 18.5.2), and the communities of Essenes (Philo, *Omn. Prob. Lib.* 12.75, 76; Josephus, *War* 2.8.2-13) and Therapeutae (Philo, *Vit. Cont.*), and probably many others, lived a life that was well-known, and recognized as religiously significant. Had Paul chosen a similar eremitic existence, therefore, he would have had precedents and models from within the Jewish apocalyptic tradition for a life of eschatological anticipation on or beyond the fringes of society.

The aftermath of religious conversion has not received due attention in the psychology of religion. The findings of Starbuck indicate a variety of possible responses and reactions to the conversion experience (1914: 118-20). The cognitive dissonance theory developed by Festinger (1956, 1957, 1964) would seem the most appropriate paradigm for analysing the post-conversion situation, and Gager and

---

1. Cf. Festinger 1956; Festinger 1957; Snow and Machalek 1983: 276.

Segal have previously applied the insights derived thereby to Paul.[1]
Gerhardsson's depiction of Paul discarding an old, Pharisaic, body of
knowledge in order to take on a new, Christian, set of ideas (1961:
289) bears a striking resemblance to the process of dissonance reduction. This is not to suggest that Paul divested himself of all his
Pharisaism, but rather that he redefined it in accordance with his
Christian convictions, or at least began the process of doing so (cf.
Festinger 1956: 264; 1964: 64). Other of the possible techniques of
dissonance reduction[2] may not have been feasible. Paul's persecuting
activities would not have made the Christians of Damascus receptive
to his overtures, so he may not have been able to join a group that
shared his convictions, and be integrated into it and derive a new
dyadic identity from this social reorientation (cf. Malina 1979; Straus
1979). Proselytization would not have been possible until Paul had
sufficiently reordered his mind to his new convictions to attempt
converting others (cf. Gerhardsson 1961: 289; Dunn 1970: 76).[3]
Recourse to solitude rather than resocialization may therefore have
been Paul's only practicable option for dissonance reduction.

How Paul's time was spent in Arabia, and how long he originally
intended to stay there, must remain largely uncertain. A period of withdrawal from society for the purpose of contemplation of his recent
conversion experience and reordering his mind to his new convictions
would seem particularly plausible in the light of cognitive dissonance
theory. This view may be supported by Gal. 1.17, to the extent that
Arabia is contrasted to Jerusalem, in which case Paul, instead of consulting authoritative Christian leaders in Jerusalem, sought further
divine guidance and inspiration in Arabia. Whether Paul envisaged his
withdrawal as preparation for an evangelistic career, or the latter was
the outcome of his meditations, is unclear. However clearly Paul sees
the course of his life as having been predetermined at the time of writing Gal. 1.15-17, it is most improbable that he sensed such certainty at
the time of these events. In order to consider these questions, and
relate them to the issue of Paul's relationships with other Christians,
we need to return to the question of chronology raised previously.

1. Gager 1981: 702; Segal 1990: 295-300.
2. Festinger 1956: 264-66; Jecker 1964; Walster 1964.
3. For social-scientific treatments of analogous phenomena, see reports of
Festinger's collaborators, 1964: Allen; Canon; Jecker; Walster.

According to Acts 9.20, Paul, within a few days of his conversion, ἐκήρυσσεν τὸν Ἰησοῦν ὅτι οὗτός ἐστιν ὁ υἱὸς τοῦ θεοῦ. κηρύσσω can mean 'to acknowledge publicly'[1] rather than specifically 'to preach', and the text could indicate merely that Paul announced, and perhaps explained, in the synagogues his conversion to Christianity. If this took place before he went to Arabia, it would indicate that Paul had already joined the Damascus church (Dunn 1970: 73-78), and would have shared whatever relationship that community may have had with the Jerusalem church. Paul makes no mention of this, however, and it is not what he seems to indicate in Gal. 1.17. If Lightfoot, Burton and Longenecker are correct in arguing that εὐθέως (Gal. 1.16) governs the three following phrases,[2] including ἀλλὰ ἀπῆλθον εἰς Ἀραβίαν (Gal. 1.17), then Paul's immediate response to his conversion was to travel to Arabia. This view would be strengthened further if εὐθέως has connotations of directness as well as of immediacy (cf. Liddell and Scott 1940: 716). If this was the case, then Paul went to Arabia without having formed any relationship with any Christian community. It would have been when he returned from Arabia that Paul first made contact with the church in Damascus, perhaps through the mediation of Ananias, as suggested above (cf. Hengel 1979: 84). His preaching in the synagogues (Acts 9.20-22) would then have belonged to the stage in his life subsequent to his return to Damascus (Gal. 1.17).

Acts 9.18b-26 makes a plausible sequence of events, which is consistent with that of Gal. 1.17b-18a. Luke omits Paul's journey to Arabia, and it is incompatible with the narrative of Acts 9 as it stands. A journey to Arabia (however that region be defined) after Paul's time in Damascus, is most unlikely if the circumstances of his departure in Acts 9.25 were those indicated in 2 Cor. 11.32-33, in which case it is more likely that Paul would have fled from, and not into, the Nabataean kingdom. Paul's journey into Arabia must therefore predate his time in Damascus. This would be consistent with Gal. 1.16-17, which indicates that Paul's immediate response to his conversion experience was to avoid human contact, and to travel to Arabia.[3] His

1.   Bauer 1957: 432; Bauer 1988: 878; cf. Friedrich 1939: 703.
2.   Lightfoot 1890: 83; Burton 1921: 53-55; Longenecker 1990: 33. For the contrary view, see Betz 1979: 72.
3.   While the aorist tense of the relevant verbs in Gal. 1.16-17 does not exclude

subsequent return to the city in whose vicinity his conversion had taken place would have been the prelude to his involvement with the Christian community there.

After an overtly individual conversion experience, independent of any Christian missionary or community and involving the acceptance of no authority other than that which derived from his experience, Paul returned to Damascus and sought membership of the Christian community there. The social integration would have involved acceptance of the relationships and authority which being a member of a community requires. Cognitive dissonance theory can usefully illuminate Paul's decision. Festinger identifies as two possible courses of action to reduce dissonance, seeking confirmatory information, and the company of people who also hold firmly to the dissonant convictions (1956: 164-165). If solitary contemplation had not resolved the tension between Paul's Pharisaic and Christian convictions, he would have been impelled to seek further information, available only from a Christian community. The social support of other Jewish Christians would not only have expedited reduction in Paul's post-conversion dissonance, but social integration into their community would have provided him with a new dyadic identity.[1] If the suppression of Christianity had been a correlative obligation of Paul's Pharisaism, then his conversion would have alienated him from his social base, and group embeddedness, within his particular strand of Judaism. His conversion was not through the agency of any Christian evangelist, and therefore did not provide immediate entry into a community that could have been the basis of his new self-identity and social integration. The consequence of Paul's conversion would therefore have been isolation and lack of social identity, until such time as he joined a Christian community (cf. Malina 1979: 128). Berger and Luckmann express this need for social integration as a corollary of

the possibility that Paul engaged in missionary work in Arabia, while based in Damascus, to which place he returned on several occasions, this does not appear to be what Paul is saying. The implication, in the context of Paul's account of his career, would seem to be that Arabia and Damascus represent two consecutive stages in Paul's life. Had the contrary been the case, Paul would surely have expressed himself differently, in terms of working in Damascus and Arabia, with similar phrasing to that with which he refers in Gal. 1.21 to his period working in Syria and Cilicia.

1. Cf. Festinger 1964: 64; Jecker 1964: 66.

Paul's conversion: 'Saul may have become Paul in the aloneness of religious ecstasy, but he could *remain* Paul only in the context of the Christian community' (1966: 158). I would suggest that it was for this purpose that Paul returned to Damascus, as recorded in Gal. 1.17.

Ananias would appear from the Lukan accounts to have played a crucial part in Paul's integration into the Christian community in Damascus (Acts 9.10-19; 22.12-16). The details of the two narratives vary regarding the role of Ananias. While this may affirm that he indeed played an important role in Paul's life during this period, it also means that we cannot be certain as to what this role entailed, and questions about both accounts remain unanswered.[1] For the present, therefore, I shall omit Acts 9.10-19a and 22.12-16 from our reconstruction, and return to them subsequently. This provides a gap in the narrative into which Paul's journey to Arabia could plausibly be placed, immediately after his conversion experience recorded in Acts 9.3-5. In omitting the journey to Arabia, if he was aware of it, Luke is able to portray Paul's conversion–initiation experience as a single event, in close conformity to what was normative in the Church of his own day. If, however, I am correct in arguing that Paul's journey to Arabia was the immediate sequel to his conversion, then his conversion–initiation experience would have been more protracted, and his return to Damascus from Arabia would have been the occasion of Ananias's role in introducing him to the church by baptism (Acts 22.16; cf. Dunn 1970: 73-78), so enabling his social integration and acquisition of a new dyadic identity. This, and the transmission of Christian traditions,[2] would have enabled Paul to reduce his post-conversion dissonance. Ananias's mediating role may well also have included effecting reconciliation between Paul and the community he had persecuted, or intended persecuting (Hengel 1979: 84).

If this reconstruction is correct, then Paul's initial response to his conversion experience was to withdraw from the area of Damascus for Arabia. We can assume that this would have involved a journey of some distance, however the boundaries of Arabia may be defined. While in Arabia, Paul contemplated the implications of his conversion, and in doing so began to reduce the cognitive dissonance between his Pharisaic and Christian convictions. On his return from Arabia,

1. Dunn 1970: 75; Wilson 1973: 162-65; Gaventa 1986a.
2. Cf. Fuller 1971: 28; Wilson 1973: 164.

this process was continued with Paul's reception into Christian fellow-ship in Damascus, where he remained for some time, possibly as long as three years (Fitzmyer 1968: 219). How he occupied himself is not recorded, except in so far as Acts 9.20-22 reflects this period in Paul's life. Those scholars who believe that Paul was the apostle to the Gentiles from the moment of his conversion would of course maintain that he was engaged in this work in Damascus (cf. Bornkamm 1971: 27). Others, however, would argue that at this stage Paul preached only to Jews (cf. Watson 1986: 29-30). Whatever the ethnic origins of his audience and converts, Paul undoubtedly gained a degree of notoriety in the community at large, to the extent that he was forced to flee the city to escape the agent of the Nabataean king (2 Cor. 11.32-33; cf. Acts 9.23-25). There is no reason to doubt that it was Paul's activities in promoting the Christian gospel which, directly or indirectly, incurred the wrath of the secular powers. This view would be confirmed, were the role attributed to the Jewish community in Damascus attested independently of Acts 9.23.[1] However, for the present purpose it is sufficient to note that Paul was actively involved in the life of the church at Damascus, from and in which he derived his dyadic identity. This would have entailed his accepting the authority and discipline that being part of a community involves, and, by extension, whatever relationship the Damascus church had at that time with the church in Jerusalem. Of the nature of this relationship, however, we have no record. While Paul would have shared in this corporate relationship, there is no indication whatever that he sought independent contact with the leaders of the Jerusalem community until his journey there, to which we shall direct our attention in the following chapter.

1.   On the function of this episode in Luke's narrative, see Petersen 1978: 83-85.

Chapter 2

PAUL'S INITIAL CONTACT WITH THE JERUSALEM CHURCH

Consideration of Paul's first contact with the Jerusalem church needs to take into account the nature of the sources, and in particular Paul's purpose in writing Galatians. Paul's relationship with the Jerusalem church at the time he wrote Galatians will be considered more fully in Chapter 6, and it is sufficient for the present to note that he was anxious both to emphasize his unity with, and his independence of, the Jerusalem church and its leadership (cf. Dunn 1982: 469). Paul's journey to and sojourn in Jerusalem, recorded in Gal. 1.18-19, has been identified with that of Acts 9.26-30, and both accounts must be considered.

I argued in the previous chapter that Paul's conversion did not immediately bring him into any form of Christian community. He subsequently joined the church at Damascus and it was some years after this that he made his initial contact with the Jerusalem church (Gal. 1.18). That this community occupied a central place in Christianity, is not disputed, however scholars may differ in their understanding of this centrality.[1] The fact that Paul moved from the outside towards the centre is potentially significant, especially in the light of the preoccupation of modern scholarship with his much-vaunted independence of the Jerusalem church in later life. Paul was at this stage in his life becoming increasingly, and not decreasingly, drawn into the life of the Church which he had previously persecuted.

Paul's reasons for travelling to Jerusalem at this stage need consideration. The theological significance of Jerusalem, bound up with its centrality in the Jewish religious tradition as well as in the events of the Christian gospel, was at least of potential significance for Paul's

---

1. This question is discussed at length in Holmberg 1978, with copious references to previous work. The debate therefore need not be rehearsed here.

journey. The narrative of Acts indicates that Paul's flight from Damascus took place immediately before his journey to Jerusalem (9.25-26), which could indicate that it was not entirely premeditated. Paul's intentions at the time are not recorded, but cannot be assumed to have been that subsequently given in Gal. 1.18. Whether Paul intended a brief visit, to become acquainted with Peter or for whatever reason, or whether, after fleeing Damascus, he wished to settle in Jerusalem, as Acts 9.26-28 may indicate, must remain uncertain. The widespread inference on the basis of Gal. 1.18 that a brief visit was all Paul intended assumes that the fifteen days Paul spent with Peter were coterminous with his stay in Jerusalem. Fifteen days' discussions with Peter are not incompatible with a sojourn in Jerusalem of considerably longer duration, and the length of Paul's stay cannot be determined on the basis of Gal. 1.18. Furthermore, if Acts 9.29-30 is correct in relating that Paul went to Tarsus after fleeing Jerusalem (cf. Lüdemann 1989: 119), this suggests that he had intended a longer stay in Jerusalem. A journey from Damascus to Tarsus via Jerusalem does not make geographical sense. This strongly indicates that Paul had definite reasons for going to Jerusalem, and that more than a brief visit was intended. Furthermore, if Paul was forced to flee Jerusalem (Acts 9.29-30) as he had fled Damascus, the implication would be that he had not envisaged leaving as soon, if at all. While the flight may confirm the relative brevity of Paul's stay in Jerusalem, it does not justify the assumption that his sojourn was coterminous with his discussions with Peter.

The reasons for Paul's decision to travel to Jerusalem must therefore remain unknown. If, however, the activities of the Jewish community in Damascus (Acts 9.23-25) were in any way the reason for Paul's being sought by the agent of the Nabataean king (2 Cor. 11.32), Jerusalem would not have been the obvious place to which to flee. In that case, Paul must have made a deliberate, and quite possibly theologically motivated, decision to travel to Jerusalem and to seek acquaintance with the leadership of the church there, and fellowship in the community over which they presided. While Paul may have been motivated by a sense of religious pilgrimage, he may also simply have moved to a place that he knew, and which was close to, but a safe distance from, that from which he had fled.

Paul's conversion would have been demonstrated by his membership of the Damascus church, and integration into a Christian community would have provided a social dimension to his Christian life. It would also have bestowed on Paul an unmistakably Christian identity in the eyes of his fellow Christians and other Jews. The Damascus church could verify Paul's conversion, and a letter from that community, if not the verbal repute of Paul's membership thereof (cf. Gal. 1.22-24), would have been able to establish some credibility for him with the Jerusalem church. If, as Acts 7.58, 8.1-3 indicates and ὁ διώκων ἡμᾶς in Gal. 1.23 may confirm, Paul's persecuting activities had taken place at least partly in Jerusalem (Hengel 1979: 74),[1] he may have felt it appropriate that he seek some form of reconciliation with that community. The fact of his having demonstrated the veracity of his conversion by joining and participating publicly in the life of the church at Damascus would have made a visit to the Jerusalem church feasible, especially if the former community had also been victim to his persecution. The eschatological and salvation-historical significance attached to the Jerusalem church would not therefore necessarily have been Paul's only motive for travelling there.

The only reason Paul gives for visiting Jerusalem is to meet Peter (Gal. 1.18), and that this was the only reason is asserted categorically by Hofius: 'Der Besuch in Jerusalem war von keiner anderen Absicht bestimmt als der, *Petrus* persönlich kennenzulernen' (1984: 85). His principal argument is that ἱστορέω implies no purpose other than making acquaintance (1984: 77-84), in which he opposes Dunn's argument that ἱστορέω implies the purpose of gaining information (1982: 465).[2] However, the significance of this encounter is not determined by the connotations of ἱστορέω, and a detailed discussion of the views of these two scholars is therefore not necessary. Irrespective of whether Paul was motivated by salvation-historical and related concerns in travelling to Jerusalem, the significance of the place and the church in the Christian tradition was unavoidable, and his meeting with Peter would have been meaningful only in the context of the Christian tradition to which they both adhered, and in which Peter enjoyed a particular pre-eminence (cf. 1 Cor. 15.5). Whether Paul's journey was undertaken in order to be near a place of eschatological

1. For the contrary view, see Conzelmann 1973: 61; Watson 1986: 27.
2. For an assessment of both Dunn and Hofius's arguments, see Walter 1989: 64-66.

Paul, Antioch and Jerusalem

significance, or to become a member of the community that bore
witness to the gospel events which had taken place there, or to
associate with a particular witness to those events who enjoyed pre-
eminence in that community, does not substantially alter the significance of the contact. The events, the community and the person
coincided (and not coincidentally) in Jerusalem, and could not have
been separated entirely from each other. In no sense was Peter a
person arbitrarily selected by Paul as a potential acquaintance.[1]
Furthermore, as a diaspora Jew, Paul would have known Jerusalem as
the focal place of national and religious life, and accordingly a place
of pilgrimage, and the place where he had studied the authoritative
texts and traditions of the faith (Hengel 1979: 82) for him now
radically redefined. He could not have been unaware of this when he
made this journey, whatever his reasons for going to Jerusalem, or
have failed to consider how the significance of Jerusalem for him had
been changed by his conversion (cf. Bowker 1971: 159, 167).

There can be little doubt that Peter was at the time of Paul's visit
the predominant figure in the Jerusalem church (Cullmann 1953: 39;
Schmithals 1971b: 85), and their encounter must be viewed in this
light. Paul had no relationship with Peter apart from their common
allegiance to Christ, and no reason to visit him other than in connection with the Christian gospel. For the purposes of their meeting,
therefore, Peter, and, for that matter, Paul, had no capacity other than
their respective standing in the Church. Their meeting in Jerusalem
must be understood in terms of the basis on which they related to each
other.

Gerhardsson's depiction of the first meeting of Peter and Paul as
that of two teachers exchanging ideas and interpretations of the traditions of their faith with the Torah conceptually between them (1961:
298), while undoubtedly somewhat stylized, forms a sound basis on
which to build an understanding of this event. It might perhaps be
argued that it was the Gospel rather than the Torah which stood
between Peter and Paul, but Gerhardsson's depiction of their meeting
is nevertheless helpful. Whatever Paul's initial purpose in travelling to
Jerusalem, he would certainly have sought to meet Peter and discuss
matters relating to the Christian gospel with him. If Paul had not yet
developed any distinctive or controversial theological ideas (Watson

1. Cf. Campenhausen 1969: 69; Betz 1979: 76; Hofius 1984: 85.

1986: 29),[1] or come to believe himself uniquely called to and endowed for apostleship to the Gentiles (Gal. 1.16; Rom. 1.5; cf. Dunn 1990: 89), he would not have had anything at stake in this encounter with Peter, as he relates was the case in his subsequent visit to Jerusalem (Gal. 2.2). It was common allegiance to Christ that brought Peter and Paul together, and it was in terms of the Christian gospel that they could relate to each other.

There can be no doubt that Peter was the senior partner to their discussions (Bruce 1968: 6). Paul was the one who had undertaken the journey and initiated the contact, and Peter occupied a position of undisputed pre-eminence in the Christian community. He was the primary, though not the only, custodian of the tradition of the Christian gospel (1 Cor. 15.3-5). While, at the same time, Paul was undoubtedly the more highly educated in *torah* and *halakhah*, it had been precisely on the basis of his understanding of his ancestral traditions that he had persecuted the Church. We cannot assume that Paul had at this stage the confidence in his Christian application of these skills which he displays in his letters written well over a decade later, and which he was to exercise in controversy with Peter at Antioch (Gal. 2.11-14). The tradition in terms of which he had defined his opposition to Christianity, and his skill in interpreting it, cannot but have been brought into question as a consequence of his conversion experience. Walter argues that Paul actively sought Peter's authoritative opinion in order to 'confirm to him that he was justified in appealing to the Lord Jesus as the authority for the course he was following' (1989: 78). While this may be both anachronistic and too specific, it is nevertheless clear that Paul had acquired convictions in terms of which his understanding of the Jewish tradition needed to be redefined. In Chapter 1 reference was made to Paul's need to reduce post-conversion dissonance, in which seeking appropriate information can play a significant role. Paul's encounter with Peter can in all probability be understood as a continuation of this process, in which greater familiarity with the Christian traditions, and with the people most closely associated with them, would enable him to diminish further the tension between his Pharisaic and his Christian convictions.[2]

---

1.   For the contrary view, see Hengel 1979: 86.

2.   For sociological treatment of analogous situations, see Davidson 1964; Jecker 1964.

Bornkamm's assertion that it is a 'fantastic idea' that Paul sought information he lacked, or anything else in which Peter was the recognized authority (1971: 28), is not supported by more recent scholarship. Dunn has shown that ἱστορέω means more than simply to make acquaintance with another person, and implies the definite purpose of making enquiries and gaining information (1982: 463-64). Whatever lexical grounds Hofius may have for disputing the connotations of the word (1984: 77-84), there can be no doubt that Dunn's interpretation correctly reflects the historical reality. Peter's acquaintance with Jesus was a source of authority, not in terms of personal status, but in terms of his memory of what Jesus had said and done (Gerhardsson 1979: 59), and to deny this is effectively to deny that the Christian traditions of which Peter was the primary custodian were relevant to his meeting with Paul. Dunn argues that it was information specifically about the pre-Easter Jesus that Paul sought from Peter (1982: 472). However, Peter was the primary witness to the resurrection (1 Cor. 15.5), and Fuller argues that Paul received the tradition of Christ's resurrection appearance to Peter and the twelve in these discussions (1971: 27-28). Given the comprehensive nature of Peter's authority and first-hand knowledge concerning Jesus, it is doubtful whether a distinction between the historical Jesus and the risen Christ would have been significant either to Peter or to Paul. This is not to deny that it would have been the historical aspects with which Paul was unfamiliar, especially if he had received the doctrinal traditions from Ananias in Damascus, as argued above (cf. Fuller 1971: 27-29), but the former were but part of a belief system which both parties would have understood as an integral whole.

Paul states that he spent fifteen days with Peter (Gal. 1.18). He may have stayed in Jerusalem for a considerably longer period, and perhaps have intended to remain longer, or even permanently.[1]

1. Rom. 15.19 may indicate that Paul preached the gospel while in Jerusalem. Dunn suggests that this verse refers to Paul's defence of the gospel of uncircumcision at the Jerusalem conference (1988: 863). It would seem more plausible, however, that, as with other places between there and Illyria, Paul is referring to preaching the gospel to non-Christians in Jerusalem. This sojourn would be a more likely occasion for such preaching (cf. Acts 9.29) than the conference visit, during which Paul would not have sought controversy with non-Christian Jews. This would not conflict with even the most literal interpretation of Gal. 1.22 (for discussion of which see below), as preaching to non-Christians would not necessarily involve

Whether his sojourn in Jerusalem was terminated on account of the
hostility of Hellenistic Jews, as Luke suggests (Acts 9.29-30), we
cannot be certain, and Paul does not supply any information on this.
However, Paul remained in Jerusalem at least for long enough to
acquaint himself with such traditions as Peter could impart and to
form a sound relationship with him (cf. Roloff 1965: 68). His claim to
have met none of the other apostles, except James the brother of Jesus
(Gal. 1.19), is therefore significant, irrespective of whether Gal. 1.19
implies that Paul recognized James as an apostle or not.[1] Whether or
not Paul's meeting with James was more than a courtesy visit (Dunn
1982: 465),[2] his claim to have met no one whom, at the time of
writing Galatians, he recognized as an apostle,[3] cannot be insignificant. Paul spent at least two sabbaths and two Sundays in Jerusalem
without encountering such people even in the context of worship. We
do not know enough about the worship patterns of the Jerusalem
church during this period to appreciate the full significance of the
limited scope of Paul's acquaintance with the Christian leadership in
Jerusalem. It may be that Paul worshipped with a Greek-speaking
congregation (cf. Acts 9.29), and that Peter and James were the only
leaders of the Palestinian Christians whose acquaintance he sought. If
Paul had intended a longer sojourn in Jerusalem (cf. Acts 9.30), however, his not having met other Christian leaders by the time of his
unpremeditated departure would not be so significant. If, however, he
had envisaged only a brief visit, which is the impression Paul intends
to convey in Gal. 1.18-19, then his not having acquainted himself with
other apostles, whomsoever these might have been, becomes significant, and we must now consider this matter.

Paul does not state that he chose not to see any other apostles, and
that leaves open the very real possibility that they chose not to see him
(cf. Acts 9.26-27). Hengel argues that this was the case, on account of
Paul's already controversial theological views and missionary policy

contact with Christians in the same place.

   1.   For discussion of this question, see Lightfoot 1890: 34, 35; Schmithals
1971b: 64-65; Trudinger 1975; Howard 1977; Betz 1979: 77-78; Longenecker
1990: 38.

   2.   Cf. Fuller 1971: 27-28, who argues that Paul received the tradition of the
resurrection appearance to James and all the apostles in this meeting.

   3.   See discussion of Paul's concept of apostleship in Gal. in Chapter 6 section 3
below.

(1979: 86). This, however, must surely be anachronistic, especially as there are no indications of controversy before Paul's subsequent visit to Jerusalem recorded in Gal. 2.1-10 (Watson 1986: 29).[1] If Paul had travelled to Jerusalem to acquaint himself with the church there, and his views had already been regarded as errant by the leadership, they would have chosen to meet him together, so as to be better able to impose their corporate authority on him.[2] It is more likely, therefore, that Paul's past record as a persecutor had made the Jerusalem church wary of him, and only Peter and James, of those whom he subsequently recognized as apostles, were willing to meet him.

Our reconstruction of Paul's initial contact with the Jerusalem church is complicated by his statement that he remained ἀγνοούμενος τῷ προσώπῳ to the Christian communities in Judaea (Gal. 1.22). Paul does not say whether or not Jerusalem is to be included in these churches, but the majority of scholars favour inclusion.[3] If this is the correct interpretation, and is historically accurate, it may indicate that Paul was snubbed by the Jerusalem church, but it cannot mean that he met no members of the Jerusalem church other than Peter and James.[4] The expression may imply that Paul did not form a personal relationship with the members of the Judaean churches (Wood 1955: 277). If so, this would apply primarily to Jerusalem as the place Paul specifically mentions having visited. However, especially if his visit was terminated prematurely (cf. Acts 9.29-30), the significance of the statement may lie in the fact that Paul did not become integrated into the Christian community in Jerusalem. His pre-conversion dealings

1.   If Paul had already become a controversial figure in the early Church, on account of his views on the Mosaic law or for any other reason, he would not have been chosen to represent the Antiochene church at the Jerusalem conference. See further discussion in Chapter 4 below.

2.   Cf. Trudinger 1975: 202, who argues that Gal. 1.19-24 implies that Paul met the apostles, but no other members of the Jerusalem church, on account of the circumstances reflected in Acts 9.26-27.

3.   Eckert 1970: 182; Betz 1979: 80; Bruce 1982a: 104. It is possible that Paul, unable to claim no acquaintance with the Jerusalem church specifically, makes a more general claim to no acquaintance with the Judaean churches in the interests of his rhetorical purpose in Gal. (for which see Chapter 6 section 3 below).

4.   Fuller 1971: 27-29 argues that Paul received the tradition of the resurrection appearance to the five hundred (1 Cor. 15.6) from one of their number during this visit to Jerusalem.

with the church may have left a legacy of distrust and suspicion (cf. Acts 9.26), which could be overcome only gradually. Winning the confidence first of Peter and James may have been a prerequisite to acceptance by the leadership and community as a whole. If this was the case, it would appear from Gal. 1.18 that the process had to be aborted after Paul's initial meeting with James. Paul's subsequent ability to discuss matters of controversy with the leadership of the Jerusalem church (Gal. 2.1-10; Acts 21.17-25)[1] indicates that at least the foundations for a sound relationship between him and the Jerusalem church were laid. While he may not have achieved full integration into the community, Paul would at least no longer be hindered in his dealings with the Jerusalem church by the legacy of his pre-conversion activities.

To summarize, therefore, Paul's initial contact with the Jerusalem church, while creating a relationship between them on the basis of common allegiance to Christ, did not result in his full social integration into the Christian community. Furthermore, if Paul had intended to settle in Jerusalem, he was, for the second time in a short period, homeless and a fugitive. There is no reason to doubt that the initial contact, through Peter and James, accomplished its purpose. Paul was presumably able to increase his understanding of the Christian gospel through apparently lengthy discussions with Peter, and perhaps to a lesser extent with James. While serving to reduce his post-conversion dissonance, the insights Paul gained through these encounters may have contributed to the further development of his thought in a direction that was, ironically, to bring him into conflict with Peter and James, on quite the opposite grounds to those which had impeded his acceptance into the Christian community in Jerusalem.

1. I shall be arguing in Chapter 4 that Paul participated in the Jerusalem conference, not in a personal capacity but as a delegate of the church of Antioch. The point I make here nevertheless stands, as the Antiochene church would not have included Paul in their delegation had his presence compromised their bargaining position with the Jerusalem church.

SUMMARY TO PART I

To sum up, in Part I we have considered the period in Paul's life between his conversion to Christianity and his association with the church of Antioch, to which Part II will be devoted. This is a phase in Paul's life of which very little is known, and probably very little can be known. It has, however, tended to be passed over too briefly in previous treatments of Paul and this has meant that assumptions about both his conversion and his later work have not been subjected to sufficient scrutiny. The uncertainties, of which many have been identified in these two chapters, have been overlooked, with the result that Paul's career has tended to be seen as an uninterrupted continuum from the moment of his conversion.

I argued that Paul's conversion had taken place without the agency of any Christian missionary or community and that his religious reorientation was therefore not accompanied by any social reintegration. Paul was therefore in a state of social dislocation until he joined the church in Damascus, which, I suggested, took place after rather than before his sojourn in Arabia. Joining the Damascus church completed Paul's conversion–initiation process, in the latter part of which Ananias appears to have played a significant role. Paul's social integration in Damascus provided him with a new dyadic identity and brought about a reduction in his post-conversion dissonance.

Paul was forced after a time to flee Damascus, and made his way to Jerusalem. How long a sojourn he intended there is not clear, but this contact was significant in that his discussions with Peter would have resulted in further reduction in his post-conversion dissonance and therefore further development in Paul's theological thinking. Paul did not become fully integrated into the Christian community in Jerusalem, however, before, according to Acts 9.30, he was forced once again to flee.

The evidence scrutinized above strongly indicates a very unsettled period in Paul's life in which any clearly formulated plans he may have had were liable to frustration. There is no evidence of Paul's having possessed a concrete self-conception as apostle to the Gentiles, but rather the impression of a convert seeking a new identity, and a new clarity of thought in terms of which the dissonance between old and new convictions could be reduced, and new goals and a new agenda set for a life, whose direction had changed radically and, despite any uncertainties, irreversibly. If this is not appreciated, then our understanding of the subsequent, and more fully documented, stages in Paul's life will be inadequate. It is my contention that Paul's apostolic formation was the product of his association with the church at Antioch, and was subsequently and radically transformed into the apostolic self-conception reflected in his letters in response to his break with that community in the aftermath of his confrontation with Peter.

Part II

PAUL'S WORK IN AND FROM ANTIOCH

In Part I we considered the period in Paul's life from his conversion to Christianity to his first subsequent sojourn in Jerusalem. According to the Lukan account Paul made his way from Jerusalem to Tarsus, his birthplace (Acts 9.30). It would appear, therefore, that after having within a short period to flee Damascus and Jerusalem, two cities with Christian churches, Paul sought refuge in his place of origin, and possibly with his family. Whether or not this was a time of 'retirement' (Lightfoot 1890: 303), the indications are that it did not last long.[1] Paul states that he went from Jerusalem to Syria and Cilicia (Gal. 1.21), the latter of which included Tarsus. However, Paul's principal base during this period of his life was Antioch where he worked in association with Barnabas (cf. Acts 11.22-26), and it is to this association, the importance of which is greatly underappreciated in New Testament scholarship, that we must now direct our attention.

1.   For the contrary view, see Conzelmann 1987: 75.

Chapter 3

BARNABAS AND PAUL, AND THE MISSION FROM ANTIOCH

According to Acts 11.25-26 it was on Barnabas's initiative that Paul left Tarsus to begin his lengthy association with the church at Antioch, during which their partnership evidently met with considerable missionary success (cf. Acts 13–14). The evidence of the events to be considered in the next chapters strongly suggests that the Antioch church was firmly bonded to the Jerusalem church, while exercising considerable independence of thought and practice, particularly with regard to association between Jews and Gentiles unhindered by the requirements of the Mosaic ritual purity laws, and especially in waiving the requirement of circumcision for Gentile converts to Christianity (cf. Lüdemann 1989: 139). I have already intimated in the Introduction that the Graeco-Roman institution of κοινωνία or *societas* provides a model whereby we can understand this relationship, and I shall argue in the following chapters that the disputes and controversies which ensued were resolved according to the conventions of such informal, but nevertheless contractual, relationships.

The relationship of κοινωνία is most apparent in Gal. 2.9, as has previously been recognized by Sampley (1980: 24-28). I shall argue, however, that Sampley errs in identifying this κοινωνία as a relationship between individuals. Hauck had earlier identified the relationship as one between Paul and all earlier Christian believers (1939: 808, 809), a view which is both too sweeping and mistaken in identifying the relationship as one between individuals. Haenchen has pointed out that the gathering, and therefore the agreement, concerned not the individuals mentioned but those whom they represented (1971: 466). It is in these terms that the events to be considered in these chapters are to be understood. The κοινωνία was between the churches of Jerusalem and Antioch, and not merely between the five individuals named in Gal. 2.9, as I shall argue more fully in the following chapter. The Jerusalem conference resolved the dispute within the framework analogous to, if not constituted by, a κοινωνία. While Paul gives the impression that this relationship was first formed at the Jerusalem conference (Gal. 2.9), there must already have been some mutually recognized basis upon which the problem could be addressed and resolved. While the κοινωνία was undoubtedly strengthened through the (apparently mutually satisfactory) resolution of the controversy, the relationship which provided the procedural framework for the discussion must already have existed (cf. Goppelt 1970: 75), in recognizable if embryonic form, well before the dispute that gave rise to the events to be discussed in the succeeding chapters.

From the time that Paul joined the Antioch church and derived his dyadic identity from membership of that community, he would have shared corporately in the relationship between his church and the Christians of Jerusalem, even if he was not personally involved in the contact between them. Notwithstanding his personal acquaintance with Peter and James, and others in the Jerusalem church, Paul's relationship with that community would have been participation in the κοινωνία between the Jerusalem and Antioch churches. With the exception of the misplaced reference in Acts 11.27-30 (12.25-26), there is no indication of direct contact between Paul and the Jerusalem church from his joining the church of Antioch until the Jerusalem conference.

Barnabas is associated both with the close contact between the Jerusalem and Antioch churches (cf. Acts 11.22-23) and with the independence of thought and practice in the Antioch community. He is described by Bornkamm as 'the apostle of Christianity without the Law to Antioch' (1971: 30) and Haenchen argues that it was he who made the decision to waive the requirement of circumcision for Gentile converts to Christianity in Antioch (1971: 370-72; cf. Holmberg 1978: 63). The significance for Paul and his subsequent work of this association with Barnabas is crucial, and its significance has not previously been sufficiently appreciated.

Whether Barnabas chose Paul to participate with him in the work of the Christian community in Antioch (cf. Acts 11.25-26) on the recommendation of the Jerusalem Christian leadership (Lightfoot 1890: 303), or precisely because these leaders would not have approved the work he was doing in Antioch (Knox 1925: 159), or on the basis of personal acquaintance (cf. Acts 9.27), or of reputation, we are not told. The suggestion of Knox, however, is most unlikely, as will become apparent in the discussion in the following chapters. According to Acts 13.1, Barnabas was pre-eminent among the leaders of the church in Antioch and, according to Acts 11.26, he formed a particular partnership with Paul.[1] We need to consider the development in this relationship from one within the church at Antioch (Acts 11.26; 13.1), but which did not necessarily exclude outreach to the local population, to one committed to mission beyond Antioch itself (Acts 13.2-4).

After the first year of their association spent in Antioch (Acts 11.26), Barnabas and Paul undertook evangelistic work in Asia Minor (Lüdemann 1989: 157). Acts 13–14 depicts this activity, illustrating the nature of their work as Luke saw it rather than recording the precise events (cf. Conzelmann 1987: 98). This is the first recorded occasion on which Paul functioned as an apostle and therefore requires particular consideration. With the exception of a text to be considered below, Paul gives no account of when he became an apostle (cf. Gal. 1.1, 16), and the widespread assumption defended most recently by Longenecker and McLean[2] that Paul's vocation to apostleship coincided with his conversion experience[3] has rightly been questioned by Dupont, Gaventa and Segal.[4] According to Acts 13.3 the Antiochene church ἀπέλυσαν Barnabas and Paul and, in the following verse, they are described as having been ἐκπεμφθέντες by the Holy Spirit. While it may be significant that ἀποστέλλω is not used in this pericope, Barnabas and Paul are nevertheless twice described as ἀπόστολοι in the narrative (Acts 14.4, 14) and they are depicted as performing in the course of their travels the work associated with apostleship in Paul's letters.[5] I would suggest therefore that Acts 13.4 represents the commencement of Paul's apostolic ministry, as the delegate of the Christian community in Antioch, accompanying

---

1. Holmberg 1978: 63; Lüdemann 1989: 138.
2. Longenecker 1990: 32; McLean 1991: 67. Cf. also Hahn 1965: 97; Georgi 1965: 22; Kim 1981: 55-66; Dunn 1990: 89.
3. Cf. also Stendahl 1976: 7-11 and others who assert that Paul's vision was a vocational, but not a conversion, experience.
4. Dupont 1970: 193; Gaventa 1986a: 11; Segal 1990: 8. Cf. also Best 1986: 6.
5. Acts 13.16, 41; 14.1, 3; cf. Rom. 1.5; 11.13; 1 Cor. 1.17; Gal. 1.16; Acts 14.8-10; cf. 2 Cor. 12.12.

Barnabas on the outreach of that community.[1] If the chronological calculations in the Introduction are correct, this would have taken place in c. 40 or 41 CE.

In 2 Cor. 12.2-4 Paul recounts in the third person an ecstatic experience which the majority of scholars attribute to Paul himself rather than to a third party.[2] 2 Corinthians 10–13 dates from c. 54 CE, almost exactly fourteen years after Paul's departure from Antioch.[3] While the majority of scholars have declined to identify it with any other recorded event in Paul's life,[4] others have ventured such identification. Giet understands 2 Cor. 12.2-4 as an allusion to the vision Paul mentions in Acts 22.17-21 which resulted in the commencement of Paul's apostolic ministry to the Gentiles (1957: 40-42; cf. Conzelmann 1963: 187-88). Zahn and Allo have located the vision of 2 Cor. 12.2-4 at Acts 11.25-26, Zahn suggesting that it prompted Paul to join Barnabas in Antioch, and Allo seeing a connection with the commencement of Paul's apostolic ministry.[5] The connection between 2 Cor. 12.2-4 and the beginning of Paul's apostolic ministry has therefore been recognized, but the connection with Acts 13.1-4 appears to have been suggested without attribution, only to be dismissed without consideration (Hughes 1962: 300-301; Martin 1986: 399). It is a possibility which merits fuller consideration, and I would suggest that 2 Cor. 12.2-4 represents Paul's individual recollection of the corporate experience related in Acts 13.2-3. Commissions received in the course of apocalyptic heavenly journeys, or accompanied by the revelation of cosmic secrets, are attested in the intertestamental literature,[6] which suggests that apocalyptic revelatory journeys were recognized as an appropriate context for vocational oracles in the Jewish world of the time. Since Paul had already received the Christian gospel, there is no contradiction between his

1. Cf. Mosbech 1948: 171; Schmithals 1971b: 90-91.
2. Knox 1954: 77, 78; Allo 1956: 303-305; Wilckens 1959: 274; Bowker 1971: 167; Barrett 1973: 307; Saake 1973: 154; Dunn 1975: 214; Schütz 1975: 236; Bultmann 1985: 219-220; Jewett 1979: 54-55; Lincoln 1979; Rowland 1982: 375; J.J. Collins 1984: 208; Lyons 1985: 69; Martin 1986: 390; Tabor 1986: 114; Halperin 1988: 6; Segal 1990: 35-38.
3. Cf. Lincoln 1979: 211. See discussion in Introduction, sections 4a and 5.
4. Hughes 1962: 300-301; Jewett 1979: 55; Martin 1986: 388-90; Segal 1990: 37-38.
5. Zahn 1909: 462; Allo 1956: 304-307.
6. *T. Lev.* 5.1-2; *1 En.* 81; *2 En.* 36.1-2; *4 Ezra* 14.1-18; *Jub.* 23.32; 49.22-23.

receiving cosmic secrets and a vocation to preach the Christian gospel. Paul, for whom ecstatic experiences were apparently frequent,[1] chose to cite a specific occasion, however obliquely,[2] which suggests that that experience was particularly significant for his rhetorical purpose in 2 Corinthians 10–13. Paul is defending his apostolic authority against rivals who had infiltrated the Corinthian church and ingratiated themselves with at least some of its members.[3] It is in this specific rhetorical context that Paul alludes to his vision.[4] One would therefore expect the vision cited to be directly relevant to Paul's apostolic vocation. Paul had come to see his apostolic vocation as integrally bound up with his conversion, but refrains in 1 Cor. 9.1, 15.8-9 and Gal. 1.16 from explicitly stating more than that the purpose of his conversion was that he should be the apostle to the Gentiles; he does not specifically identify the occasion of his conversion with the occasion of his apostolic vocation.[5] The close association between Paul's conversion experience and his apostolic vocation was, I shall be arguing, the product of his separation from the church of Antioch.[6] The independence of Paul's apostleship from human constraints required that his vocation be associated not with his contacts with the Jerusalem and Antioch churches, but with his conversion which preceded both. It is in identifying the former as the purpose of the latter, not in identifying the two events, that Paul asserts the independence of his apostleship. There is therefore no contradiction between Paul's stressing the unity of purpose between his conversion to Christianity and his vocation to Christian apostleship in such texts as Gal. 1.16, and his relating a vision which took place some years after his conversion in defence of his apostleship in 2 Cor. 12.2-4.

If I am correct in identifying Acts 13.1-4 as reflecting the commencement of Paul's apostolic ministry, then the importance of the

    1.   Bowker 1971: 159; Lincoln 1979: 211; Gaventa 1986a: 11.
    2.   Plummer 1915: 344; Betz 1972: 91; Barrett 1973: 308; Furnish 1984: 544; Tabor 1986: 37.
    3.   See further discussion of the situation in Corinth in Chapter 8.
    4.   Schweitzer 1931: 137; Lincoln 1979: 207; Rowland 1982: 379; Schäfer 1984: 23; cf. Hughes 1962: 429-30; Betz 1972: 72-75; Furnish 1984: 544; Tabor 1986: 21. For the contrary view, cf. Schütz 1975: 235; Baird 1984: 654.
    5.   Betz 1979: 71; Gaventa 1986a: 11; Segal 1990: 13.
    6.   See further discussion in Chapter 6 section 3.

Antioch church in Paul's Christian career becomes more apparent. It was from the Christian community in Antioch that Barnabas and Paul were sent out on their missionary work, and it was the gospel as lived and taught in Antioch that they would have preached. Most importantly, in contrast to Paul's later apostolic self-understanding (cf. Gal. 1.1), Barnabas and Paul were the apostles of a particular church, on behalf of which they carried out their particular functions. As the delegates of a community engaged in its apostolate they would have been accountable to the church that sent them (cf. Holmberg 1978: 64).

The Antioch church, therefore, seems crucial to understanding Paul's apostolic ministry. Not only did Paul's apostolic career begin under its auspices, but there are indications that the pattern and practices of his subsequent ministry continued to be influenced by the customs of the Antiochene church. As these include an issue that became crucial in Paul's later dealings with the churches he established, it is worth considering the matter further.

In 1 Cor. 9.6 Paul implies that he and Barnabas, alone of the apostles, did not draw economic support from the churches in which they were working (cf. 1 Thess. 2.7-9; 2 Cor. 11.7; 12.13-14). We would expect that this common practice originated in a community with which both were associated, and I would accordingly suggest that Barnabas and Paul's practice reflects the missionary policy of the church of Antioch during the period in which they exercised the apostolate of that congregation. Paul does not state in 1 Corinthians 9 what form the support Peter and the other apostles derived from the churches in which they worked took. Nor is it unambiguously clear from 2 Cor. 11.20 what Paul's opponents received, though 2 Cor. 12.18 may indicate that they took money. There is widescale wariness in the early Christian writings concerning financial payments to Christian workers, notwithstanding their equally widely recognized right to hospitality and subsistence.[1] It is not feasible here to discuss the origins of the various forms of the synoptic mission discourse and other relevant texts. While the origins of all have been located in or near Antioch at various stages of the scholarly debate,[2] they almost

---

1.   Mt. 10.8-10; Mk 6.8-9; Lk. 9.3-4; 10.4-5; 1 Cor. 9.4-5; *Did.* 11.6, 12; 13.1-2.

2.   Cf. Streeter 1930: 500-503; Kilpatrick 1946: 134; Leaney 1958: 3-4; Filson 1960: 15; Fuller 1966: 107, 115; Hill 1972: 51-52; Lohse 1981: 145; Kümmel 1975:

certainly reflect conditions subsequent to the period under discussion, and the later policy of the Antiochene church may well have been influenced by Peter (cf. Gal. 2.11-12). I would suggest, therefore, that the policy Paul reflects in 1 Corinthians 9, where the right to support is asserted in principle but not exercised in practice,[1] derived from that of the Antiochene church during the period of his association there, and indicates the continuing importance of this period in Paul's subsequent career.

There can be little doubt that Barnabas was the senior partner in the Antiochene apostolate, despite the fact that, at least partly on account of Luke's preoccupation with him, Paul is mentioned first on each occasion in the Acts narrative after the first episode (13.6-12), and Barnabas is frequently not mentioned at all. It is not inconceivable that Paul's (perhaps not always willing) subordination to Barnabas may have led to tension between the two of them and germinated the atmosphere in which a clash between them would later end their partnership (Gal. 2.11-14; cf. Acts 15.36-41). Nevertheless, Barnabas would have been the leader of the mission in the eyes of the Antiochene community that sponsored them, and which was later to support Barnabas against Paul (Gal. 2.11-14). Barnabas and Paul would both have been accountable to the community from which they had been sent out (Acts 13.1-3; cf. Holmberg 1978: 64), even if Barnabas himself, and, to a lesser extent Paul, held a position of pre-eminence in that community.

To sum up, therefore, Paul's life between his conversion to Christianity and his joining the Christian community in Antioch, as reconstructed in Part I, was unsettled and unstable. Membership of the Antiochene church provided him with a dyadic identity and with it stability and social support. He shared both in the corporate relationship of developing κοινωνία between his community and the church at Jerusalem, and in the freedom of Christian thought and expression exercised by the Antiochene Christians within that broader unity. Paul's apostolic work, I have argued, began during this period, when he was commissioned, along with Barnabas, for the evangelistic

119; Fitzmyer 1981: 53; Nickle 1981: 122; Brown and Meier 1983: 22, 53, 84; Niederwimmer 1989: 80.

1. Cf. the discussion in Introduction section 3a as to whether (Bierstedt 1954) or not (Friedrich 1958) authority can exist in a state of latency within a relationship without being exercised.

outreach of the Antiochene church beyond Antioch itself. The form this apostleship took is immensely important, as will become clearer in the discussion of Paul's later apostolic self-conception to be considered in Chapter 6. Developments independent of the Jerusalem church, which took place in Antioch during this period, cannot but have been formative for Paul's thinking and practice in his later work. It was these developments, and the reaction to them, that led to the crucial Jerusalem conference, the accounts of which provide our most useful insights into the relationships with which this book is concerned. It is the question of the continuing significance of the Mosaic law for Christians, and especially Gentile Christians, and attempts to resolve it, that must now be considered, insofar as they illuminate the issues with which we are concerned.

Chapter 4

THE QUESTION OF THE LAW, AND THE JERUSALEM CONFERENCE

It is generally accepted that, during the period prior to the Jerusalem conference, Paul worked with Barnabas in and from the church at Antioch. While the conference was undoubtedly a watershed in Paul's career, it would be anachronistic to assume that its consequences were fully apparent to Paul, or to anyone else, at the time. It was only after the subsequent confrontation between Peter and Paul at Antioch that Paul's association with Barnabas and the Antiochene church was ended. The Jerusalem conference therefore belongs strictly to the period in Paul's life when he was associated with the church at Antioch. However, the conference and the issues it discussed are of such significance as to require separate treatment, which is the purpose of this chapter.

In the Introduction, the gathering related by Paul in Gal. 2.1-10 was identified with that recounted by Luke in Acts 15.6-29. The prevailing scholarly consensus is that the 'Apostolic Decree' of Acts 15.19-20 and Acts 15.23-29 was not promulgated at this conference, but subsequently, and in Paul's absence. The 'Apostolic Decree' will therefore not be discussed in this chapter, but in an Excursus at the end of Part II.

A problem raised in the Introduction, and which is nowhere more apparent than with regard to this chapter, is that of the relative reliability of the primary sources, Acts and Galatians. Most scholars tend to prefer the latter text where discrepancies are detected and their position, as Betz sums it up, is that

> Paul's own account in Galatians 2 is that of a first-hand witness and it must have priority in case of doubt, but the circumstance and function of the defence in his letter to the Galatians have coloured his account (1979: 81).

Nickle expresses this view with less balance, describing Galatians as 'more trustworthy' than Acts, and citing the oath in Gal. 1.20 in support of this (1966: 41).[1] The very fact that it is a first hand account is cause for scepticism on a number of points, and the passage has rightly been described by Holmberg as 'tendentious' (1978: 14). Similarly, Mussner has recognized the 'gegenwärtigen Standpunkt' of Paul's account (1974: 131), and Räisänen has remarked that the 'naive trust on a man's testimony about himself is a curious fundamentalistic survival within critical scholarship' (1983: 232). Watson has unambiguously challenged the plausibility of Paul's account (1986: 53-56), while Holmberg has noted a tendency towards greater recognition of the historical reliability of Acts (1990: 65). Notwithstanding the critical problems surrounding Acts 15 (cf. Dibelius 1956: 96), there is no justification for uncritical acceptance of Galatians 2. I hope therefore to reconstruct the events, drawing on the evidence of both tendentious accounts, and subjecting them equally to rigorous critical scrutiny.

Linton has drawn attention to similarities between traditions reflected and opposed by Paul in Galatians 1–2, and those recorded in Acts.

> There exist perhaps certain affinities between an early representation of St Paul's person and activity, an account contested by the Apostle himself, and the later literary image drawn in Acts (1949: 80).

The corollary of this is that Paul's account of the events is not necessarily an older and more authentic tradition than that later incorporated into Acts. The parallels Linton identifies may or may not be convincing, but the principle nevertheless stands that the objective historical truth cannot be presumed to be recorded in any particular source, and the evidence of all available material must be critically examined in order to reconstruct the events as accurately as possible. This will be the approach taken in this chapter, as elsewhere in the study.

1. *Circumstances Giving Rise to the Conference*

Acts 15.1-2 relates that Barnabas and Paul travelled to Jerusalem from Antioch in order to discuss matters of Jewish observance that Judaean

---

1. Sampley 1977 argues that the oath is in fact a sign of weakness in Paul's argument.

Christians who had come to Antioch wished to impose on Gentile Christians. The circumstances mentioned by Luke may well be those reflected by Paul in Gal. 2.3-5. Watson accordingly argues that the events of Gal. 2.3-5 took place in Antioch before, and not in Jerusalem during, the conference (1986: 50-51).[1] Paul, however, indicates further matters, albeit not unrelated, which were discussed (Gal. 2.2, 6-10), and an apparently very different reason for going to Jerusalem than response to a crisis in Antioch (Gal. 2.2). We need therefore to consider further the reasons for the conference.

Baur asserts that the Jerusalem apostles had sent the Judaean teachers to Antioch to impose the Law (1878: 52), and Holl affirms that this was a claim on their part to oversight of the Antioch church (1921: 57). Burton, however, argues that Paul was seeking to avoid potential opposition to his projected work, rather than dealing with a crisis (1921: 72), but subsequent scholarship has tended to follow Baur and Holl. Hengel understands the visitation from Judaea as being symptomatic of the increasing legalism in the Jerusalem church at this time, in response to increased pressure from the Jewish community, not without nationalistic overtones, and accompanied by the ascendancy of James at the expense of Peter and the other disciples of Jesus (1979: 113).[2] Barnabas and Paul were sent to Jerusalem by the Antiochene church in response to this attack on what had been their practice for many years, as Hengel and Koester argue.[3] Watson argues further that Paul's own position in the Antiochene church was threatened on account of the activities of the Judaean Christians, and that referral of the question to Jerusalem was a gamble aimed at restoring his position (1986: 51).[4] While it would be anachronistic to distinguish too radically between Paul's position and that of Barnabas and other leaders of similar persuasion in the Antiochene church, Watson's reconstruction does account for Paul's regarding his entire work as at stake in his journey to Jerusalem (Gal. 2.2). The situation becomes clearer if a relationship of, or analogous to, a κοινωνία operated

1. Cf. Geyser 1953: 132 for a different interpretation.
2. For discussion of political conditions in Judaea, and their implications for the Christian community there, see Brandon 1957: 88-100; Jewett 1971: 202-206; Reicke 1984.
3. Hengel 1979: 114; Koester 1982: 105. Cf. Holtz 1974: 139, who argues that Barnabas and Paul sought consent for innovations they were contemplating.
4. See Dibelius 1956: 93 for a contrary view.

between the churches of Antioch and Jerusalem. The primacy of the Jerusalem church, as the more ancient and eschatologically more significant, and led by the principal witnesses to the gospel events, could not be ignored, and was not ignored by the Antiochene Christians (cf. Schütz, 1975: 138). It would therefore have been necessary that Barnabas and Paul reach agreement with the Jerusalem church and its leadership before the controversy became unmanageable. If the church at Antioch as a body was willing to submit to the demands of the Judaeans, then the authority of Barnabas in that community, at least as much as that of Paul, was threatened.

The immediate cause of Barnabas and Paul's travelling to Jerusalem was the activity in Antioch of Christians from Judaea (Acts 15.1), and probably specifically from Jerusalem, who represented a more legalistic, and particularistic, understanding of the gospel than had been the prevailing view previously both in Jerusalem and in Antioch. The Antiochene church had previously recognized the authority of the Jerusalem leaders, within their relationship of κοινωνία, and the community evidently was unwilling to ignore the views of teachers from Jerusalem at this time, despite the requirement that they abandon the practices which they had maintained for several years. A great deal more than the customs of one Christian community was seen to be at stake, so much so that Paul could state that he ἀνεθέμην ... τὸ εὐαγγέλιον ὃ κηρύσσω ἐν τοῖς ἔθνεσιν (Gal. 2.2). It was not so much a case of seeking belated approval (Betz 1979: 86), still less of discussing innovations in doctrine and discipline (cf. Holtz 1974: 139), but rather of defending the established customs and practices of the Antioch church which had been challenged for the first time. The future of the gospel as lived and preached in and from Antioch depended on the outcome of Barnabas and Paul's negotiations (cf. Schütz 1975: 139).

We need to consider, before discussing the conference itself, the precise nature of the demands made by the Judaean teachers in Antioch which, according to Acts 15.5, were shared by converted Pharisees in Jerusalem. The demand as recorded in Acts 15.1 was that ἐὰν μὴ περιτμηθῆτε τῷ ἔθει τῷ Μωϋσέως οὐ δύνασθε σωθῆναι. A similar requirement is reflected in Gal. 2.3-5. It would be a mistake, however, to understand the position of the Judaean Christians as simply requiring that Gentile Christians be circumcised. περιτομή is metonymous and connotes the Mosaic law as a whole, and Jewish nationhood, and not merely physical circumcision. Such usage is frequent both in Paul's letters and in Acts.[1] The wider connotations of περιτομή are reflected also in the demands of the Pharisaic Christians in Jerusalem (Acts 15.5). What was at stake in Antioch, therefore, was not simply the initiation procedures into the Church but the whole way of life of the community. Furthermore, for Jewish Christians circumcision would not have been part of the conversion–initiation process marking the beginning of a new life discontinuous with their old one, but rather a rite of passage that was part of the continuum of their national and cultural, as well as religious, life-cycle (cf. Eckert 1971: 53). Jewish Christians would therefore not have understood circumcision in terms of initiation, but in terms of the whole way of life of the covenant community (cf. Borgen 1983b: 88). This is not to deny that physical circumcision had acquired particular significance in Jewish religion and culture. The prohibition of the rite by Antiochus Epiphanes (1 Macc. 1.48) had elevated circumcision to the status of fundamental principle, worthy of martyrdom (cf. 1 Macc. 1.60-61), and it had accordingly become definitive for Jewish identity in a way that had not previously been the case.[2] This, however, is not to claim that there was complete unanimity on the place of circumcision in Jewish life during this period.

Jub. 15.33-34 indicates that for some Jews circumcision was no longer an essential rite. Philo would not have had occasion to assert the continuing obligation of physical circumcision (*Migr. Abr.* 92; *Spec. Leg.* 1.304-306), had the spiritual understanding of circumcision he advocates elsewhere (*Spec. Leg.* 1.1-11) not come to be regarded by some Alexandrian Jews as a substitute for the physical rite. In another context, the Babylonian Talmud records disagreement on the subject of proselyte initiation. R. Joshua argued that immersion alone was adequate, while R. Eliezer argued that circumcision alone was sufficient, but the consensus of the sages was that both rites were required (*Yeb.* 46a). Collins argues that the issue was not whether circumcision of proselytes was obligatory or not, but whether it was a requirement of becoming a Jew, or a consequent obligation (1985: 174). It should, furthermore, be noted that the view widely ascribed

---

1. Acts 7.8; 10.45; 11.2; Rom. 2.25-29; 4.9-12; 15.8; Gal. 2.7-9, 12; 5.2-6. For discussion of this issue, see Dunn 1988: 120.

2. Cf. Dunn 1988: 119; Cohen 1989: 27.

to Hillel that circumcision of proselytes was not obligatory in fact applies only to proselytes who were circumcised before conversion, and is ascribed by the tradition to the Beit-Hillel, and not to Hillel himself (*t. Šab.* 15.9; *b. Šab.* 135a). *Sib. Or.* 4.163-65 is interpreted by Meyer as advocating immersion in place of circumcision (1959: 79), but this seems most unlikely. The φάσγανα in line 164 are more likely to be the weapons of ἀνδροκτασίας τε καὶ ὕβρεις, mentioned in the same line, than the instruments of circumcision. The lustrations in rivers mentioned in line 165 are akin to the baptism of John and do not involve incorporation into any community (J.J. Collins 1983: 388; Collins 1985: 169). The question of proselyte initiation therefore does not arise. Epictetus (*Disc.* 2.9.19-21) may reflect an isolated situation where baptism was the only normative form of initiation into Judaism (cf. McEleney 1974: 332).

This fluidity on the question of circumcision in first century Judaism must, however, not be overemphasized. While the patterns of Gentile God-fearing varied considerably (cf. Cohen 1989), and while there were exceptions to the normative practice of circumcision of all male Jews, the 'irreducibly fundamental importance of circumcision' for the Jewish nation cannot be denied (Dunn 1988: 119).[1] Cohen has shown, furthermore, that not even circumcised proselytes could be assured of full recognition as Jews (1989: 29). Though it was perhaps the ultimate expression of conversion to Judaism, proselyte circumcision did not guarantee acceptance as a Jew. This raises questions as to the intentions of those who demanded circumcision of Gentile Christians and the significance they attached to the rite they demanded.

Paul makes no explicit reference to the circumcision question, except in the section Gal. 2.3-5. The phrase παρεισάκτους ψευδαδέλφους οἵτινες παρεισῆλθον (Gal. 2.4) clearly implies that the persons concerned were outsiders to the community, but nonetheless Christians, which strengthens the case for identifying them with the Judaean teachers in Antioch at Acts 15.1-2, rather than with any group within the Jerusalem church (Watson 1986: 50). Even assuming Watson to be correct, however, we need to consider Paul's assertion that he went to Jerusalem κατὰ ἀποκάλυψιν (Gal. 2.2). Whatever the nature of the religious experience which, Paul says, preceded his decision to travel to Jerusalem, there can be no doubt that the

---

1. Cf. McEleney 1974: 323; Berger 1977; Segal 1990: 194.

historical circumstances that gave rise to the journey were those in the Antiochene church discussed above. By citing a particular revelation as having occasioned his journey, however, Paul implies that this was a particular occasion, and not a precedent for further journeys to Jerusalem in which his authority and teaching would be subjected to the judgment of the Jerusalem church. Paul is claiming independent authority for his journey, rather than denying that it was occasioned by the ecclesiastical controversy in Antioch (Betz 1979: 85).

The fact that Paul found it necessary subsequently to deny having been summoned to Jerusalem may indicate that it was the suggestion of the Judaean teachers that the question of Jewish observance be referred to Jerusalem, as Dibelius argues (1956: 93).[1] Whatever the precise circumstances, however, there can be little doubt that Paul was the junior partner of Barnabas in a delegation from the Antiochene church to Jerusalem (Holmberg 1978: 18).[2] This view is reinforced by Paul's statement that he travelled μετὰ Βαρναβᾶ, which does not explicitly state the nature of their relationship, but, in contrast to συμπαραλαβὼν... Τίτον (Gal. 2.1), which explicitly subordinates Titus to Paul, suggests that Barnabas was the principal actor. Any lack of clarity must indicate that Paul was subordinate to Barnabas.[3]

In travelling to Jerusalem on behalf of the church at Antioch, Paul was actively participating in the relationship between the two churches. This meant that Paul recognized the primacy accorded by the Jerusalem church and its apostles to the Antiochene Christians (cf. Dunn 1983: 6). According to Gerhardsson, Jerusalem enjoyed unquestioned doctrinal authority, but Stuhlmacher and Mussner understand the primacy of Jerusalem in terms of prestige rather than authority, a distinction perhaps more subtle in theory than in reality.[4] There can be little doubt that, however the relationship was theoretically

1. Cf. Watson 1986: 51 for a contrary view.
2. Cf. Hahn 1965: 77; Georgi 1965: 14-16; Schütz 1975: 140. For a different view cf. Lüdemann 1989: 118-19.
3. The contrary position, that the apparent neutrality of the expression μετὰ Βαρναβᾶ implies Paul's equality with, if not leadership over, Barnabas, has been argued by Burton (1921: 69) and Longenecker (1990: 46). However, in a text where Paul is emphasizing his authority as far as possible, the absence of an explicit statement of leadership must imply the opposite.
4. Gerhardsson 1961: 276; Stuhlmacher 1968: 88; Mussner 1974: 91. Cf. also Schmithals 1971b: 84.

conceived, in reality the Jerusalem church was the senior partner in what was at least an incipient κοινωνία and in a position of considerable authority, and could determine the outcome of the issue (Schütz 1975: 139).

To summarize, therefore, Paul accompanied Barnabas to Jerusalem, representing the church at Antioch, in order to seek resolution to the crisis in their community that had arisen as a consequence of the activity there of Judaean teachers. These Judaeans had demanded that Gentile Christians observe the Mosaic law to a degree contrary to what had been the custom of the Antiochene church for some time (cf. Segal 1990: 194-200). There can be no question that the demand was for the circumcision of all male Christians and their adherence, with whatever degree of rigour, to Jewish ritual and dietary, as well as moral, laws. The way of life and the missionary outreach of the Antiochene church were in jeopardy (cf. Gal. 2.2). The esteem in which the community held the Jerusalem church required that the leadership recognize a degree of authority in that body, as implied in their κοινωνία, and refer the question there for arbitration and adjudication.

2. *The Conduct of the Conference*

The designation 'Apostolic Council', frequently applied to the gathering under discussion, is something of a misnomer. Especially in the light of later ecclesiastical developments the expression has acquired connotations of a legally convened synod or ecumenical council, by implication at least summoned by the highest authority in the Church. Such an interpretation of the event would be both anachronistic and misleading. There is no indication in either record of the gathering that the Jerusalem leadership knew the delegation from Antioch were coming before they arrived, and absolutely no evidence that they summoned them to Jerusalem. The contact was initiated from Antioch, notwithstanding the role of the Judaean teachers in precipitating it. There is no reason to believe that any church other than those of Jerusalem and Antioch was involved. The conference was essentially an *ad hoc* gathering, within the context of a κοινωνία between the two churches, at which Barnabas and Paul, and any who accompanied them, raised with the leadership of the Jerusalem church matters pertaining to the crisis in Antioch. This is not to deny the importance

of the conference, but its significance rests on that of the two participating churches, and of the issue discussed, and not on any notion of
catholicity or magisterium that may be attributed to it anachronistically.

Gerhardsson models his reconstruction of the conference on
rabbinic *yšybh* and compares it also with the Qumran *mwšb hrbym*
(1961: 247). While it would be erroneous to formalize the gathering
too much, the procedure whereby issues were discussed in contemporary Judaism may be of help in illuminating the records of the
deliberations. Gerhardsson argues that the apostles and elders
discussed the question, speaking in reverse order of seniority, so that
James spoke last (1952: 252). However anachronistic the identification
of apostles and elders may be, the fundamental problem with this
hypothesis is that the order of speeches in the Acts narrative does not
conform to seniority. Peter spoke first (Acts 15.7), then Barnabas and
Paul (Acts 15.12), presumably in that order, and James last (Acts
15.13), whereas, if Gerhardsson were correct, then presumably Paul
and Barnabas, in that order, would have spoken before Peter and
James, in whichever order. The formality Gerhardsson ascribes to the
conference is therefore questionable.

An alternative model whereby the proceedings of the conference
are understood is that of a business meeting of a voluntary association,
as proposed by Judge (1960: 46). He argues that the initial proposition
was made from the floor of a meeting of all church members (by
Barnabas and Paul), and that the management committee and its advis-
ers (the 'apostles' and 'elders') thereupon withdrew to consider the
proposals in detail. When they had reached their decision they
returned to the assembly, and those who had instigated the discussion
(Barnabas and Paul) presented a full report on the circumstances
which had given rise to the issue. A member of the management
committee (James) other than the one who had proposed the resolution
in their closed meeting (Peter) then presented a formal motion, which
was approved by the assembly. We do not need to identify this motion
with the Apostolic Decree in order to gain from Judge's insights. A
major weakness in Judge's reconstruction, for the purpose of this
book if not his own work, is that it is entirely dependent on Acts 15,
and makes no reference to Gal. 2.1-10, and leaves open the question
whether Luke anachronistically imposed the conventions with which
he was familiar on the deliberations. This is particularly crucial in
that the procedures of voluntary associations were evolved in the

Graeco-Roman republican milieu, as Judge himself points out (1960: 46), and we therefore require somewhat firmer evidence that they applied in Jerusalem. Furthermore, as will be discussed further in this and the succeeding chapter, it would appear that Luke compresses a rather more protracted debate in the early Church into a single conference for the purpose of conciseness. Nevertheless, Judge does account for the order in which speeches are recorded in Acts 15 and for the fact that Barnabas and Paul's contribution is not recorded. He could also account for the discrepancy between Paul's assertion that the deliberations were conducted privately (Gal. 2.2) and the more public gathering alluded to in Acts 15.12. This question requires further attention.

Gerhardsson and Judge's assertion that the deliberations took place in the presence of the community[1] is problematic. Such a meeting may be indicated by τὸ πλῆθος in Acts 15.12 (Bauer 1957: 674; Aland 1988: 1343), but is not a necessary connotation of the word. Delling questions this position in the light of the usage of ἐκκλησία in contrast to τὸ πλῆθος in Acts 15.22 (1959b: 278). The balance of probability must favour the identification of τὸ πλῆθος in Acts 15.12 with the Jerusalem church as a whole, however, in the light of the connotation of great numbers and of the notion of the corporate whole as opposed to the ruling group.[2] This brings the Lukan account into apparent contradiction with Paul's assertion in Gal. 2.2 that he conducted his business κατ' ἰδίαν δὲ τοῖς δοκοῦσιν (cf. Conzelmann 1987: 116). The precise numbers involved are not stipulated in either account, but the apparent contradiction remains. A number of scholars, however, argue that Paul alludes, however obliquely, to a gathering of the church, as well as a private meeting, in Gal. 2.2.[3] There can nevertheless be little doubt that Barnabas and Paul's first approach was to the leadership, and they may well have hoped to keep the discussions discreet in order to avoid any pressure nomistic factions in the church might have brought to bear upon the leadership (cf. Bruce 1982a: 110). It is not improbable, however, that the

1.   Gerhardsson 1961: 252; Judge 1960: 46.
2.   Cf. Liddell and Scott 1940: 1417; Delling 1959b: 274-76; Lampe 1961: 1092.
3.   Schlier 1971: 66; Mussner 1974: 104-105; Betz 1979: 86; Lüdemann 1989: 171; Longenecker 1990: 47-48.

leadership would have wished to consult a wider body before coming
to a decision. It seems most likely, therefore, that the initial contact
and discussions were conducted between Barnabas and Paul on the one
hand, and on the other James, Peter, John, and whoever else is to be
included in the leadership group in Jerusalem, loosely defined by Paul
as τοῖς δοκοῦσιν (Gal. 2.2), and by Luke more rigidly as ἀπόστολοι
and πρεσβύτεροι (Acts 15.6). It cannot be assumed that the deliberations were conducted in accordance with the procedures described by
Gerhardsson or Judge, but the more general norms in terms of which
business was conducted in the ancient world at that time can illuminate
our understanding of developments.

Paul's version of the business of the conference is anachronistically
egocentric (cf. Schütz 1975: 140) and apparently inconsistent with the
issue of Jewish observance stated in Acts 15.1-5 (cf. Gal. 2.3-5). If,
however, we recognize Paul's rhetorical situation in Galatians, and the
personalization of the account which this necessitates, then the discrepancy between the two accounts can be understood.[1] Paul participated
in the Jerusalem conference as a representative of the Antiochene
church,[2] and therefore when he writes ἀνεθέμην... τὸ εὐαγγέλιον ὃ
κηρύσσω (Gal. 2.2) he is in fact describing the gospel as lived and
taught by the church at Antioch, which he as a member and apostle of
that church shared. The gospel of the Antiochene church and the way
of life and missionary outreach of that community were threatened by
the demand that stricter Jewish observances be imposed on Gentile
Christians. Paul had come to identify the law-free gospel for Gentile
Christians specifically with himself (Gal. 1.16; cf. Rom. 1.5) and
clearly does not do justice to earlier developments in this direction,
particularly in the church at Antioch (cf. Gal. 2.12; Acts 11.20-23).
The applicability of the Jewish law for Gentile Christians was the issue
under discussion in Jerusalem, although far more was at stake for the
church at Antioch, so much so that Paul could write μή πως εἰς κενὸν
τρέχω ἢ ἔδραμον (Gal. 2.2). If Barnabas and Paul did not win the
support of the Christian leadership in Jerusalem, then the cohesion and
unity of the Antiochene church, and the functioning of its apostolate,
would be in jeopardy.

1.	See further discussion in Chapter 6 section 3 below.
2.	Cf. Haenchen 1971: 466; Hahn 1965: 77; Georgi 1965: 21; Schütz 1975:
147; Holmberg 1978: 18; Betz 1979: 85; Dunn 1982; Brown and Meier 1983: 37.

The relationship between the Jerusalem and Antioch churches is illustrated by the use of ἀνατίθημι in Gal. 2.2. Behm, Bauer, Stuhlmacher, and Holtz understand the verb as meaning 'to present for approval'. Dunn, however, argues that the word means 'to submit for consideration and opinion', without any connotation of religious authority.[1] There can be no doubt that, irrespective of the degree of authority accorded to the Jerusalem church, their decision, whether opinion, directive, or instruction, would determine the solution to the crisis in Antioch. If the Jerusalem church did not approve the gospel as preached and lived by the church at Antioch, then the work of that church would have been in jeopardy. Barnabas and Paul sought affirmation for their gospel and reaffirmation of the κοινωνία between the two churches (Goppelt 1970: 75), because the future of their work depended upon it.

There is no indication that Barnabas and Paul received an unsympathetic hearing from Peter and James,[2] or that they were not accorded full participation in the deliberations.[3] Paul does not give the impression in Gal. 2.1-10 of having been silent, and Luke, while not writing his and Barnabas's speeches for them, nevertheless confirms that they participated in the discussion, even if at the level of citing evidence in support of their case rather than of expounding the principles involved (Acts 15.12). Nevertheless, there can be little doubt that it was Peter and James, and not Barnabas and Paul, whose role was decisive. While Barnabas and Paul were not mildly supplicant (Betz 1979: 86), they did not share the prestige or influence of Peter and James with the leadership of the Jerusalem community, even if Barnabas was highly respected there (cf. Acts 9.27; 11.22-23). Peter was the primary witness to the resurrection of Christ, and accordingly enjoyed considerable eminence and authority in the Church. Furthermore the Christian community in Jerusalem was situated in an eschatologically significant position, and undoubtedly included among its members other witnesses to the resurrection, as well as to the ministry of Jesus. The potential of the Jerusalem church and its leadership to assert authority over other Christians, particularly those

1.   Behm 1933: 353; Bauer 1957: 123; Stuhlmacher 1968: 87; Holtz 1974: 121; Dunn 1982: 466. Cf. also Longenecker 1990: 47.
2.   Schoeps 1961: 66; Eckert 1971: 226.
3.   Conzelmann 1973: 85; Betz 1979: 86; cf. Judge 1960: 46.

less endowed with traditions and witnesses to the events enshrined in those traditions, and less secure within the broader Jewish community, would therefore have been considerable. Furthermore, Barnabas and Paul were outsiders to the Jerusalem church and would not have been able to influence the mind of the community in the decision making process to the same degree as its own leadership. While they undoubtedly related to the Jerusalem leadership as the leaders of one church to another, their influence would have been less, both with the leaders and with the community, especially as the Antiochene church they represented recognized a degree of primacy in the Jerusalem church. The referral of an issue of grave concern through the delegation of Barnabas and Paul was in itself symbolic of the subordination of the Antiochene Christians to the authority of the Jerusalem church, within their relationship of κοινωνία.

The decision of the conference was essentially that sought by the Antiochene delegation. Paul could write ἐμοὶ...οὐδὲν προσανέθεντο (Gal. 2.6). If we were to substitute ἡμῖν for ἐμοί, we would probably have a substantially accurate understanding of the outcome of the conference (cf. Schütz 1975: 147). The Jerusalem leadership, the effective decision-makers at the conference, affirmed the gospel as lived and preached at Antioch and imposed no further obligations on that community (Stuhlmacher 1968: 87). Circumcision and other Jewish legal observances would not be imposed on Gentile Christians in Antioch. The clear implication that the Jerusalem leadership could have decided otherwise, however, is not to be ignored. The decisive voices were those of Peter, James, and John (Gal. 2.6). Barnabas and Paul, and similarly other participants who could have held a very different point of view (cf. Acts 15.5), may have been able to argue persuasively, but their voices were not decisive. The decision was that sought by the Antiochene delegation, quite probably in the face of concerted opposition from within the Jerusalem church. The decision was not simply assent to the Antiochene practice and relinquishment of authority on the part of the Jerusalem leadership. Rather, the decision was an assertion on the part of the Jerusalem leadership of authority that was recognized by all parties, both in affirming the Antiochene teaching and practice and in suppressing the attempted imposition of Jewish legal observances on Gentile Christians.[1]

---

1. Cullmann argues the contrary position, that the decision of the Jerusalem

At the conclusion of the discussions, when the agreement had been reached, James, Peter and John gave Barnabas and Paul δεξιὰς... κοινωνίας (Gal. 2.9). This fellowship, not between the five people mentioned, but between the two churches they represented,[1] is a relationship of unity, though not necessarily equality (Hauck 1939: 802). Barnabas and Paul had succeeded not only in obtaining the ruling of the Jerusalem church which they needed but also in maintaining the unity between the two churches. Within that κοινωνία, the primacy of Jerusalem was recognized, but also the freedom of the Antiochene church to preach and to live its own interpretation of the gospel, albeit subject to the approval of the Jerusalem leadership.

Sampley has portrayed the deliberations of the conference as evidence of consensual *societas* between Paul, Barnabas, Peter, James, and John (1980: 26-32). While he may be correct in saying that this is the interpretation put on the conference by Paul (1980: 29), as an accurate reflection of the historical meeting it seems inadequate. Rather than forming a contract between five individuals, the conference reaffirmed the κοινωνία between the two churches those individuals represented. The issues discussed involved the life of the Christian communities, and not only the work of five missionaries (cf. Sampley 1980: 27-32). The collection, which Sampley cites as an obligation in terms of *societas* (1980: 32), clearly involves the members of the church at Antioch, and those which had been established by missionaries from there, as well as Barnabas and Paul themselves (cf. Georgi 1965: 21-22). That the relationship in terms of which the conference was conducted was one between churches, and not individuals, will become clearer in the discussion which follows in this and succeeding chapters.

The conference strengthened the authority of the Jerusalem church in its relationship with the Antiochene church. It also strengthened the authority of the leadership of the Jerusalem church. The fact that the ruling they gave was the one sought by the Antiochene delegation does not alter this. As will become clear from discussion of subsequent

conference entailed the relinquishment of authority on their part (1953: 46). I hope to show in subsequent chapters, however, that this was far from being the case.

1. The former position is argued by Sampley (1980: 26), but, as Haenchen (1971: 566), Goppelt (1970: 75) and others have argued, the people mentioned carried out a representative function.

events in Antioch in the next chapter, the Jerusalem leadership, far from conceding a point through weakness, created a precedent for further assertions of authority in their relationship of κοινωνία with the church at Antioch. The assertion of greater authority, however, involved the greater risk of defiance, and the greater danger of successful resistance. Defiance of this authority was a major factor in subsequent developments, as I hope to show in the next chapter. First, however, we need to consider the ruling of the conference in greater detail.

3. *The Ruling of the Conference*

We have seen that the Jerusalem conference reached the decision sought by the Antiochene delegation led by Barnabas. In reaching this decision the leadership of the Jerusalem church asserted its authority both within their own community and in the relationship of their church with that at Antioch. We need to consider this decision now, not only specifically in terms of the obligations of Gentile Christians with regard to the Mosaic law, but also in terms of the missionary work of the two churches, and the obligations accepted by the Antiochene church.

The agreement entered between the Antiochene and Jerusalem churches on the basis of the ruling of the conference would have applied only to those two churches, and others established under their respective auspices. However, the importance of these two communities in early Christianity was such that the ruling of the conference was a significant precedent, both for the application of the principles of the ruling elsewhere than in the churches directly or indirectly involved, and also for the assertion of jurisdiction by the Jerusalem church over other Christian communities. This would have been the case particularly if Betz is correct in identifying political language in Gal. 2.7-9, which would have involved legal connotations to the agreement for both parties (1979: 86).[1] When the issue of Gentile observance of the Jewish law arose elsewhere, as was inevitable, the ruling reached at Jerusalem, and the authority that the leaders of that community exercised in reaching it, could form the basis for universalization both of the principle itself and of the authority that

1. Cf. Sampley 1980: 28; McLean 1991: 69-71.

formulated it. The conference decision was therefore potentially, if not inevitably, more sweeping in its application than originally envisaged.

a. *The Applicability of the Law for Gentile Christians*
Since it was the central issue at the Jerusalem conference, the question of the obligations of Gentile Christians with regard to the Mosaic law has been mentioned in the preceding sections, and there is no need to repeat the discussion here. A number of observations should, however, be made.

In the Introduction I recorded my acquiescence in the prevailing scholarly consensus that the 'Apostolic Decree' was not formulated at the conference under discussion, but subsequently.[1] The decision of the Jerusalem conference is therefore not to be identified with the 'Apostolic Decree', which will be considered later.[2]

We can, and must, assume that the decision of the Jerusalem conference was less detailed than the subsequent 'Apostolic Decree', or else the latter would have been redundant. The question of the applicability of the requirements of the Mosaic law for Gentile Christians must therefore have been defined and decided in fairly simple terms, which stands to reason, as the conference, rather than expounding new principles, essentially affirmed the prevailing customs of the Antiochene church. The Gentile Christians were not obliged to be circumcised. So much is clear, but the full implications of this are not. Whether all the observances associated with circumcision were waived, or the specific requirement of circumcision itself, must remain uncertain, and the agreement may have been open to a variety of interpretations from the beginning, if interpreted on the basis of different presuppositions. Paul's statement in Gal. 5.3 that circumcision requires obedience to the entire law reflects his thinking at a later period, and in a particular polemical context, and cannot be assumed to be relevant to the detail

---

1.   In recent years, the most significant reconstruction which does not accept this view is that of Achtemeier, who identifies the conference of Gal. 2.1-10 with that of Acts 11.1-18, while the subsequent conference of Acts 15 was that at which the 'Apostolic Decree' was promulgated (1987: 50-61). For our present purpose, Achtemeier's reconstruction does not differ fundamentally, in that the nature of the conference of Gal. 2.1-10 is unaltered, and the 'Apostolic Decree' was formulated subsequent to it.

2.   See the excursus at the end of Part II.

of the agreement reached at the Jerusalem conference. Clearly, however, no fundamental changes were required in the life of the Christian community at Antioch (cf. Gal. 2.6). That the issue was not so straightforward as might appear, and as Paul succeeds eloquently in portraying it, will become apparent in the discussion of subsequent events.

b. *The Missionary Work of the Two Churches*
The gospel preached and lived in Antioch was for Gentile Christians a gospel without at least one of the requirements of Jewish observance. This made it essentially different to that preached at Jerusalem, in terms of which all Christians were bound to observe the Mosaic law (cf. Segal 1990: 194). The decision not to impose circumcision on Gentile Christians in Antioch therefore involved the recognition by the Jerusalem leadership of a form of the Christian gospel which was distinct from their own (cf. Haenchen 1971: 466).

The Jerusalem leadership had recognized that the Antioch church had been entrusted with τὸ εὐαγγέλιον τῆς ἀκροβυστίας, while they had been entrusted with [the gospel] τῆς περιτομῆς (Gal. 2.7). According to Betz, ἰδόντες denotes theological insight (1979: 96). The Christian leadership in Jerusalem recognized that Barnabas and Paul's teaching, and the practice of the church at Antioch, were theologically tenable, even if they were not going to adopt either the theory or the practice themselves. The gospel of uncircumcision, preached by Barnabas and Paul, and by which the Antiochene church lived, was a legitimate interpretation of Christianity, as was the gospel of circumcision, preached by Peter, and to which the Jerusalem church conformed. The Jewish community of this period was not unaccustomed to differences of opinion, or incapable of accommodating them within a wider whole, and we have no reason to suppose that the early Christians did not share this capacity for diversity. There would therefore be no inconsistency in the Jerusalem leadership recognizing the validity of the Antiochene gospel, while at the same time themselves adhering to the gospel of circumcision as more appropriate to their own circumstances (cf. Longenecker 1964: 220).

The rationale for this mutual recognition of diversity, as Paul relates it, is that God was working through Peter εἰς ἀποστολὴν τῆς περιτομῆς, and through himself εἰς τὰ ἔθνη (Gal. 2.8). Paul does not repeat ἀποστολή with reference to himself, and Betz suggests that this indicates that Paul is here citing the actual words of the agreement, in terms of which he was not recognized as an apostle (1979: 98).[1] We cannot be certain, however, as to how clearly or rigidly defined apostleship was at this time (cf. Schmithals 1961: 90-92). The word ἀποστολή is clearly being used in terms of Christian mission, rather than as a personal title or designation. The conference was between churches, and its agreement concerned the life and work of the two churches, to which the personal status of the individuals concerned was secondary. The personalization of the account by Paul into a dichotomy between himself and Peter reduces its historical reliability considerably. There is no reason, other than Paul's polemical purpose in Galatians, to understand the apostolate in terms of anybody's particular status (cf. Holmberg 1978: 18). This was not at issue at the conference and should not be read into any conference statement which Paul may be citing. Since the question of apostleship was not at issue at the conference, there is no significance in the non-repetition of ἀποστολή, other than that it makes more lucid Greek.

Paul briefly paraphrases the practical implication of the agreement: ἡμεῖς εἰς τὰ ἔθνη αὐτοὶ δὲ εἰς τὴν περιτομήν (Gal. 2.9). This has been variously interpreted, usually in terms of allocation of missionary spheres to the two parties, either along ethnic or geographical lines. The fundamental problem with these notions of dividing the world between Peter and Paul is that it assumes that the conference took place on a more grandiose scale than was the case, and that every missionary and every church was party to the deliberations. As seen above, the conference involved only Jerusalem and Antioch and churches under their respective auspices. Important though these two churches were, they could not divide all Christian missionary work between them. Not only would neither be in a position to honour the obligations involved, but such an arrangement would ignore the work of other Christian missionaries. The weight of scholarship behind this view, however, requires that it be examined more closely.

A substantial number of scholars argue that missionary tasks were allocated along ethnic lines.[2] Watson disputes the historicity of the

1. Cf. Dinkler 1953: 270-82; Klein 1969: 90-128; Dunn 1982: 473; Longenecker 1990: 56; McLean 1991: 67.
2. Campenhausen 1969: 33; Cullmann 1953: 43; Schmithals 1965a: 48-49; Georgi 1965: 21; Stuhlmacher 1968: 97; Conzelmann 1973: 86; Eckert 1971: 190;

agreement and asserts that Paul no longer had any intention of preaching to Jews anyway, as the fundamental premise of the Gentile mission was that such an exercise would be futile (1986: 53). The interpretation of the agreement in ethnic terms, when the practical implications are considered, does not, however, seem feasible. Not only was Antioch a mixed church (cf. Gal. 2.11-13), but the dispersion of the Jewish nation throughout the eastern Roman empire and beyond, and the Gentile settlement of Palestine, would have made such an arrangement unworkable. Furthermore, godfearing Gentiles, a principal source of Christian converts, would have been left in a grey area between Jews and Gentiles,[1] and it is unlikely that either party would have agreed to this. Paul clearly cites the agreement with approval, shortly before relating his criticism of Peter for involvement in racial separation within the church, and in the same letter in which he wrote οὐκ ἔνι ’Ιουδαῖος οὐδὲ ῞Ελλην... ἐν Χριστῷ ’Ιησοῦ (Gal. 3.28). Paul's declared policy in 1 Cor. 9.20, which he would not have stated if it was no longer his practice (Wilson 1983: 65-68),[2] implies unambiguously that he preached to both Jews and Gentiles. Division of missionary work along racial lines is therefore clearly untenable.

The territorial division of mission areas, the precise parameters of which are uncertain, but in terms of which most or all missionary work outside Palestine would be conducted from Antioch, has also been argued.[3] Holmberg argues that this division constituted a theological rather than a practical reality and was not as rigid as Paul suggests (1978: 30-31). The geographical hypothesis, however, is more fundamentally problematic than this, in that, like the ethnic hypothesis, it does not take into account other missionaries already operating inside and outside Palestine who were not represented at the conference, or party to its agreement. Even if the agreement was not to be understood as though Paul was the only missionary to Gentiles (Holmberg 1978: 70), as was undoubtedly the case, a division along geographical lines would still have been too rigid to be workable. This

Wilson 1973: 185; Betz 1979: 100; Lüdemann 1984: 72; Lüdemann 1983: 62; Kim 1981: 272.
    1.   On the place of godfearers, see J.J. Collins 1985: 175; Cohen 1989: 14. Cf. also Kraabel 1981, 1982.
    2.   Cf. Countryman 1988: 100; Segal 1990: 239-240. For the contrary view, see Schmithals 1965a: 48; Sanders 1983: 185-186; Watson 1986: 29.
    3.   Burton 1921: 98; Munck 1967: 150; Bruce 1968: 11.

is not to deny a possible geographical corollary to the agreement, but the division of territory cannot have been primary.

The meaning of the agreement is to be found not in elaborate or simple delimitation of missionary areas or targets, but in the mutual recognition, the κοινωνία between the Jerusalem and Antioch churches.[1] The Jerusalem church recognized the authenticity of the Antiochene gospel and maintained its κοινωνία with the community despite the significant differences, and the Antioch church remained the subordinate partner in the κοινωνία that bound the two churches together. The essential content of the agreement was recognition of 'the basic character of the missionary preaching of the two groups' (Bornkamm 1971: 39-40), and of 'the main emphasis and purpose of the missionary activity' of the two churches (Hahn 1965: 81). Barnabas, Paul and the Antiochene church would continue to preach and practise their form of Christianity, in which Gentiles were not obliged to be circumcised, but they would not compel Jewish Christians to desist from observing the Law. The gospel of uncircumcision might apply only to Gentiles, but this did not mean that the Antiochene church and those engaged in mission from there, would not preach to Jews. Similarly, the gospel of circumcision would apply only to Jews, and the Jerusalem church would not impose circumcision and legal observance on Gentile Christians. Both churches would preach to and welcome all who would listen, but the gospel of circumcision, represented by James, Peter and John, would be obligatory only for Jews, and the gospel of uncircumcision, represented by Barnabas and Paul, would apply only to Gentiles.

Rather than delimitation of territory, or racial division, I would argue, therefore, that the Jerusalem conference agreed that the two churches would adhere to the gospel as they understood it, and neither would attempt to impose its views on the other. This would apply both to their lives and to their mission, and their diversity of belief and practice would be maintained within the κοινωνία that had been affirmed at the conference.

---

1.   Haenchen (1971: 467) argues that the agreement consisted entirely in the assent of the Jerusalem church to the Antiochenes that they would continue not to require Gentile converts to Christianity to be circumcised.

c. *The Obligations Accepted by the Antiochenes*
The only obligation which Paul acknowledges having accepted, was
τῶν πτωχῶν...μνημονεύωμεν (Gal. 2.10). Betz correctly points out
that Paul portrays this as supplementary rather than integral to the
agreement (1979: 101; cf. Sampley 1980: 32). The fact that this is not
mentioned in Acts 15 may support this interpretation, but it must also
be observed that Luke ceases to be concerned with the church at
Antioch, on whose behalf this undertaking had been given, after Paul
ceased to operate from there (Acts 15.40).[1] However, whatever the
cause of Luke's silence, and whether the obligation to remember the
poor was integral or supplementary to the agreement between Antioch
and Jerusalem, it was something the former could not decline, and
Paul is quite clear that, at the time (cf. Wedderburn 1988: 39), he had
no desire to do so.

The obligation to remember the poor is frequently identified with
the collection (cf. Betz 1979: 103). The connection between the obligations assumed by the Antiochene church through its delegates at the
Jerusalem conference and the collection Paul raised for the Jerusalem
church in the final years of his ministry, however, is neither direct
nor straightforward, as will become increasingly clear in subsequent
chapters.[2] The connection is at least as tenuous as Paul's links with the
church of Antioch during the period subsequent to the Antioch incident, and direct identification between the Jerusalem agreement and
Paul's collection would be erroneous. We therefore need to consider
the obligation to remember the πτωχοί in its own right, without presupposing a connection with Paul's later activities. This can best be
accomplished through a consideration of the implications of
μνημονεύω and πτωχός.

μνημονεύω means to call to mind.[3] This can imply simply to
remember, or to mention, but it is quite clear that the act of remembering envisaged in the Jerusalem agreement entailed rather more

1. Acts 11.27-30 relates the delivery of a collection from Antioch to Jerusalem,
in which both Barnabas and Paul were involved. Luke conflates Barnabas's delivery
of the Antiochene collection with Paul's independent project, and places his account
in the section of Acts where he is concerned with the life of the Antiochene church.
See further discussion in Introduction 4b and 5 and in Chapter 7.
2. Wedderburn 1988: 37-41 has shown to some degree how tenuous the
connection is between Gal. 2.10 and Paul's collection.
3. Liddell and Scott 1940: 1139; Michel 1942: 682; Lampe 1961: 874.

than this. It can also be assumed that more than intercessory prayer is implied. Elsewhere, Paul uses μνημονεύω to remind his readers of his own labours (1 Thess. 2.9), of his sayings (2 Thess. 2.5) and of his chains (Col. 4.18). The intention is that his readers should remember Paul, the one from whom they had received the gospel, with a sense of obligation which influences their behaviour (Michel 1942: 682), and the same principle of obligation towards those from whom the faith had been received, however indirectly, is involved in Gal. 2.10 (cf. Rom. 15.27). Similarly, in 1 Cor. 11.2, remembering Paul implies adhering to his teaching. Remembering therefore involves action motivated by a sense of moral obligation (cf. Georgi 1965: 27-28). Significantly, in 1 Thess. 3.1, μνείαν is a matter of attitude, and implies, at least in principle, the maintenance of sound relations (cf. Michel 1942: 678). Recollection clearly is intended to evoke a response, but quite what action is implied in the particular case in Gal. 2.10 is not stated in the text. The identification of this obligation with the collection is dependent upon the association of the object τῶν πτωχῶν with a later reference to Paul's collection project in Rom. 15.26. Therefore, the sense in which πτωχός is used, must be considered briefly before the implications of remembering with obligation can be understood.

πτωχός is used in the LXX for a number of Hebrew and Aramaic words, most notably *'ny*, which designates a victim of unmerited impoverishment, and came to acquire a religious significance. Other words rendered πτωχός include *rš*, which conveyed only social and economic connotations in the biblical literature, and *'bywn*, which denotes a beggar. It is in the post-biblical literature that poverty came to acquire a positive religious significance, over and above the Old Testament conception of the poor enjoying a degree of divine protection. In the *Psalms of Solomon*, πτωχός came to be equated with δίκαιος and ὅσιος (Hauck and Bammel 1959: 896). This understanding of poverty is taken further in the Qumran writings. In 1QH 5.1 the author, possibly the Teacher of Righteousness, calls himself *kpš 'ny wrš 'ny*. He also calls himself *'bywn* (1QH 5.13, 16, 18). These expressions are also applied, in plural form, to other members of the community (1QH 2.32; 5.21; 18.14, 22). The expression *nwy rwḥ* (cf. Mt. 5.3) occurs in 1QM 14.7. All these texts refer to the poor as the objects of God's dealings in the world (Hauck and Bammel 1959: 897). Clearly, the religious connotations of poverty attested at

Qumran and in the Matthaean version of Q cannot be presupposed in the Pauline writings, or in the usage of the Jerusalem church at the time of the conference. However, if, as Bammel suggests, Paul's use of πτωχός in connection with the collection is a quotation of the self-designation of the beneficiaries thereof (Hauck and Bammel 1959: 909), then the question of theological connotations to the expression requires further consideration. While there appears to be no spiritual-ization of the concept of poverty in the Pauline writings, except in connection with the collection in Rom. 15.26-27 (Hauck and Bammel 1959: 910), it is possible that πτωχοί is a translation of 'bywnym, a self-designation with religious as well as, or rather than, material connotations. Schlier argues that πτωχοί is to be equated with ἅγιοι (1971: 80; cf. Keck 1965), and Longenecker identifies them with the Jewish Christians of Jerusalem (1990: 60), in which case the material circumstances of the persons concerned are at most of secondary importance.

If Paul quotes the self-designation of the beneficiaries of the collec-tion, it does not necessarily imply that he or Barnabas shared their understanding of the term, or even recognized the spiritual qualities associated with poverty. Paul deplored the sanctification of laziness, and condemned wanton idleness unequivocally (cf. 1 Thess. 4.11-12; 2 Thess. 3.6-12), and clearly recognized no virtue in self-inflicted poverty. If raising money, with the single motive of charity, was all that was envisaged, therefore, it is clear that the deprivation to be alleviated was unmerited; a likely, if not almost certain, state of many in the Jerusalem church. Gal. 2.10, however, does not state that the sole beneficiaries of the collection would be the Jerusalem church or the poor among its membership. If, as is generally assumed, the collection would benefit the Jerusalem church exclusively, then quali-ties other than poverty are at issue. μνημονεύω implies obligation, and not merely voluntary charity, as has been shown above. Further-more, it would not have been the material poverty of the πτωχοί that created the obligation of the Antiochene Christians, but the position of the Jerusalem church at the fountainhead of the gospel, and the κοινωνία between the two communities (cf. Rom. 15.26-27). Even if the collection was earmarked for those members of the Jerusalem church who were economically impoverished, and even if not all members of the Antioch church contributed, the project was never-theless conceived on the basis of a corporate relationship between the two communities, that is, on a basis other than their relative and respective economic circumstances.

That remembering the poor at least partly took the form of financial aid would appear to be the unanimous view of contemporary scholarship.[1] However, if this financial support was to be directed exclusively to beneficiaries in Jerusalem, which seems an equally widely held view, although one not supported in the text of Gal. 2.10, then qualities other than material poverty, a widespread phenomenon in the world of the time, were criteria of receiving this aid (Betz 1979: 102). These qualities need to be identified if the obligation assumed by the Antiochene church is to be understood correctly. Holmberg argues that the Jerusalem church would have felt entitled to the collection by virtue of its eschatological position (1978: 39).[2] Schoeps argues that it was a means of appeasing the Judaists who had been overruled at the conference (1961: 68). Berger argues that almsgiving was looked upon in some Jewish circles as almost a substitute for circumcision for Gentile adherents as a means to righteousness (1977: 187), and Betz similarly points to the association of gifts with ritual sacrifice in the thought-world of the time (1985: 42). However, in none of the cases Berger cites does the righteous Gentile actually become part of the covenant community of Israel, and this Segal identifies as the crucial issue, rather than circumcision (1990: 194).[3] There is therefore no apparent precedent for regarding almsgiving as a complete substitute for circumcision, and, unless Gentile Christians were to be regarded as righteous, but not part of the covenant community, Berger's argument seems inapplicable. Furthermore, if the collection was conceived and mutually understood as a substitute for circumcision, to a degree unprecedented in Judaism, it would not have been supplementary to the agreement, but an integral part of it. If, however, remembering the poor was regarded as a lesser obligation on Gentile Christians, which presumably implied even less recognition and acceptance than circumcision (cf. Cohen 1989: 29), then presumably it represents a concession in respect of

1. Cf. Schlier 1971: 80; Mussner 1974: 124; Betz 1979: 102-103; Longenecker 1990: 60.

2. Cf. Holl 1921: 60; Stuhlmacher 1968: 104; Betz 1979: 103.

3. For a treatment of the status of proselytes in the Jewish community, see Cohen 1989.

Mosaic observance. If the practice of almsgiving was not currently observed by the Antiochene church, but was accepted as a new obligation at the Jerusalem conference,[1] this would imply a greater degree of Jewish observance in the Antiochene church than hitherto had been the case. If the almsgiving was directed specifically to the Jerusalem church, or those of its members in greatest need, this would involve further recognition of the pre-eminence of the Jerusalem church, with probable eschatological overtones (cf. Isa. 2.2; 60.5-17).

Given the tenuous link between Paul's later collection and the obligation accepted at the Jerusalem conference (Wedderburn, 1988: 37-41), however, we cannot simply reduce remembering the poor to financial support, and still less to financial support for the Jerusalem church. If something more specific than general almsgiving is implied, as the overwhelming majority of scholars assume, then the significance of the obligation lies not in the poverty of the beneficiaries but in their politically motivated and theologically legitimated claims on other Christians. A criterion other than poverty for receiving financial support implies other factors in the relationship between the parties. This can consist either in the exchange of services for money, or in the recognition of the right to some form of tribute on the part of those receiving the money. Financial support for the Jerusalem church for reasons other than poverty would therefore imply recognition on the part of the donors of a legitimate claim to such payment. That the Jerusalem church exercised some degree of authority over the Antiochene church, recognized in terms of their κοινωνία, has already been shown. This authority extended beyond the right to financial support and included the right to regulate the conduct of the Antiochene Christians. We therefore need to consider the possibility that the obligation to remember the poor was an aspect of the right of the Jerusalem church to regulate Christian life in Antioch.

I would suggest that the obligation to remember the poor, accepted by the delegation of the Antiochene church, involved more than simply remembering in kind the material poverty of the Jerusalem church. The Jerusalem Christians, and their mission, could be compromised if people associated with them, such as the Christians of Antioch, exercised liberties in their observance of the Law such as could not be tolerated in Jerusalem and would have scandalized some

---

1. Cf. Berger 1977; Cohen 1989: 18-19.

non-Christian Jews. If the Jerusalem church had recognized the freedom of the Antiochene church from at least some of the constraints of
the law, one would expect that in return they would ask that this
liberty be exercised with consideration, and, when appropriate,
restraint. Longenecker argues that the Antiochene Christians undertook to exercise their liberty in a manner that would not undermine
the viability and credibility of the missionary work of the Jerusalem
church (1990: 60), but there seems good reason to believe that
the safety of the Jerusalem Christians themselves was also at stake
(cf. Gal. 6.12; 1 Thess. 2.14-16).[1] The Jerusalem church would be
compromised not merely in its mission but in its security if the
liberties exercised by the Antiochene Christians, with whom they were
associated in a κοινωνία, incurred the wrath of the Temple authorities. A condition of the Antiochenes' freedom, that it be exercised
with due regard for its consequences for the Jerusalem church, would
therefore seem plausible. Not only would such a stipulation provide
the basis for responding to a situation in which the safety of the
Jerusalem Christians was compromised, but it would also constitute a
significant concession to those within the Jerusalem church whose
activities had precipitated the conference, and who would have
opposed the decision reached. The leaders of the Jerusalem church
would naturally be concerned that the Antiochene practices, already a
cause for considerable apprehension, would, if given their explicit
approval, lead to further marginalization of the their community in
Jerusalem, and seriously jeopardize their security.

I would suggest, therefore, that, in return for recognition of their
gospel by the leadership of the Jerusalem church, the Antiochene
Christians undertook to exercise their freedom and independence with
due consideration for the implications of their conduct for Christian
communities in Judaea. More than simply raising money to support
the Jerusalem Christians, and expressing whatever was implied in that
gesture, the delegation from Antioch undertook in terms of their
κοινωνία with the Jerusalem church, to exercise their freedom with
consideration for the effects of their behaviour on the Christians of
Jerusalem, and recognizing the right of the Jerusalem church to call
for modifications in the Antiochene Christian customs, should the

1.   Jewett 1971: 202-206; Reicke 1984. For a contrary view, see Brandon 1957: 88-100.

former deem them appropriate in the light of their own circumstances, as well as of more general considerations of propriety. The authority of the Jerusalem church to regulate conduct in the church of Antioch was at least implicit in the κοινωνία and was exercised in the decision of the Jerusalem conference. That this authority was subsequently exercised with these considerations in view I intend to argue in the following chapter.

To sum up, therefore, the Jerusalem conference was a decisive event in the early history of Christianity. Two of the most significant churches of that period formed an understanding whereby their theological diversity, and its implications for their way of life and missionary outreach, could be accommodated within the κοινωνία that bonded them together. The church at Antioch initiated the contact which resulted in the conference, thereby affirming its subordination to the community in Jerusalem, but at the same time establishing its right to a degree of independence of thought and action. The authority of the Jerusalem church was at the same time entrenched, and its leadership strengthened their position within the community by deciding in favour of the Antiochene delegation. This assertion of authority carried with it the potential for greater defiance, a factor which will be evident in the discussion in the next chapter, which will concern the confrontation between Peter and Paul at Antioch.

Chapter 5

PETER AND PAUL AT ANTIOCH

The majority of recent scholars locate the altercation between Peter
and Paul at Antioch (Gal. 2.11-14) during the period shortly after the
conference described immediately before in the Pauline narrative
(Gal. 2.1-10), which is to be identified with that of Acts 15. This
consensus has been challenged in four principal ways. Munck argues
that Paul places the incident after the conference in his narrative in
order to demonstrate the independence of his apostleship (1959: 100,
102, 106). Bruce (1982a: 128) and Longenecker (1990: lxxxiii) place
the confrontation before the conference of Acts 15 by identifying
Paul's visit to Jerusalem recorded in Gal. 2.1-10 with that of Acts
11.27-30. Lüdemann argues that the situation giving rise to the
episode in Antioch would have been conceivable prior to the conference, but not after (1984: 75). Achtemeier argues that the conference
of Gal. 2.1-10 is to be equated with that of Acts 11.1-18, and that the
conference of Acts 15 was held subsequently, without the participation
of Peter, Barnabas, or Paul, and formulated the Apostolic Decree
(1987: 51-52). The delegation from James brought the Apostolic
Decree to Antioch, giving rise to the confrontation between Peter and
Paul. The decree was therefore the cause of the conflict, not the
resolution thereof (1987: 58). It will, I hope, be clear from this
chapter that the scholarly consensus represents the most plausible
reconstruction.

At the Jerusalem conference, discussed in the previous chapter, the
delegation of the church at Antioch won recognition for its distinctive
version of the Christian gospel which did not require circumcision of
Gentile converts to Christianity, and possibly waived other ritual
and dietary requirements also, which could not have failed to affect
the observances of Jewish Christians. The Jerusalem church would
continue to preach its gospel of circumcision, while the Antiochenes

preached their gospel of uncircumcision. The Antiochenes undertook, in return, to remember the poor. This, it was argued, involved not only intercessory prayer and the collection of funds, but also the obligation of the Antiochenes to consider the effects of their exercise of freedom from the Law on the circumstances of the Christian community in Jerusalem and their mission.

The Jerusalem church had entrenched its jurisdiction over the Antiochene community through the conference and its exercise of decision-making authority. The decision was not reached without opposition from within the Jerusalem church, and the assertion of jurisdiction by the Jerusalem leadership generated increased potential for resistance to them, both in Jerusalem and in Antioch. While their authority was uncontested, as it was at the conference, to the point of having been actively appealed to by the Antiochene church, it was secure, and could be asserted and entrenched through precedent. However, when authority cannot be reinforced by means of coercive power it is vulnerable to defiance.[1] Successful defiance can result in the disintegration of authority. Therefore, in extending their jurisdiction over the Antiochene church, the leadership of the Jerusalem church increased the risk of defiance and the potential for resistance to undermine their authority. This is important in considering the events which followed in Antioch, and particularly Paul's role in them.

1. *Circumstances Giving Rise to the Confrontation*

How long after the conference the events recorded in Gal. 2.11-14 took place is uncertain. Reicke suggests that it was several years (1953: 178), but the majority of scholars prefer a shorter period, and it is unlikely to have been more than a few months. Peter evidently visited the church at Antioch shortly after the conference (cf. Gal. 2.11), whether as a fugitive (cf. Acts 12.17), or to reciprocate the visit of Barnabas and Paul to Jerusalem and build up further the κοινωνία between the two churches, is uncertain. It is most improbable that the purpose of Peter's visit to Antioch was to ensure that the agreement was being observed. As argued in the preceding chapter, the conference had confirmed the gospel as preached and lived by the

---

1. See discussion in the Introduction section 3a.

Antiochene church and therefore did not require enforcement. The obligations accepted by the Antiochene delegation were supplementary to the agreement and not easily quantifiable, and it would probably not have been regarded as helpful by either party for anyone from Jerusalem to have been involved in the implementation of these. Therefore, while a demonstration of authority in some form as the purpose of Peter's presence in Antioch cannot be excluded entirely, it cannot be identified with enforcement of the decision of the Jerusalem conference.

Peter participated fully in the life of the Antiochene church, and conformed to its customs, evidently quite willingly (Gal. 2.12). Quite what happened when τινας ἀπὸ 'Ιακώβου (Gal. 2.12) arrived in Antioch is difficult to reconstruct. It is clear that Peter withdrew from table fellowship with the Gentile Christians, and that the Jewish Christians, including Barnabas, followed his example (Gal. 2.12-13). Table fellowship between Jewish and Gentile Christians is therefore clearly involved in this episode. This does not imply that it was necessarily the principal issue in the debacle (cf. Segal 1990: 194), but it nevertheless requires consideration.

The Jerusalem conference had clearly ruled that Gentile Christians need not be circumcised, but the precise implications of this, and the extent to which such details were discussed, is far from certain. Paul certainly claims that no requirements were stipulated (Gal. 2.6), which implies that no ritual or dietary observances not already practised in the Antiochene church were imposed by the conference. Preoccupation with circumcision, and confusion on account of the metonymous nature of the expression, may have led to oversight of lesser details, or mutual misunderstanding, but nevertheless the Antiochene custom was affirmed, by implication at least, in all its aspects. The conference did not consider the implications of this for table fellowship with Gentile Christians for Jewish Christians who did not assent to the Antiochene version of the gospel (Holmberg 1978: 21; cf. Schoeps 1961: 68). This was evidently not an issue for the Jewish Christians at Antioch (Gal. 2.12-13; cf. Acts 11.20-21), and Barnabas and Paul would have assumed that this aspect of the life of the Antiochene church, along with the gospel they preached, had been affirmed. Those who had wished to change the Antiochene practice were Judaeans and would have had no interest in further contact with the Antiochene church if it did not adhere to the gospel of circumcision. The question of table fellowship in Antioch would therefore have been of no concern to them.

Dunn has shown that Jewish practice regarding table fellowship with Gentiles was not uniform, but that the laws were applied with varying degrees of rigour during the period, and that it was the food consumed, as well as the company, that were determinative in such matters (1983: 14), and Gaston has shown that there was no legal prohibition of table fellowship (1986: 43).[1] The implication of this would seem to be that only the most rigorous forms of Jewish observance excluded all social intercourse with Gentiles. Whatever the nature of Jewish observance, however, the economic factors bearing upon the situation in Antioch require consideration. Since the Jewish community in Antioch was substantial,[2] it may be assumed that it had its own food markets, and that food which conformed to Jewish ritual requirements was therefore obtainable in Antioch, at a price. However, it cannot be assumed that the standards of legal observance in these markets were the same as those which prevailed in Jerusalem. Furthermore, we can be certain that food bought in the Jewish markets in Antioch would have been more expensive than food not subject to the specific requirements of the Law. Not only would tithes have had to have been paid on it to conform with the Law, but it is a universal economic reality that any produce required to meet specifications over and above what is normative in the market will accordingly be more expensive. The economics of legal observance therefore cannot be ignored, and this is a factor which will have to be considered further below.

An observation which needs to be made at this point is that the refusal of fellowship, or withdrawal therefrom, has definite implications for the relationship between the parties. Deliberate separation is never between parties who consider themselves equal. The act of separation is at least implicitly hostile and constitutes a claim to privilege (cf. Segal 1990: 194), and the assertion of superiority over the rejected party. Weber has drawn attention to the role of rituals in demonstrating and maintaining status distinctions (1948: 188-189),

1. Cf. *m. Ber.* 7.1. For the contrary position, see Esler 1987: 77. See also Dunn's response to Esler (1990: 180-81). Cf. also Howard 1990: xx.
2. For a treatment of the Jewish community in Antioch, see Meeks and Wilken 1978: 2-4. Cf. also Brown and Meier 1983: 30-32.

and dietary laws and table fellowship are social rituals which reflect assertions of relative status, as well as communion or separation. In the case of Jewish Christians declining table fellowship with Gentile Christians who do not observe Jewish dietary laws, the gesture is, at the very least, an implied assertion of superiority.[1] This is important in considering the attitudes of the parties to the confrontation in Antioch.

The Christian community in Antioch appears to have abandoned full conformity with Jewish dietary regulations, at least in the context of meetings of the church, and in so far as was necessary to maintain the unity of the community (Dunn 1983: 31-34; Watson 1986: 34). Whatever Jewish Christians did in their own homes, and whatever food they provided for gatherings of the church, their conduct did not conform to the more rigid interpretations of the Jewish dietary laws. Paul describes Peter as having lived ἐθνικῶς (Gal. 2.14), when Peter had been doing nothing other than conform to what was the custom of the Antiochene church (Gal. 2.12).[2] While Paul may simply have been wishing to cast a slur on Peter's character or credentials as an observant Jew (cf. Watson 1986: 33) in order to undermine his moral authority, the fact that it did not result in his winning the confrontation, as will become clear in the discussion below, would seem to indicate that Paul was referring specifically to Peter's conduct in relation to the issue in Antioch. The implication of this would seem to be that the prevailing practice in the Antiochene church was, from the point of view at least of those who had earlier opposed the custom of the church (Gal. 2.3-5; Acts 15.1-2), not lax observance of the dietary laws, but disregard thereof.[3] However, Paul's polemical purpose in Galatians means that we cannot be certain that this was the case. What we can be certain of, though, is that Jewish and Gentile Christians in Antioch had found an accommodation whereby they could eat together. That this did not conform to the more rigorous interpretations of Jewish law is clear from the events which took place, and to which we must now give attention.

1. For anthropological discussion of the issue, see van Gennep 1960: 29. For treatments of the particular topic, see Sanders 1977: 155-56; Rowland 1985: 70; Segal 1990: 124.
2. For discussion of the phrase, see Dunn 1983: 32.
3. Cf. Dunn 1983: 31-33; Watson 1986: 29.

2. *The Position and Conduct of the Parties*

What took place at Antioch shortly after the Jerusalem conference was far more complex than simply a confrontation between Peter and Paul. What happened was triggered by neither of the chief protagonists, but by the visitors from Jerusalem. The outcome was determined not by Peter or Paul, but by the response of the Antiochene Christians to conflicting assertions of authority in their community. Peter's response to the visitors from Jerusalem, and the effects of his conduct on the church as a whole, brought him into confrontation with Paul. We must therefore consider the roles of the various parties before reconstructing the event as a whole.

a. *The Delegation from James*
Paul identifies the catalysts in the incident only as τοῦ... ἐλθεῖν τινας ἀπὸ ʼΙακώβου (Gal. 2.12). There can be no doubt that the James mentioned is the brother of Jesus, a leading figure in the Jerusalem church. The implication is, therefore, clearly that the visitors came from Jerusalem and in some sense represented James. Bornkamm argues that they were not an official delegation from James (1971: 33). The majority of scholars, however, take a different view. Mussner argues that the direct role of James depends on how the grammatical structure of the clause is understood.[1] Nickle argues that the visitors were on a specific mission from James (1966: 64), and Gerhardsson presents a rather more elaborate theory that the visitors represented the corporate authority of the apostolic body in Jerusalem (1961: 318; cf. Holl 1921: 57). It is unlikely that the visitors were in Antioch for any reason other than having been sent there by James and the group around him in the Jerusalem church. This does not exclude the possibility that James was constrained to despatch his delegates to Antioch, for whatever purpose, by pressure from the nomistic faction within the Jerusalem church, but the precise reason for their visit is difficult to identify. Unless it was not known that Peter was in Antioch, the visitors cannot simply have been reciprocating Barnabas and Paul's visit to Jerusalem. It is unlikely that they were ensuring

---

1.	If ἐλθεῖν is more closely linked with ἀπὸ ʼΙακώβου than with τινας, then James is to be understood to have been more directly responsible for the conduct of the visitors than would otherwise be the case (Mussner 1974: 139). Cf. Betz 1979: 108.

that the agreement was being observed, as the Jerusalem conference had essentially affirmed the *status quo* in Antioch. They may simply have been passing through Antioch *en route* elsewhere, but it is generally believed that their visit to Antioch had a specific purpose, and that they made demands concerning the life of the community. The probability is therefore that the visit was a deliberate demonstration of authority.

Esler is alone among recent scholars in arguing that the visitors effectively demanded circumcision of Gentile Christians (1987: 88).[1] This would have been a complete breach of the agreement between the Jerusalem and Antiochene churches in which James had played an important role. It is most unlikely therefore that James sought reversal of the agreement, or that he believed he could enforce such a reversal, especially with Peter's being in Antioch at the time. The authority of the Jerusalem church in Antioch may have been entrenched by the Jerusalem conference, but James would have been jeopardizing this authority had he attempted to reverse the decision of the conference without reference to Peter, and while Peter was in Antioch. Furthermore, there is no evidence that this is what James sought to accomplish.

Schmithals argues that the separation between Jewish and Gentile Christians, which Peter initiated, was what the visitors sought (1965a: 69). It is unlikely, however, that this could have been a premeditated demand, as it would have had no basis in the Jerusalem agreement. I have argued above that the separation of Jews from Gentiles in the Church was not part of the agreement and was in fact quite contrary to it.[2] The Jerusalem conference sought to maintain unity not to create division. If, however, the visitors did demand separation, it could only have been on the basis of circumstances they discovered in the church at Antioch, presumably to do with dietary observances.

Watson argues that the delegation from James demanded the observance of the Mosaic law (cf. Gal. 2.14) and disputes Paul's contention that the Jerusalem leadership had ever waived the requirements (1986: 53-56). Dunn argues that the demands specifically concerned the dietary laws and required that they be observed to the standard that had been assumed to prevail in Antioch when the Jerusalem agreement

---

1. Cf. Dunn 1983: 35; Dunn 1990: 180-81; Howard 1990: xx.
2. See discussion in Chapter 4 section 3b.

130   *Paul, Antioch and Jerusalem*

was reached (1983: 31-34). As the response of Peter and the Jewish
Christians in Antioch specifically concerned table fellowship, it is
likely that the demands of the visitors were so directed. If, however, a
higher standard of Jewish dietary observance had been assumed by the
Jerusalem leadership to prevail in Antioch, then the visitors' demand
could not have been premeditated, but rather a response to conditions
they found in Antioch. Dunn also points to the deteriorating political
situation in Judaea which may have motivated the action of the
visitors, with the accompanying nationalistic overtones to the demand
for compliance (1990: 176). Pressure on the church in Jerusalem
(cf. Gal. 6.12; 1 Thess. 2.14)[1] may therefore have constrained them to
curtail the liberty of other Christians with whom they were associated.
In this case, the actions of the visitors from Jerusalem are to be
understood in terms of the Jerusalem agreement and the κοινωνία
which bound together the churches of Jerusalem and Antioch.

To sum up, therefore, the visitors from Jerusalem appear to have
been sent to Antioch by James, quite possibly with a definite intention
of asserting further the authority of the Jerusalem church. As agents
of James, who was presumably in a position of unrivalled dominance
in the Jerusalem church in Peter's absence, they would have been in a
position to exercise the authority of the Jerusalem church in Antioch,
either with specific instructions issued by James, or with discretionary
powers as agents to act as they saw fit. It is most unlikely, however,
that they would knowingly have chosen a time when Peter was in
Antioch and could complicate their attempts to exercise authority in
that church, if a demonstration of authority through contravening the
terms of the Jerusalem agreement was in itself the purpose of the visit.
It is more likely that they were responding to changing circumstances
facing the church in Jerusalem. If the Jerusalem church was claiming
jurisdiction over other Christian communities, it stood to be held
accountable by the Temple hierarchy for what happened in those
communities. This may have motivated the request to remember the
poor, discussed in the previous chapter. Schmithals argues that the
delegation from James visited Antioch in the aftermath of the martyrdom of James, the son of Zebedee, recorded in Acts 12.2 (1971b: 68).
There are further indications that the Jerusalem church was facing

1.   Cf. Jewett 1971: 202-206; Reicke 1984. For the contrary view, see Brandon
1957: 88-100.

persecution at this time in 1 Thess. 2.14-16 and Gal. 6.12 which date from shortly after the incident under discussion. If the community felt itself to be compromised by the conduct of the Antiochene church, James would have felt entirely justified in invoking the agreement, and seeking, in terms of, and not in violation of, the conference decision (cf. Schütz 1975: 154) to bring a greater degree of conformity to the Jewish law into the life of the Antiochene church, with whatever repercussions for the relations between Jewish and Gentile Christians in Antioch. It would seem most likely, therefore, that the visitors' request for conformity to Jewish dietary regulations, to whatever standard, took place fully within the context of κοινωνία between the churches. It is important to recognize, however, that Paul does not actually attribute any demands to the visitors, although he clearly blames them for causing Peter's change of practice. The issue cannot be resolved without attention to Peter's role in what happened.

b. *Peter*
According to Paul, Peter withdrew from table fellowship with the gentile Christians in Antioch on account of the visitors from James (Gal. 2.12), and his example was emulated by the Jewish Christians (Gal. 2.13). We are not told whether it was at the visitors' behest that Peter acted, or whether he merely acted in response to their presence and the pressure, direct or indirect, that they exerted on him. We therefore do not know who initiated the sequence of events in the Antiochene church, although it is clear that the visitors from James were at the least a catalyst, and Peter a major protagonist.

Peter changed his behaviour from conformity with the practice of the Antiochene church to eating apart from the Gentile Christians, and presumably eating only food which conformed to Jewish ritual requirements.[1] As noted above, it was primarily the food, and not the racial origins of the people, that determined Jewish dietary observance. The implication of this is that Peter would not have withdrawn from table fellowship with the Gentile Christians because they were Gentiles, but because the food consumed did not meet the requirements of the Law, presumably as understood by the visitors from Jerusalem. There is no indication of any attempt to impose Jewish dietary laws upon the Gentile Christians (Räisänen 1983: 259). This

---

1. Cf. Räisänen 1983: 259; Howard 1990: xx.

may indicate that Peter's action was intended as a temporary measure, for the duration of the visit, so that the people from Jerusalem would be able to eat with at least him, if nobody else in the Antiochene church, without compromising their own standards of observance.[1] Another possibility is that separation was envisaged as a temporary measure while the Jerusalem church was threatened with persecution. It would probably not have been economically or practically feasible to impose dietary observances on Gentile Christians, which would have made them dependent upon the Jewish markets and the willingness of non-Christian Jewish traders to deal with Gentiles. It would presumably also have been regarded as a breach of trust, and contrary to the Jerusalem agreement, for Peter and the visitors unilaterally to impose dietary laws in Antioch, even if the issue which had arisen had not previously been discussed. Temporary separation may therefore have been seen as the least offensive option available (cf. Sanders 1955: 139). The connotations of inequality between Jewish and Gentile Christians in such action would probably not have occurred to people accustomed to such attitudes (cf. Cohen 1989: 29). The possible implications of separation for future developments could probably not have been foreseen by those not engaged in missionary work among the Gentiles and would probably have been overlooked on account of preoccupation with the more familiar and more urgent situation in Jerusalem.

It is unclear whether Peter intended his behaviour to be followed by the Jewish Christians in Antioch. If Peter was responding to intimations from the visitors that his credibility as a Christian missionary to the Jewish people was compromised by his behaviour in Antioch,[2] then he may not have intended his behaviour to influence that of anybody else. While Peter himself may have needed to maintain his credibility as a preacher of the gospel of circumcision, this would not have been the case with the Jewish Christians of Antioch. Gal. 2.13 seems to indicate spontaneity rather than obedience to a directive, which could support Holmberg's suggestion that it was the force of Peter's example that led to his emulation by the Antiochene Jewish Christians (1978: 34). This possibility will be considered further below, when the role of Barnabas and the church is discussed.

1. Cf. Bauckham 1979: 64; Bruce 1982a: 131.
2. Cf. Dunn 1983: 35; Longenecker 1990: 60.

If Peter's motive was not simply hospitality, it remains unclear whether he was party to any conscious decision that Jewish Christians in Antioch should not eat with Gentiles, or simply acquiesced in a decision which had been made in Jerusalem, or in Antioch by the delegation from Jerusalem. The implication of Gal. 2.12-13 would seem to be the latter, particularly as Paul attributes Peter's action to cowardice, φοβούμενος τοὺς ἐκ περιτομῆς. Whether the objects of Peter's alleged fear are those who preach the gospel of circumcision, the visitors from Jerusalem and those they represented, or non-Christian Jews, those responsible for persecution of the Jerusalem church, is neither clear nor, for the present, relevant. The widescale uncritical acceptance of Paul's ascription of cowardice to Peter[1] is itself highly questionable. Whatever the historicity of the Passion narratives in the Gospels, and Peter's less than heroic role therein, the fact that on one occasion of potentially mortal peril his survival instinct overcame the sentiments which had previously produced extravagant bravado is far from sufficient evidence upon which to base the assumption that Peter was a habitual coward (cf. Nickle 1966: 65-66), and is no basis for believing that Peter was motivated by cowardice on this particular occasion. Furthermore, if fear was the motive for what happened, this fear would presumably have been shared, at least in part, by others who followed Peter's example, in which case there would probably have been good reason for it, such as persecution of the church in Jerusalem (cf. Longenecker 1990: 74-75). Paul's ascription of ὑπόκρισις to Peter (cf. Howard 1990: xx) likewise cannot be taken as reliable or objective in reconstructing the event, but reflects Paul's subjective, polemical, and anachronistic, perspective on the episode.

Meier suggests that Peter was a moderating influence rather than Paul's opponent in the confrontation (Brown and Meier 1983: 41). In this case, Paul's real antagonists would have been the visitors from Jerusalem. This may be an accurate reflection of Peter's theological position in relation to Paul and James, but Paul is unequivocal in Gal. 2.11-14 that it was Peter whom he had confronted. It may have been that Peter's attempt to effect a compromise led to his being accused by Paul of succumbing to pressure from James, a common method of manipulating would-be mediators, and one to which those who hold

---

1.   Burton 1921: 107; Schmithals 1963: 66; Nickle 1966: 66; Bruce 1982a: 131.

moderating positions are prone. Peter may, moreover, as the more prominent figure, have played a more public role in the debacle, while James's emissaries made their overtures discreetly, in which case it would have been Peter who incurred the wrath of those who opposed the developments.

Many unanswered questions regarding Peter's action in Antioch remain and will require further attention, when the positions of the other parties have been reconstructed.

c. *Barnabas and the Antiochene Christians*

Barnabas appears to have been the most eminent of the leadership in the Antioch church (cf. Acts 13.1). His role in the debacle would therefore have been crucial, even if Paul does appear to suggest that Barnabas merely followed the crowd when the Jewish Christians discontinued table fellowship with the Gentile Christians (Gal. 2.13). Given Barnabas's position of leadership in the community, however, he would have been expected to play a more active role, and it is unlikely that the Jewish Christians would have acted without consulting him, especially as he had represented them in formulating the agreement with the Jerusalem church. It is more plausible, therefore, that Barnabas exercised leadership in this episode and was largely responsible for determining what action would be taken by the Christians of Antioch to resolve the dilemma. The role of Barnabas, and of the church as a whole, can therefore appropriately and conveniently be considered together.

Bauckham plausibly attributes Barnabas's decision to withdraw from table fellowship with Gentile Christians to consideration for the scruples of the visitors (1979: 64). Bruce argues similarly that this was an exceptional deviation from normal practice, motivated by considerations of courtesy and hospitality rather than change of principle (1982a: 131). It seems clear from Paul's account that Barnabas and the Antiochene Christians took their lead in this matter from Peter (Gal. 2.12-13), and Schütz argues that this would not have happened had Peter's action been in breach of the Jerusalem agreement (1975: 151; cf. Holmberg 1978: 32). I argued above that any action James was taking in Antioch through the visitors was in terms of, and not contrary to, the agreement, and this would seem to be confirmed by Barnabas and the Antiochene Christians' response to the situation (cf. Schütz 1975: 147-151). They were following the directive of an authority which was recognized in terms of the κοινωνία between the churches (cf. Dunn 1983: 35). Peter and James, and the Jerusalem church, were acknowledged as authoritative by the Antiochene Christians in matters affecting their faith and life. They seem to have been quite willing accordingly to adapt their customs, however temporarily, when prevailed upon by James, supported by Peter, to do so. It is most likely that Barnabas, far from following the crowd as he is depicted by Paul as having done, was instrumental in negotiating with Peter and the visitors how the Antiochene Christians would respond to the situation in Jerusalem (cf. Longenecker 1990: 76). The Antiochenes were willing to consider the effects of their freedom of association, and other customs which deviated from standard Jewish practice, on the Jerusalem church and to curb their liberty when its exercise imperiled that community.

d. *Paul*
Paul was quite clearly isolated in and through his confrontation with Peter and resistance to the authority of the Jerusalem church. In Gal. 2.11-14 he gives no indication at all that anybody supported his position at the time or subsequently. The Gentile Christians are conspicuously silent and passive in Paul's account, and the fact that Paul did not form a separate Gentile church in Antioch may indicate that they accepted, however willingly or unwillingly, the decision of the leadership and the response of the Jewish Christians in following the lead of Peter in withdrawing from table fellowship with them. There are grounds to believe that Silvanus and Titus, Paul's future colleagues, supported him,[1] but neither is mentioned in Paul's account of the episode, and the impression that Paul was isolated in the community stands.

Paul's action, whether he sought to convince Peter, persuade the Jewish Christians, or rally the Gentile Christians, was evidently motivated by theological considerations, for he saw the action of Peter and the Antiochene church as conflicting with τὴν ἀλήθειαν τοῦ εὐαγγελίου (Gal. 2.14). Paul took his stand on principle in a matter on which James, Peter, and Barnabas exercised pragmatism rather than dogma (Bornkamm 1971: 47). This would seem to be the

---

1. Cf. Sanders 1955: 141; Ollrog 1979: 18; Achtemeier 1987: 59. See further discussion in Chapter 6 section 1.

fundamental difference between them. All assented to the principle of a Christian gospel in terms of which Gentiles were included in the Church without being circumcised, and those who did not preach it were pledged to maintain unity with those who did. This was not at stake, or in question so far as Peter and the visitors were concerned, but Paul saw their withdrawal from table fellowship with Gentile Christians as a threat to that principle (cf. Segal 1990: 194). For Paul it was a great deal more than concessions to their own freedom by one church on one occasion for the sake of another. Not only would it set a precedent, both for future occasions on which Jewish and Gentile Christians could be separated within a single church and for the further extension of the authority of the Jerusalem church in other communities, but the criteria for Gentile Christian fellowship with Jewish Christians would become more rigorous than those required for salvation. Furthermore, separation is a form of exclusivism, and the implication of separation of Jewish from Gentile Christians could only be that the latter were inferior. This would denigrate both the Gentile Christians themselves and the gospel in terms of which they were received into the Church without observance of the Jewish law. Gentile Christians would either accept inferior standing within the Church, which would seem to have happened, at least for a time, in Antioch, or be coerced into observing the Jewish law. Paul therefore saw the feasibility of the Christian mission to Gentiles as in peril, and with it the integrity of the gospel he preached.

The fact that Barnabas and the Antiochenes did not share Paul's perception of the situation and were evidently convinced more by the harsh realities of persecution in Jerusalem than by the theological truths articulated by Paul, or the consequences of their action which he foresaw, does not mean that Paul was single-mindedly absorbed in dogma and theory, or that the others were correspondingly swayed by sentiment. The question of authority also influenced the course of events through deciding the stand of Barnabas and the Antiochene Christians. The Antiochenes had previously recognized the authority of the Jerusalem church, and it would have been most unlikely that they would have defied that authority when it was reinforced by the presence and example of Peter in their midst. In terms of the relationship of κοινωνία between the two churches, a directive from Jerusalem, or given on the authority of the leadership of that community, was sure to be effective unless it was so repressive as to become intolerable. Resistance in this case would undoubtedly have been successful, since the Jerusalem church had no coercive power by which to enforce its authority and could exercise jurisdiction only by consent.[1] The compliance of the Antiochene Christians must therefore have been willing for the Jerusalem church was able to exercise its authority despite its lack of power and to maintain, and possibly strengthen, its authority over the church at Antioch.

Paul, however, found the directive from Jerusalem so repressive, and so alien to his understanding of the gospel and endangering to his work, that he rebelled against it. He failed to convince the Antiochene church, still less Peter and the visitors, and his repudiation of the authority of the Jerusalem church therefore applied to his own life and work only. In this respect, Paul could in Weberian terms be compared to a failed charismatic whose message and leadership were not accepted or recognized by those whom he sought to convince.[2] His action brought him into conflict with the authority structures on which church life in Antioch was based, and his failure to convince the Antiochenes placed him outside those structures.

That Paul failed to convince Peter or anyone else, with one or two possible exceptions, such as Silvanus and Titus, to adopt his position in Antioch is quite clear. The contrary view has been defended most recently by Lyons (1985: 134-135)[3] but it is quite clearly not compatible with the account. Paul would certainly have recorded any victory he had scored over Peter in Antioch in his account in Galatians, and the conspicuous absence of any such evidence and the absence of any indication of support for Paul from within the Antiochene community must demonstrate strongly that Paul's confrontation with Peter ended in defeat and isolation for him, as the majority of recent scholars argue.[4]

To sum up, therefore, the sparsity and partiality of the evidence

1. See discussion in the Introduction sections 3a and 3c.
2. See the Introduction section 3c.
3. Also Knox 1925: 193; Munck 1959: 102; Roloff 1965: 75; Hainz 1972: 125, 248; Oepke 1973: 88-89; Bruce 1982a: 132.
4. Haenchen 1971: 476; Georgi 1965: 31; Nickle 1966: 66-67; Stuhlmacher 1968: 106-107; Robinson and Koester 1971: 122; Eckert 1971: 227; Holtz 1974: 124; Mussner 1974: 186-87; Catchpole 1977: 439-440; Dunn 1977: 254; Dunn 1983: 39; Holmberg 1978: 34; Bauckham 1979: 64; Brown and Meier 1983: 39; Achtemeier 1987: 59; Longenecker 1990: 79.

makes reconstructing the incident at Antioch very difficult. While the main parties can be readily identified, their actions and motives are a matter of speculation, assisted only by unreliable aspersions by Paul in his account of the episode. It seems clear, though, that the visitors from Jerusalem were acting on behalf of James and that their action was conceived in terms of the agreement recently reached between the Jerusalem and Antioch churches and the κοινωνία between those communities. Persecution of the church in Jerusalem, or the threat thereof, may well have given rise to the visit. The Jerusalem church, accountable for and compromised by the conduct of Jewish Christians in Antioch, needed to demonstrate to the Temple hierarchy and other potential persecutors its capacity to curb the liberties exercised by the Antiochene Christians. The visitors sought therefore to seek the curtailment, temporarily or permanently, of unrestricted table fellowship between Jewish and Gentile Christians in Antioch. In this they were evidently supported by Peter and Barnabas who would almost certainly have been consulted before action was taken. The Antiochene Christians evidently complied quite willingly with the decision and Paul's resistance led to his own isolation in Antioch and beyond. The consequences of the incident require further consideration.

3. *The Consequences of the Incident*

The immediate consequence of the confrontation between Paul and Peter, and the failure of the former to convince the latter to reverse his decision to withdraw from table fellowship with Gentile Christians, was the continued separation between Jewish and Gentile Christians in Antioch. Holmberg argues that this includes separate celebrations of the Eucharist (1978: 33). This would almost certainly have been the case had the bread and wine not all been acquired on the Jewish markets. That this was not the final resolution to the problem will become clear in the discussion below.

The conflict between Paul and Peter did not affect the agreement between the Jerusalem and Antioch churches.[1] Paul had not been a party to the agreement in his personal capacity, but as a representative of the Antiochene church (Schütz, 1975: 140-51).[2] The church

---

1. Cf. Munck 1959: 101-102; Schoeps 1961: 68.
2. Cf. Sampley 1980: 24-32.

maintained the agreement, as mutually understood by them, Peter, and the visitors. The κοινωνία was strengthened, in that it withstood the pressure applied to it by Paul, and the authority of the Jerusalem church in Antioch was entrenched. The gospel of uncircumcision was undoubtedly compromised, but the agreement stood.

It is generally agreed that the confrontation between Peter and Paul, in which Barnabas supported Peter, brought an end to the partnership between Barnabas and Paul, and also to the latter's association with the church at Antioch.[1] It was therefore a crucial turning point in Paul's life which fundamentally altered the entire basis of his Christian being and activity. Separation from the Antiochene church deprived Paul of his dyadic identity in that community as well as of his commission as an apostle of that community. In order to compensate for the loss of identity and support Paul was forced to substitute new structures which would support and legitimate his activities. As will become clear in the following chapter, dependence on the church at Antioch was replaced with dependence entirely on God. Paul came to derive his apostolic vocation directly from God and to identify his very being with his vocation to preach the Christian gospel to the Gentiles, so that, in a sense, he derived his dyadic identity also from God.

---

1. Holmberg 1978: 65; Brown and Meier 1983: 39; cf. Conzelmann 1987: 123; Bauckham 1979: 67.

Excursus

The Apostolic Decree

It is generally accepted that the Apostolic Decree was formulated in response to the situation which arose in Antioch as a result of separation between Jewish and Gentile Christians.[1] Paul was not involved in this and may not have known about it until informed by James at Acts 21.25.[2] It is more likely that Paul learnt of the Apostolic Decree when he returned to Antioch for the visit recorded in Acts 18.22, but there is no indication that it influenced his subsequent work.[3] The Apostolic Decree is therefore not relevant to Paul's ministry but nevertheless merits some consideration.

It would seem that it was the recognition that the ending of table fellowship between Jewish and Gentile Christians in Antioch was not a satisfactory resolution to the peril facing the Jerusalem church that led to the formulation of the Apostolic Decree. In this it was to some extent a vindication of Paul's position (cf. Segal 1990: 194), irrespective of whether or not he approved of the provisions, or would have been willing to abide by them and enforce them in his churches.

The precise provisions of the Apostolic Decree vary in the different accounts, Acts 15.29 and Acts 21.25 agreeing against Acts 15.20; in addition there are textual variants (cf. Achtemeier 1987: 83-84). For the present purpose it is not necessary to discuss the details of these variations, since it is sufficient to establish that provision was made for table fellowship between Jewish and Gentile Christians in the aftermath of its suspension at Antioch and the rupture between Barnabas and Paul on that account. Borgen has argued, on account of the textual variations, that there never were specific provisions to the Apostolic Decree (1988: 135). The essential purpose of the Decree was to confirm that circumcision was not integral to Christian teaching (1988: 137; cf. Dibelius 1956: 97) and this was embellished with various versions of the catalogues of pagan vices which proliferated in the Jewish world at the time. The degree of agreement there is between the various accounts, however, and the relatively narrow range of behaviour covered indicate something rather more definite, even if the provisions were general rather than specific. Schoeps argues that the Apostolic Decree reflects the Noachic obligations, traditionally regarded as incumbent

1.   Nickle 1966: 67; Brown and Meier 1983: 42; Dunn 1983: 38.
2.   Sanders 1955: 140; Nickle 1966: 55; Hengel 1979: 117; Brown and Meier 1983: 42; cf. Bornkamm 1971: 42; Conzelmann 1973: 89; Esler 1987: 99.
3.   For the contrary view, see Hurd 1965: 246-67, 289, 294.

upon sojourners in Israel as well as Israelites (1961: 66-67; cf. Dunn 1983: 32). In this case, the Decree would represent the minimal level of observance of the Jewish law needed for Gentiles to enter the Church and enter table fellowship with Jewish Christians. Wilson, however, argues that, as the Decree nowhere mentions foods forbidden to Jews, it provides for common worship rather than table fellowship (1973: 189; cf. Dunn 1983: 31-36), and is directed against Gentile Christian participation in pagan cults (1983: 94-99). It is questionable whether Wilson's distinction is applicable, at least to the extent that eating formed part of worship. Countryman has also argued that the Apostolic Decree was devised to prohibit Christians' participation in pagan cults, but identifies provision for table fellowship between Jewish and Gentile Christians as its objective (1988: 71-77). The wider application is more likely as all three accounts of the Apostolic Decree prohibit consumption of the meat of strangled animals (Acts 15.20, 29; 21.25), which may apply to meals in the context of which the Eucharist was celebrated but not to the Eucharistic elements themselves (cf. 1 Cor. 11.20-34). Likewise, the proscribed foods of Leviticus 11 are all the meat of unclean animals. Meat was normally accessible only to the wealthy, and is therefore unlikely to have featured prominently in the communal meals of early Christian churches. The specific applicability of the Apostolic Decree to common worship must therefore be doubtful and, furthermore, the Jewish prohibition on eating pork was sufficiently well-known to have been symbolic of the Jewish food laws,[1] and for eating pork to be symbolic of apostasy and paganism (cf. Isa. 65.4; 1 Macc. 1.47). It would therefore not have required specific mention in a document produced by Jewish Christians which would have presupposed a prohibition on pork for table fellowship between Jewish and Gentile Christians. Other forbidden foods were less symbolic of all that was opposed to Jewish beliefs and values and would therefore have been less likely to provoke Jewish sensibilities if and when they were served at corporate Christian meals. The Apostolic Decree could therefore have provided a basis for table fellowship between Jewish and Gentile Christians, through prescribing guidelines for Gentile dietary observance, without expounding every prohibition in full.

Whether the Apostolic Decree was intended for all churches (Geyser 1953: 138), or only for those centred on Antioch (Bruce 1968: 14; Dunn 1990: 258), it had no bearing on Paul's work, as shown above. I have argued that the Apostolic Decree represents primarily a further development in the relationship of κοινωνία between the churches of Jerusalem and Antioch, rectifying inadequacies in the previous state of mutual recognition which had been revealed through the confrontation between Peter and Paul. The Apostolic Decree, I would suggest, was formulated by James, Peter, and Barnabas in consultation with the leaders of their churches in order to create a basis for table fellowship between Jewish and Gentile Christians in Antioch, which would offend the sensibilities neither of nomistic Jewish Christians, nor of the Temple hierarchy. The freedom of the Antiochene church to preach and live by their gospel of uncircumcision was undoubtedly curtailed, but no more than was

1. Jagersma 1985: 52; Achtemeier 1987: 84. See also Plutarch, *Sept. Sap.* 4.4; 5.3.

considered necessary to maintain the κοινωνία between the two churches without compromising the safety of the Christian community in Jerusalem. The Jerusalem church therefore entrenched further its jurisdiction over the Antiochene church, while the relationship between the churches was maintained.

There can be little doubt that the precedents set in the relationship between the churches of Jerusalem and Antioch could influence or even perhaps determine the outcome of analogous situations elsewhere. The Jerusalem church had a precedent on the basis on which to demand obedience from other Christian communities, and the specific provisions of the Apostolic Decree, as of previous agreements between the two churches, concerned issues that would unquestionably have arisen elsewhere. The potential for universal applicability of the Apostolic Decree is therefore not to be ignored, even if it was not realized at the time.

Paul's period of association with the church at Antioch began after he had been forced to flee Damascus and Jerusalem, and brought stability after an unsettled period in his life. It would appear from the records that he worked closely with Barnabas, both in Antioch and in missionary outreach from there in Asia Minor. As well as dyadic identity, membership of the Antiochene church gave Paul a role in the community, both in Antioch and, perhaps more significantly, in the apostolate of that church beyond its own confines. During this period, I have argued, Paul was fully integrated into the life of the Antiochene Christian community and became one of its leaders, though the junior partner to Barnabas in their missionary activities.

Paul shared in the relationship of κοινωνία between the churches of Antioch and Jerusalem in which the latter was the dominant partner. It was in the context of this relationship that the Jerusalem conference took place, at which Barnabas and Paul, representing the Antiochene church, sought clarity on the obligations of Gentile Christians with regard to the Mosaic law, and specifically the question of circumcision. The gospel as lived and preached in Antioch and the churches its missionaries had established elsewhere was at stake, and the viability both of the communities and of their missionary work would have been jeopardized had circumcision become obligatory for gentile Christians.

At the Jerusalem conference the Antiochene gospel was affirmed in the context of mutual recognition between two disparate expressions of the one Christian gospel, a gospel of circumcision to which the Mosaic law was integral, and a gospel of uncircumcision to which certain provisions of the Law were axiomatic, while others, most notably circumcision of Gentile converts, were waived. While this was the ruling sought by the Antiochene delegation, it nevertheless entrenched the predominance of the Jerusalem church in the κοινωνία in that it created a precedent whereby controversial questions of doctrine and practice were settled in Jerusalem, effectively by the leadership of the Jerusalem church. Furthermore, the obligations accepted by the Antiochene delegation reinforced the inequality in the relationship between the two churches and provided the basis for further encroachment upon the liberty of the Antiochene Christian community.

The sequel to the Jerusalem conference was the confrontation between Peter and Paul at Antioch. The episode was precipitated by the intervention of a delegation from Jerusalem, sent by James, to assert further the authority of the Jerusalem church in the κοινωνία which bound the churches of Jerusalem and Antioch. In response to persecution of the Christian community in Jerusalem, the delegation sought curtailment of table fellowship between Jewish and Gentile Christians in Antioch. The decision that Jewish Christians should withdraw from table fellowship with Gentile Christians was agreed between Peter and Barnabas on the one hand, and the delegation from Jerusalem on the other. Paul saw this as a threat to the life of the community and to its missionary outreach. He accordingly confronted Peter but was not supported by the community in doing so, and the acrimony with which the episode was conducted was apparently such that Paul could no longer function within the Antiochene church and its missionary outreach.

While the Antiochene Christians resolved the problem of table fellowship between Jewish and Gentile Christians through the promulgation of the Apostolic Decree in further consultation with the Jerusalem church, Paul departed from Antioch and began a career of independent missionary work. Neither the Antioch incident nor the departure of Paul substantially affected the κοινωνία between the churches of Jerusalem and Antioch. Rather, resolution of the problem strengthened the bond between the communities and entrenched the predominance of the Jerusalem church in their relationship. It is to Paul's work subsequent to his separation from the church of Antioch that we must now direct our attention.

Part III

PAUL'S INDEPENDENT MISSION

I argued in Part II that Paul's work during the period of his life between his first post-conversion visit to Jerusalem and the Antioch incident must be understood within the context of his membership, and later apostleship, of the church of Antioch. Paul shared in the κοινωνία that bound the churches of Jerusalem and Antioch. I have interpreted the texts of Paul's allusions to this period in this light and questioned the individualistic account of the events related in Galatians. We turn now to the subsequent period in Paul's life, that during which this account, and all Paul's extant correspondence, was written. Paul's departure from Antioch resulted in the transformation both of his self-identity and of the nature of his apostolic ministry. In seeking to demonstrate the degree of this transformation I shall illustrate further the importance of the church of Antioch in Paul's Christian career, and particularly his apostolic formation, and shall argue that the self-image Paul projects in his letters is fundamentally a response to the severance of his association with the Antiochene church and an adaptation to the resultant change in his social and ecclesiastical circumstances.

Chapter 6

THE AFTERMATH OF THE ANTIOCH INCIDENT

Paul's confrontation with Peter at Antioch left him isolated in that church and alienated him also from the Jerusalem church. He accordingly repudiated the authority of those communities, which cost him the support of the structures upon which his missionary work had been founded. He was therefore obliged, if he was to continue his work of Christian mission, to form his own structures which would provide the support to which he no longer had access. That he did so, and with considerable missionary success during the ensuing period, is abundantly clear from the sources.

We are concerned in this chapter with Paul's relationship with the Jerusalem church during his period of independent Christian missionary work between the incident at Antioch and his return there recorded in Acts 18.22. This is the period during which 1 Thessalonians, Galatians, and possibly also 2 Thessalonians, were written, and is reflected also in Acts 15.40–18.22, the so-called 'second missionary journey'. However inappropriate that designation, it nevertheless demarcates a distinct phase in Paul's career. We begin our discussion by assessing the evidence for contact between Paul and the Jerusalem church during this period.

1. *Contact between Paul and the Jerusalem Church*

There is no evidence that Paul visited Jerusalem during this period, except and until the doubtful visit of Acts 18.22. A significant number of scholars argue that Paul did visit Jerusalem at this point,[1] including those who identify the Jerusalem conference (Gal. 2.1-10) with this

---

1. Filson 1964: 246; Nickle 1966: 61-62; Munck 1967: 181; Schneider 1982: 254.

visit.[1] Haenchen argues that Paul visited Caesarea unintentionally, on account of the prevailing winds, while intending to travel to Antioch, but did not travel to Jerusalem, even if Luke thought he did (1971: 544). Conzelmann similarly argues that the text refers to a visit to Jerusalem, but states that such a visit is historically improbable (1987: 156). Haenchen and Conzelmann's arguments seem more plausible in the light of consideration of the sources and chronology, and a journey by Paul to Jerusalem between the conference and his final visit must therefore be regarded as most unlikely. Following Haenchen and Conzelmann, therefore, I would maintain that the visit to Antioch recorded in Acts 18.22 is historical but no visit to Jerusalem took place at this point.[2]

We know of no meetings outside Jerusalem between Paul and the leaders of the Jerusalem church, and these must be regarded as unlikely. Nor have we any evidence that letters were exchanged between these parties, which leaves the impression that there was no direct contact between them during this period. In Rom. 15.31 Paul indicates a degree of apprehension at his forthcoming visit to Jerusalem, which corroborates the indications of such evidence as there is that there was no contact between Paul and the Jerusalem church after the Antioch incident. This view may be substantiated by James's telling Paul of the Apostolic Decree, as though for the first time, in Acts 21.25, implying that there had been no direct contact between them since its promulgation.[3] This is not to say that Paul heard of the Apostolic Decree for the first time on his final visit to Jerusalem, since he could not have failed to have heard about it on his visit to Antioch at Acts 18.22, but Acts 21.18-25 represents the first meeting between Paul and the leadership of the Jerusalem church since the promulgation of the Apostolic Decree.

One possible form of contact between Paul and the Jerusalem church during this period, lies in the role of Silvanus in Paul's missionary work. Recent scholarship is unanimous in identifying the Silvanus (Σιλουανός) who participated in the mission to

1. Knox 1954: 68-69; Jewett; 1979: 78-80; Lüdemann 1984: 149; Lüdemann 1989: 206-207; Hyldahl 1986: 82.
2. See discussion of chronology in the Introduction section 5.
3. Cf. Haenchen 1971: 606-608; Georgi 1965: 88-89; Holmberg 1978: 42. Cf. also Conzelmann 1987: 180-81, who disputes the historicity of Acts 21.

Corinth (2 Cor. 1.19; cf. Acts 18.5), and who is a co-author of the Thessalonian letters (1 Thess. 1.1; 2 Thess. 1.1), with the Silas (Σίλας) introduced in Acts 15.22, a prominent member of the Jerusalem church, who was despatched to Antioch with the Apostolic Decree, and became Paul's partner after his break with Barnabas, apparently for the duration of the 'second missionary journey' (Acts 15.40).[1] Haenchen, Ollrog, and Schneider, while accepting this identification, doubt Silvanus's connection with Jerusalem, the last-mentioned suggesting he was an Antiochean.[2] The narrative of Acts 15.32-40 is the sole authority for identifying Silvanus as a member of the Jerusalem church and this text therefore requires closer examination.

I argued at the close of Part II that the Apostolic Decree belongs to the period subsequent to the incident at Antioch, and not to the Jerusalem conference. This raises questions about the narrative and chronology of Acts 15.32-40 in which Silas travelled to Antioch, from where, with the exception of some texts of Acts 15.34,[3] he is recorded as having returned to Jerusalem, before being chosen as Paul's colleague after the latter's split with Barnabas. It is not inconceivable, but there is no indication that any members of the Jerusalem church accompanied Barnabas and Paul on their return to Antioch in Paul's account; Peter's arrival in Antioch occurred some time later (Gal. 2.11). Those whom Luke describes as accompanying Barnabas and Paul are, in any event, recorded as having returned to Jerusalem after completing their task, according to the most reliable texts.

By the time the Apostolic Decree was brought to Antioch Paul would have departed with Silvanus for missionary work in Asia Minor in the aftermath of his confrontation with Peter. The only delegation of which we know from Jerusalem to Antioch between the conference and that incident was the one which occasioned the confrontation between Peter and Paul. It is most unlikely that Paul would have chosen one of James's delegates as his partner after the incident, as Lietzmann argues (1937: 141; cf. Ollrog 1979: 18). It is

---

1.   Schmithals 1971b: 66; Filson 1964: 218; Munck 1967: 143; Conzelmann 1973: 160; Best 1972: 61; Barrett 1973: 77; Holmberg 1978: 66; Bruce 1985: 22; Furnish 1984: 135; Wanamaker 1990: 8, 67-69.

2.   Haenchen 1971: 397, 423; Ollrog 1979: 18-19; Schneider 1982: 184, 187.

3.   The textual issues are discussed by Metzger 1975: 439.

also unlikely that one of James's delegates would have been willing to work with Paul after the incident, even if Paul wished it as a gesture of reassurance to the Jerusalem church, as Harnack suggests (1908: 178; cf. Bruce 1985: 26). The delegation from Jerusalem to Antioch of Acts 15.32, cannot therefore readily be identified with any known from Galatians 2, if Silvanus was a member of it. How Silvanus came to join Paul cannot therefore be explained on the basis of the records of Acts.

If Silvanus's association with the Jerusalem church is historical, he must nevertheless have been in sympathy with the gospel of uncircumcision preached at Antioch (cf. Bruce 1985: 25), to the extent that he was willing to preach it, and, despite the recent episode, to associate with Paul in doing so. Sanders argues that Silvanus supported Paul at Antioch (1955: 141), while Ollrog asserts that, if present, Silvanus did not support Peter (1979: 18). It is inconceivable that Paul would have travelled to Jerusalem in the hope of recruiting Silvanus or anybody else to work with him after the Antioch incident. It is most likely, therefore, that Silvanus was present in Antioch and supported Paul (Achtemeier 1987: 59). While, as noted in Chapter 5, there is no indication in Gal. 2.11-14 that anybody supported Paul at Antioch, this silence does not necessarily imply Paul's total isolation, as Titus, who had accompanied Paul to Jerusalem (Gal. 2.1), continued to work with him after the Antioch incident (2 Cor. 12.18).[1] It would therefore seem likely that Silvanus too supported Paul at Antioch, in which case he was probably a member of that church, rather than of the Jerusalem community. This is not to deny that Silvanus had been connected with the Jerusalem church, as indeed Barnabas had been, but, at the time of the Antioch incident, it would appear more plausible that he was a member of the Antiochene church and supported Paul against

1.   Titus is not included among those who accompanied Paul on his mission to Corinth, not long after the Antioch incident (2 Cor. 1.19). However, if the hostility of non-Christian Jews in Macedonia had precipitated Paul's departure from the region, as Acts 17.5-10, 13-14 indicate (cf. 1 Thess. 1.6; 2.2), then it is conceivable that Titus could safely have remained in Macedonia while Paul was in Achaia. It is of course also possible that Titus's association with Paul was resumed after an interval. In either event, Titus as a Gentile Christian would probably not have played a significant role in the Antioch incident, which was essentially an intra-Jewish Christian controversy. As Titus is not mentioned in Acts, no corroborative evidence is available from that source.

Barnabas, Peter, and the visitors from James.

If Silvanus had in some way represented the Jerusalem church in Paul's missionary work, this would have raised questions about the nature of Paul's relationship with that community during the period in which his independence of any human authority was most aggressively asserted. While this seems unlikely, some questions nevertheless remain, to which attention must be given.

The fact that Paul does not name Silvanus as co-author of Galatians cannot be insignificant. Paul mentions πάντες ἀδελφοί in Gal. 1.2. While these certainly could include Silvanus (2 Cor. 1.19), the indications are that they do not share with Paul in the authorship of the letter,[1] but only in the greeting (Gal. 1.3-5), since Paul reverts to the first person singular in Gal. 1.6, and is concerned in the following verses with asserting his own apostolic authority. Paul is seeking to demonstrate his unity with, as well as independence from, the Jerusalem church, and, while the latter aim may have been compromised, the former could have been immeasurably strengthened, had Paul named Silvanus as co-author and Silvanus been connected with the Jerusalem church. Wainwright suggests that Silvanus was in Galatia at the time Paul wrote the letter (1980: 69), but his thesis ignores Paul's assertion that Silvanus had participated in the mission to Corinth (cf. 2 Cor. 1.19). Wainwright contradicts both the account of Acts (18.5) and what evidence can be gleaned from Paul's letters and is therefore of little help in resolving this question. Silvanus's absence from Galatians, I would suggest, is most plausibly explained by his not having been involved in the mission to Galatia, which Paul had undertaken with Barnabas, and his therefore not having had any personal connection with the Galatian churches. He may, furthermore, have been unwilling to involve himself in Paul's dealings with churches which had been established under Antiochene auspices, and which the Jerusalem and Antioch churches would still have regarded as coming under Antiochene oversight (cf. Dunn 1990: 258-259). Silvanus's support for Paul in Antioch would not necessarily have extended to participating in the latter's attempts to assert his own authority in place of the oversight of the Antiochene church in Galatia.[2] I would suggest, therefore, that Silvanus was willing to support Paul in new

1. Lightfoot 1890: 72-73; Burton 1921: 8-9; cf. Betz 1979: 40.
2. See discussion in section 3 below.

missionary outreach, and he may have joined in sending his greetings to the Galatian Christians, but he was not willing to lend his name and authority to what he considered a subversive project.

Silvanus is named as co-author of the letters to the Thessalonians, the first of which reflects some esteem for the Judaean churches (2.14), compared with which Galatians is at best equivocal about the Jerusalem church and its leaders (2.6). Even taking into account the very different circumstances reflected in these letters, which date from much the same period, the question arises as to whether Silvanus's role in the composition of the Thessalonian correspondence influenced the more positive attitude to the Jerusalem church reflected in these letters. If Silvanus was able to moderate the tone of Paul's statements about the Jerusalem church, this could indicate that he influenced not merely other parts of the letter, but also the teaching delivered in the Pauline churches during this period. That this was not in the direction of nomism may be indicated by the contents of 1 Corinthians, unless Silvanus was in some way responsible for the formation of the Peter party in Corinth (cf. Kaye 1979: 25).[1] The latter possibility would be most unlikely, if our reconstruction of the events at Antioch is correct. It is also unlikely that the break with the synagogue in Corinth was the cause of Silvanus's leaving Paul's missionary team (cf. Kaye 1979: 24).

It is not possible to be absolutely certain as to the role of Silvanus in Paul's missionary work. His apparent connection with Jerusalem leads some scholars to see him as the representative of that church, monitoring and moderating Paul's teaching activities.[2] It seems more likely, however, that whatever Silvanus's previous connections with Jerusalem, he was active in the Antioch church at the time of Paul's confrontation with Peter there and supported Paul in that crisis. Silvanus's previous links with the Jerusalem church do not therefore constitute a link between Paul and that church during the period of their association.

Silvanus is not mentioned in Acts after 18.5. This would seem to indicate that he did not accompany Paul on his subsequent work after

1. For discussion of the Peter party in Corinth, see section 5 below and Chapter 7 section 1.

2. Cf. Harnack 1908: 178; Lietzmann 1937: 141; Bruce 1985: 26; Wanamaker 1990: 8, 67-69.

their return to Antioch in Acts 18.22 (Ollrog 1979: 20), and functioned elsewhere thereafter (cf. Holmberg 1978: 67). In the traditional
terminology, Silvanus accompanied Paul on his 'second', but not his
'third missionary journey'. It is possible that the Apostolic Decree, as
implemented in Antioch, had rectified relations between Jewish and
Gentile Christians to the extent that Silvanus was inclined to resume
his association with that church, and perhaps even with Peter (cf.
1 Pet. 5.12), rather than to continue to participate, perhaps uneasily,
in Paul's missionary work.

We have found no reason to believe that there was any direct contact between Paul and the Jerusalem church during the period under
consideration. It would seem that Paul did not visit Jerusalem, and
there is no evidence of his having written or sent messengers to the
church there. Whatever his past associations with the Jerusalem
church, it would appear that Silvanus did not join Paul's missionary
work as a representative of that community but as a supporter of
Paul's position on the relationship of Jews and Gentiles in the Church.

2. *The Evidence of 1 Thessalonians*

Discussion of Paul's potentially significant statement in 1 Thess. 2.
14-16 requires preliminary discussion of the status of the text in
question. It is precisely because Paul writes favourably of the Judaean
Christians and expresses with unusual vehemence his hostility towards
Jews opposed to the gospel that a number of scholars have questioned
the authorship of 1 Thess. 2.14-16. This position has no textual
support, but must nevertheless be considered, as it could potentially
influence the outcome of the present research.

The traditional position that 1 Thessalonians was written by the
authors mentioned in the introductory greeting from Corinth in c. 50
CE, now almost universally affirmed, was questioned by Baur, largely
on account of the text under consideration. Baur regarded 1 Thess.
2.14-16 as 'thoroughly un-Pauline', reflecting a period when accommodation was sought with the Jewish Christianity Paul had so vehe-
mently opposed (1876: 87). Baur proceeded to date the entire letter
after Paul's death (1876: 96), and after the destruction of Jerusalem in
70 CE, to which he saw allusion in 1 Thess. 2.16 (1876: 340).

A number of scholars, most notably Pearson, have followed Baur in
disputing Paul's authorship of 1 Thess. 2.14-16, but have identified

these verses as a post-Pauline interpolation rather than refuting the Pauline authorship of the letter as a whole. Pearson argues that the attack on the Jews for killing Christ and the prophets (1 Thess. 2.15) is incompatible with Paul's pride in his Jewish achievements, as expounded in Gal. 1.14 (1971: 85). The juxtaposition of these texts, however, is fallacious, even if persecution is closely linked to both.[1] In the latter Paul is not so much expressing pride in his achievements in Pharisaic observance, as confessing how misguided that pride had been before his conversion, especially in that it had led him to perse-cute the Christians (cf. 2 Cor. 11.21-23; Phil. 3.4-7). Pearson asserts that there is no evidence of persecution of Jewish Christianity between 44 CE and the outbreak of the Jewish War in 66 CE (1971: 86). Jewett, however, rightly points out that Gal. 6.12, almost contemporary with 1 Thessalonians, indicates the persecution of Jewish Christians (1986: 38), as does Gal. 4.29 (cf. Wanamaker 1990: 112-13). Pearson's con-clusion, therefore, that 1 Thess. 2.14 is both historically and theologi-cally 'incongruous' (1971: 88) is unsupported by the evidence.

Recent scholarship has tended to accept the authenticity of 1 Thess. 2.14-16.[2] The most significant recent works are those of Jewett and Wanamaker. Jewett refutes Baur's claim that 1 Thess. 2.16 necessarily alludes to the destruction of the Temple (1986: 38), and argues that the evidence for interpolation is insubstantial (1986: 36-41), and affirms the likelihood of Pauline authorship of the verses in question (1986: 46). In this he is substantially followed by Wanamaker, who concludes that the interpolation theories are unconvincing (1990: 29-33). In view of the demonstrated weakness of the arguments against the authenticity of 1 Thess. 2.14-16, we can accept their Pauline authorship and their inclusion in the original text of 1 Thessalonians. We are therefore dealing with the words of Paul, albeit co-authored by Silvanus and Timothy, but nevertheless issued on Paul's authority.

Paul describes the Thessalonian Christians as having become μιμηταί of the Judaean churches (1 Thess. 2.14) by virtue of having endured persecution. This is significant in view of Paul's generally pejorative attitude to the Jerusalem church in Galatians. The precise

---

1.   For discussion of the question of persecution of Christians in Judaea during this period, see Jewett 1971: 202-206, and Reicke 1984, who argue that there was persecution, and Brandon 1957: 88-100, who argues that there was not.

2.   Best 1972: 123; Lyons 1985: 202-207. Cf. also R.F. Collins 1984: 114.

meaning of μιμητής must therefore be established. As well as denoting conscious and deliberate imitation of another party, the word can be used in comparison, where no imitation is implied (Michaelis 1942: 664-665). If Paul is using μιμητής in the former sense, he is expressing unequivocal, if implied, praise for the Christian communities in Judaea. However, if Paul is merely expressing comparison between the experience of the Thessalonian Christians and that of the Judaeans, the implied praise of the latter does not imply that the Judaean Christians are a model for the behaviour of the Thessalonians. There is no reason at all to believe that the Thessalonian Christians' endurance of persecution was consciously modelled on that of the Judaeans. It would seem more likely that the Thessalonians' response to persecution was spontaneous and that Paul is making a comparison between the endurance of the Judaean Christians in the face of harassment from their compatriots and that of the Thessalonians, as Michaelis, Best, and Wanamaker argue.[1] Paul's implied praise for the Jerusalem church is therefore confined to the matter on which comparison is made. Paul's regard for their perseverance in the face of persecution does not imply any approval of the cultic observances and other specifically Jewish practices to which the Jerusalem church adhered, and which had been partly responsible for the conflict between them. Still less does it imply approval of attempts to curtail the liberty of other Christians, as had recently taken place in Antioch. A dichotomy therefore cannot be drawn between Paul's attitude to the Jerusalem church in Galatians and that implied in this text. Nevertheless, it is clear that Paul does not regard the Judaean Christians as so reprehensible in other ways that he cannot associate his converts with them. This is especially so if Malherbe is correct in arguing that Paul implies that the Judaean and Thessalonian Christians, on account of their endurance of persecution, belong to a 'worldwide fellowship' (1987: 75).

It is nevertheless somewhat curious that Paul should have chosen the Judaean churches, with whom his relationship was at the time under considerable strain, as the group of Christians with whom to compare the Thessalonians. 1 Thess. 2.1 and Acts 16.19-24 indicate that the Christian gospel encountered hostility in neighbouring Philippi (cf. Phil. 1.29), which, if historical in general, if not in the particulars

1.   Michaelis 1942: 666; Best 1972: 113; Wanamaker 1990: 113.

of the episode recorded in Acts, would have provided another church established by Paul with which the Thessalonians could be compared. However, Paul cites the Judaean churches rather than the church at Philippi as, if not a model, at least a type, of Christian communities which have endured persecution and remained faithful. The status of the most ancient Christian communities, with whom he compares the Thessalonians, is a factor Paul could not have ignored, even if the Thessalonians knew no Christian teaching other than his own. Antiquity was a well-known criterion for religious respectability in the Graeco-Roman world,[1] and Paul's comparison of his converts with the oldest Christian communities must be understood in such terms. The comparison does not explicitly equate the Thessalonians with the Judaean Christians but does imply a degree of parity, 'supporting the genuine character of the addressees' Christian experience of the gospel' (Johanson 1987: 96), and does not establish the Judaeans as exemplary in any respect other than their endurance of persecution. Paul is affirming the Thessalonians who excelled themselves, rather than the Judaeans, the type with which he compares them. It is significant, furthermore, that in 1 Thess. 2.15-16 Paul attributes responsibility for opposition to his preaching to Gentiles to those who persecute the Judaean Christians, who are clearly non-Christian Jews. In Gal. 6.12 Paul insinuates that those seeking to impose circumcision on the Gentile Christians in Galatia were motivated by the desire to avoid persecution. If Paul saw them as the mediators of non-Christian Jewish opposition to his preaching, then presumably he would not have included them among those whom the Thessalonian Christians emulate. This may imply a degree of qualification to Paul's approbation of the Judaeans, in that it indicates that the endurance of at least some of them was not as resolute as he would expect. A dichotomy between Paul's statement in the verses under consideration, and in Galatians, to be considered below, should therefore not be overemphasized.

3. *The Evidence of Galatians*

I have argued for an early date for Galatians (Introduction section 4a), during Paul's mission to Corinth, or shortly thereafter. It therefore

---

1.   See discussion of this question by Georgi 1986: 158-64.

belongs to this period in Paul's life, but is addressed to churches in whose foundation he had participated while working from Antioch with Barnabas (cf. Dunn 1983: 39). His relationship with Barnabas and that church had been strained to such an extent that Paul had been obliged to leave Antioch and to work on his own. In Galatians Paul makes a virtue of this necessity, and elevates his independence of the Jerusalem and Antioch churches to a principle of his vocational self-understanding (cf. Mussner 1974: 131). At the same time, he is asserting over the Galatian churches his personal authority, and in so doing attempting to supplant that of the Antiochene community which he and Barnabas had previously exercised. This aspect of the letter may account, as suggested above, for Silvanus's not being a co-author.

In asserting his authority in the Galatian churches, Paul describes himself as an ἀπόστολος...διὰ 'Ιησοῦ Χριστοῦ (Gal. 1.1). He interprets his vocation and authority in terms of this apostleship, which he defines over against that exercised by the leaders of the Jerusalem church (cf. Best 1986: 11). Paul personalizes the office of apostle which becomes the whole basis of his identity in this passage, in contrast with the concept of ἀποστολή which, as seen in Chapter 4 above, seems to have been the more general usage in early Christianity. ἀποστολή, unlike the office of ἀπόστολος, defines the work undertaken rather than the status of the people who undertake it. ἀποστολή is not limited to particular people in the way in which ἀπόστολος can be, and subsequently was by Luke, and, albeit less rigidly, by Paul himself (cf. 1 Cor. 12.28-29). This text in Galatians would seem, however, to be the earliest attempt to articulate a conception of apostleship as an office or vocation limited to particular people (cf. Schmithals 1971b: 86). Whereas Paul had previously participated in the apostolate of the Antiochene church, in which all missionaries could presumably be called ἀπόστολοι (cf. Acts 14.4, 14), he now defined himself and his work, and effectively the Christian gospel, in terms of his own vocational self-understanding as an apostle. Paul closely identifies his reception of the gospel with his vocation to preach it (Gal. 1.16), which a number of scholars understand to mean that Paul became a Christian apostle at the moment of his conversion.[1] Other scholars, however, have appreciated the need

---

1. Hahn 1965: 77; Georgi 1965: 22; Stendahl 1976: 7-11; Kim 1981: 55-59. Cf. also Dunn 1990: 89-104.

to recognize developments in Paul's career.[1] I argued in Chapter 3
that Paul's apostolic vocation came some years after his conversion,
when he was living in Antioch, and a member of the Christian community there. It was only after his break with the church of Antioch
that Paul came effectively to equate the gospel with his apostleship (cf.
Schütz 1975: 134), in order to legitimate his authority without reference to any human principal. In defending and asserting his legitimacy
as a preacher of the Christian gospel, and therefore his authority as an
apostle, Paul is forced to define, at least implicitly, his more rigid and
exclusive concept of apostleship. In identifying specific criteria of
apostolic legitimacy, where the mere fact of preaching the Christian
gospel was insufficient on account of his isolation in the Church, Paul
narrows the applicability of the term ἀπόστολος to those who could
match the credentials he offers in his own defence. Paul's personalization of the apostolate in Galatians 1–2 results also in his assimilating
into his own self-conception and apostolic vocation his account of his
association with the church at Antioch and its missionary outreach,
which Barnabas had led, and in which he had previously participated
(cf. Holmberg 1978: 14). At the same time, Paul is anxious not to
imply any hostility on his part to the Jerusalem church, but rather to
stress the unity between them, so as to discredit any suggestion that the
Jerusalem leadership supported, or were represented by, his opponents in Galatia. Paul needs to demonstrate that he still exercised
legitimately in the Galatian churches the authority which he had exercised while working from Antioch, and which, he wished to claim,
had been recognized on his terms by the Jerusalem church, without
conceding that the Jerusalem church could determine the legitimacy of
his authority. The narration and reinterpretation of events in Galatians
1–2 is accordingly complex and in many places ambiguous (cf. Dunn
1982: 469). In previous chapters I have reconstructed the history
which lies behind the narrative, so far as is possible. Our present task
is to discern Paul's attitude to, and relationship with, the Jerusalem
church at the time of writing. In doing this it is necessary to be aware
of the problem of distinguishing Paul's attack on his opponents in
Galatia from his assertions about the Jerusalem church, as Betz and
Smith have correctly argued.[2]

1. Dupont 1970: 273; Gaventa 1986a: 11; Segal 1990: 8.
2. Betz 1979: 92; Smith 1985: 191.

Paul cites no paradigm of apostleship, other than claiming for apostles pre-eminence in the Church (1 Cor. 12.28), as it is defined in terms of himself and his work. He cites further criteria of apostleship implicitly as well as explicitly (1 Cor. 9.1-5; 15.7; 2 Cor. 12.12; Gal. 1.16; 2.7-9), but it would be a mistake to seek any objective definition, or to determine too rigidly who else might qualify in terms of Paul's implicit definition. Paul could recognize another as an apostle only as he saw that person in terms of himself. At the same time, if Paul was to assert authority within the Church, as he does in Galatians, as well as establishing new churches, he needed to define himself in terms of those whom he saw to be exercising authority effectively in the various Christian communities. It was abundantly clear that the leaders of the Jerusalem church were the most effective wielders of authority in the Church, as they had recently demonstrated to Paul's disadvantage in Antioch. Paul therefore needed to assert for himself, so far as he could, the credentials from which they derived their authority, irrespective of whether the Jerusalem leaders called themselves or any other bearers of authority apostles. He had also to modify those credentials in accordance with his own experience and circumstances so as to make them credible and effective in his own specific context. Paul accordingly could not simply ignore the authority exercised by the leaders of the Jerusalem church, but he needed to define his own somewhat differently, since he had not been a disciple of Jesus and did not have the support or commission of any community on which to base his authority. Furthermore, Paul was alienated from the eschatological centre of Christianity and could derive no authority from that centre without affirming the higher authority of the Jerusalem church in communities over which he exercised authority. Paul was obliged therefore to claim for his apocalyptic conversion experience the significance attributed to other Christians' experiences of the risen Christ and, over and above that, to derive from it that authority which he defined as apostleship.[1] There is no evidence that anybody else was concerned at this time with personalizing the Christian apostolate, and Paul therefore does not need to counter one

1. Cf. Stendahl 1976: 7-11; Kim 1981: 55-66; Dunn 1990: 89. The identification of Paul's revelatory vision of the risen Christ as a criterion for apostolic authority does not, however, imply that his vocation to apostleship was received in that vision.

explicit definition of apostleship with another, but rather to match the authority exercised by others in the Church with his own, which he defined in terms of apostleship. Galatians was written early in Paul's period of independent mission and therefore early in the process in which he sought to articulate his conception of his personal apostolic vocation.

Paul opens his letter to the churches of Galatia with a very explicit statement about his apostleship. In this he is refuting the conception of apostleship as a function delegated by a church. This was the apostleship Paul had exercised in his mission to Galatia, but which office he no longer held. In order to assert authority effectively, therefore, he claims a particular apostolic vocation, identity, and authority independent of human principals. Paul is not an apostle simply in that he participates in the apostolate of a Christian church, its work of mission and evangelism. He regards his own apostleship as οὐκ ἀπ᾽ ἀνθρώπων (Gal. 1.1). He is not the agent of any human principal (cf. Burton 1921: 37-38). He has not been sent out by any church to undertake its apostolic task, and therefore does not represent any human institution. This is emphasized further by Paul's assertion that his apostleship is not δι᾽ ἀνθρώπου (Gal. 1.1). Not only did no human being appoint Paul to apostolic work, but no human being mediated his apostolic commission (cf. Burton 1921: 38-39). The Antiochene church is excluded not merely as commissioning community, but also as mediator of Paul's apostolic vocation, which comes directly διὰ Ἰησοῦ Χριστοῦ καὶ Θεοῦ πατρός (Gal. 1.1). He is sent by God, and not by any church.

Paul refutes in Gal. 1.11-12 similar contentions about the gospel he preaches to those about his apostleship which he refutes in Gal. 1.1 (cf. Betz 1979: 62). It is not possible to draw phrase for phrase parallels between the two sentences, but there is a conspicuous similarity between them. The first conception of his gospel, real or hypothetical, which Paul denies, is that it was κατὰ ἄνθρωπον (Gal. 1.11), of human origin. Paul is not simply passing on a message he had received from another human being. Just as Paul's apostleship, so does his gospel not derive from any human source, and is not to be equated merely with the teachings of the Antiochene church. Similarly, Paul states next that he did not receive his gospel παρὰ ἀνθρώπου (Gal. 1.12). Paul was not converted through the efforts of any Christian evangelist and human mediation, individual or corporate, had no part in his reception of the gospel. Just as his acquisition of Christian convictions had been without human intervention, so was Paul's apostolic vocation received without human mediation. This association of his reception of the Christian gospel with his vocation to preach it enables Paul to assert an authority for both, and particularly the latter, which transcends that of the Antiochene church. Paul received the gospel δι' ἀποκαλύψεως 'Ιησοῦ Χριστοῦ (Gal. 1.12), through direct communication between himself and the transcendental reality to which his preaching bears witness. This claim to a privileged spiritual experience enables Paul to assert that his apostolic authority in Galatia arose from an experience which transcended human authority, and was therefore independent of the church of Antioch. His apostolic authority was therefore not affected by his severance from the Antiochene church.

Paul denies that, after his conversion, προσανεθέμην σαρκὶ καὶ αἵματι (Gal. 1.16). Dunn has shown that προσανατίθημι has very specific connotations, to do with consulting authoritative interpreters of signs and portents (1982: 462). While the examples Dunn cites are all Greek rather than Jewish, this does not exclude such an interpretation of the word, especially as Paul was writing to a Gentile, Greek-speaking group of churches. Paul did not seek any interpretation of his experience, as it was self-explanatory (Dunn 1982: 463). He wishes to convey the impression that his preparation for his apostolic work was complete with his vocational experience (cf. Kim 1981: 55-59), and that at no time had he required the authority of any Christian leader to confirm or interpret his experience. This is how Paul's conversion has been widely understood, as was discussed in Chapter 1. Paul's purpose, however, in emphasizing the lack of human communication following his conversion is to reinforce his assertion of authority independent of the Antiochene church. This independence was a current reality when Galatians was written, and is retrojected into the period immediately following Paul's conversion so as to predate his membership of the church of Antioch, and further to exclude that community as the source of his authority.

Paul follows his denial of having sought an interpretation of his conversion experience from any human authority with an explicit denial of having travelled to Jerusalem to consult those who were already Christian apostles (Gal. 1.17). The mention of τοὺς πρὸ ἐμοῦ ἀποστόλους demonstrates that Paul's apostleship is the key issue. Not merely does it suggest, but not state, that Paul was already an apostle immediately after his conversion,[1] but it reinforces his claim that his apostolic authority is independent of the Jerusalem church, and by implication also the Antiochene. His authority does not depend on his having been recognized as an authentic preacher of the Christian gospel at the earliest opportunity by the leaders of the Jerusalem church. Paul is engaged at the time of writing in work which is independent of the apostolate of any Christian community, and this is legitimated by the inference that he had begun his Christian missionary work without reference to the Jerusalem church. His participation in the Christian apostolate was not contingent upon his having been commissioned by any church for that work. Antioch may have become his geographical base, where and from where his apostolic ministry was for many years to be exercised,[2] but the church was not the source of his apostolic authority.

The independence of his apostleship which Paul emphasizes in this text, is a reflection not so much on how his Christian career began, as on the circumstances in which he found himself at the time of writing Galatians (cf. Schütz 1975: 155). Paul ascribes to his conversion experience vocational connotations and can accordingly assert that not only his vocation, but his authority, derive directly from God, and are not of human origin or mediation, and antecede his membership of the Antiochene church. Paul is consequently not accountable to any human authority for the conduct of his apostolic work. Nor was his apostolic work in Galatia in reality subject to the jurisdiction of the church of Antioch. This places his authority beyond dispute anywhere he claims jurisdiction, and neither the Galatian Christians nor any other Christian authority can question it.

After arguing the basis of his independent and absolute apostolic authority, Paul outlines such contact as he is prepared to admit he had with the Jerusalem church, conspicuously neglecting to mention the Antiochene church, except by allusion in Gal. 1.21. Paul's first visit to

1.   While explicit in identifying unnamed persons in Jerusalem as having been apostles before him, Paul does not state, or necessarily even imply, that he was already an apostle at the time.
2.   Antioch is conspicuously not mentioned in Paul's autobiographical narrative until Gal. 2.11, but merely alluded to in Gal. 1.21. Paul's account of the episode in Antioch, however, in itself demonstrates that he had some standing in that community, and had expected his authority to be recognized there.

Jerusalem was in order to ἱστορῆσαι Κηφᾶν (Gal. 1.18). Any casual overtones identified in this phrase by Campenhausen, Betz, and Hofius[1] reflect Paul's anachronistic depiction of the event rather than the historical reality (cf. Dunn 1982: 463-65). Paul is anxious to demonstrate a degree of unity of purpose with Peter and James, without acknowledging for his own work the authority recognized in them by other Christians, and particularly by his opponents and the Christians of Galatia (Betz 1979: 78), any more than was necessary.

The oath in Gal. 1.20 indicates the weakest point in Paul's argument (Sampley 1977: 479). He needs to indicate that Peter and James, the principal bearers of unquestioned authority in the Church, had recognized his claim to authority comparable to theirs without implying that his authority in any way derived from theirs, or was subject to their ratification. In this, Paul is similar to, but by no means typical of, a charismatic prophet. He is dependent on the acknowledgement of his converts, as is typical of all forms of authority that cannot be imposed by force. However, Paul needs in Galatians not only the recognition of the Galatian Christians over whom he asserts authority, but also that of the Jerusalem leadership, whose superior authority the Antiochene church recognized and which the Galatian Christians would not have questioned. Paul is asserting his personal apostolic authority in communities where he had previously exercised authority as an apostle of the Antiochene church and in which the authority of the Jerusalem church and its leaders was acknowledged as having some pre-eminence, if not supremacy. Only if his authority was recognized by Peter and James, and if continuity was established in that authority between the time of the events recorded and his present circumstances, could Paul assert it successfully in Galatia, and exclude the Antiochene church from the equation. Furthermore, only if he could convince the Galatians that he had never been subject to the jurisdiction of the Jerusalem church could he successfully assert authority in the Galatian churches without reference to, if not in defiance of, Jerusalem. Paul wishes to claim acknowledgement from, while denying jurisdiction to, Peter and James, and the authority they represent. Paul's anachronistic reinterpretation of events and relationships is a weak point in his argument. His present claim is not based

1.   Campenhausen 1969: 69; Betz 1979: 76; Hofius 1984: 77-78. See discussion in Chapter 2 above.

on historical reality but represents a response to the demands of his new situation of independence, the cost of which is isolation, and denial of his authority by those who have remained within the κοινωνία between the Jerusalem and Antioch churches, which would have included the congregations established under Antiochene auspices.

Paul states that he travelled to Jerusalem μετὰ Βαρναβᾶ fourteen years later (Gal. 2.1), κατὰ ἀποκάλυψιν (Gal. 2.2). In Chapter 4 above, I argued that Paul travelled to Jerusalem as the junior partner to Barnabas in a delegation of the Antiochene church aimed at resolving the question of Gentile obligations with respect to the Jewish law, and specifically the question of circumcision. While Paul does not explicitly deny that the journey was occasioned by the ecclesiastical controversy in Antioch (Betz 1979: 85), he does reinterpret the event in the light of his situation at the time of writing Galatians. The church of Antioch is not mentioned, and Paul's purpose in travelling to Jerusalem is stated in the singular. Not only is Paul distancing himself from Barnabas and the Antiochene church on account of subsequent events, but he is also personalizing the account,[1] assuming to himself the gospel preached at Antioch and the missionary work carried out from there. The whole orientation of Paul's account of the conference is directed away from relations between Jews and Gentiles in the Antiochene church and the concomitant theological issues, to Paul's own apostolic authority and the gospel he associates therewith.

Paul states that he ἀνεθέμην the gospel which he preaches to the Gentiles (Gal. 2.2). The gospel of uncircumcision submitted by the Antiochene church becomes the gospel of Paul. The occasion on which the Antiochene gospel was vindicated and affirmed in Jerusalem is reinterpreted by Paul as an occasion on which he had demonstrated the incontrovertibility of his own preaching to, and had his apostolic authority acknowledged by, the leaders of the Jerusalem church. Paul asserts that the meeting was conducted κατ' ἰδίαν δὲ τοῖς δοκοῦσιν (Gal. 2.2), in order to give the impression that only a very few of the most eminent leaders in the Jerusalem church were consulted.[2] In restricting the encounter to the leadership Paul seeks to distinguish between them and the Jerusalem church as a whole, in order to

1. Cf. Schütz 1975: 140; Betz 1979: 81.
2. Cf. Schlier 1971: 66; Mussner 1974: 104-105; Betz 1979: 86.

repudiate any authority exercised by others from that community, and acknowledged by the Christians in Galatia. Paul wishes to demonstrate accord with the most eminent leaders in the Jerusalem church without involving the church as a whole and without conceding authority over himself and his work to anyone.

Paul gives as his purpose in consulting the Jerusalem leadership μή πως εἰς κενὸν τρέχω ἢ ἔδραμον (Gal. 2.2). This is one of the more revealing statements in Paul's defence of his apostleship, in that he explicitly states that the Jerusalem leadership were in a position to determine whether or not his teaching, and therefore his entire apostolic ministry, was valid, or, at the very least, effective. Paul is forced to concede to the Jerusalem church authority which impinges on his own. What had been a question of the viability of the gospel as preached in and from Antioch is here portrayed, and portrayed as totally vulnerable, in terms entirely of Paul's own preaching. This reflects on the circumstances in which Paul wrote and indicates that he remains vulnerable to the judgment of the Jerusalem church, and its influence over the Antiochene church and communities established under the auspices of the latter, including those of Galatia. At the same time, in acknowledging that his gospel had been scrutinized and approved by the Jerusalem church, Paul implies that his opponents in Galatia, whose authority must be less than that of Peter and James, are not in a position to question Paul's teaching, and therefore his authority, which had been recognized by those whom they themselves looked upon as the highest authority in the Church. To the same degree as he had been vulnerable, Paul claims that he had also been vindicated, and that his authority is therefore incontrovertible. Despite his recent departure from the structures of Christianity centred on Jerusalem and Antioch, Paul remains dependent upon the recognition of the leaders of the Jerusalem church. He can diminish, but he cannot deny, this dependence. At the same time as claiming for himself the acknowledgement of their gospel that had been accorded the Antiochene church, Paul is forced to concede his need of that acknowledgement. What is at stake in Galatians is not what happened at the Jerusalem conference, but Paul's authority in the present, specifically in relation to the churches in Galatia, and this depends on a measure of recognition from Jerusalem, which Paul claims.

Paul returns in Gal. 2.6 to the main thrust of his narrative, from which he has been somewhat diverted since Gal. 2.3. He refers once again to those of repute, but somewhat equivocally, as τῶν δοκούντων εἶναί τι, which, at the very least, is open to interpretations of irony (cf. Barrett 1953: 2-4). While not committing himself to declaring the high standing, and therefore the authority, of the Jerusalem leadership to be more apparent than real, Paul allows his readers this conclusion. While allowing that the Jerusalem leadership do exercise authority in the Church, Paul carefully avoids any implication that he himself is subject to that authority (Betz 1979: 92). So far as he is in accord with the Jerusalem leadership, their authority is useful in reinforcing his own, but Paul at the same time emphasizes the irrelevance of that authority in respect of his own, which derives directly from God. This is emphasized further by ὁποῖοί ποτε ἦσαν (Gal. 2.6). The implication that the pre-eminence of the Jerusalem leadership rests on events of the past, presumably their participation in the ministry of Jesus and experience of the risen Christ, rather than their current work, qualifies their authority in relation to Paul's apostleship. Their criteria for pre-eminence οὐδέν μοι διαφέρει (Gal. 2.6). The use of μοι relates the authority of the Jerusalem leadership to Paul's own apostolic authority. Whatever the significance of the authority of the Jerusalem leadership elsewhere in the Church, it did not qualify them to judge Paul's claim to apostleship or to constrain its exercise in Galatia.

After a lengthy, and somewhat convoluted, qualification of the authority of the Jerusalem leadership, Paul finally states: ἐμοὶ γὰρ οἱ δοκοῦντες οὐδὲν προσανέθεντο (Gal. 2.6). The redefining of the issue at stake in Gal. 2.2 in terms of Paul's apostolic preaching and authority is followed here by the vindication of Paul's position. Paul is able to personalize the account because the cause he had represented had been vindicated, and he claims that victory for himself. The Jerusalem church's affirmation of the gospel preached at Antioch becomes Paul's claim that his own teaching and practice, and by implication apostolic authority, were recognized by the Jerusalem leadership. If, however, the Jerusalem church was so completely behind Paul, he would not have found it necessary to qualify their authority at such length. There can be little doubt that, at the time Galatians was written, the leaders of the Jerusalem church would have regarded the conference agreement as irrelevant to the claims Paul is making concerning his personal status. Paul nevertheless claims for himself that recognition which had been accorded the Antiochene church and reinterprets it in terms of his own apostolic self-conception.

Paul proceeds to recount the corollaries to his acknowledgment by the leaders of the Jerusalem church. Far from stipulating requirements further to the gospel Barnabas and Paul preached, the Jerusalem leadership had recognized that they had been entrusted with τὸ εὐαγγέλιον τῆς ἀκροβυστίας, just as Peter had been entrusted with [the gospel] τῆς περιτομῆς (Gal. 2.7). The parallelism between the gospels preached in and from Jerusalem and Antioch[1] is coopted by Paul in defence of his own gospel and preaching. He claims for himself the degree of recognition that had been accorded the Antiochene church and its gospel, in the context of mutual recognition in a relationship of κοινωνία between the two churches. The parallelism breaks down when Paul states the practical aspects of the agreement. According to Paul, the Jerusalem leaders recognized that God operates through Peter εἰς ἀποστολὴν τῆς περιτομῆς, and through Paul εἰς τὰ ἔθνη (Gal. 2.8). Two aspects of these statements are remarkable. First, ἔθνος is used of Paul's work, whereas ἀκροβυστία had been used in the previous clause (Gal. 2.7). This would seem to emphasize the notion of a gospel and a mission directed specifically to Gentiles, rather than the gospel of uncircumcision as lived and taught by the Antiochene church and which included both Jews and Gentiles. I would suggest, therefore, that Paul amends the wording of the original agreement between the two churches, which concerned the Antiochene gospel of uncircumcision, to a phrase which reflects and emphasizes his current apostolic claims (cf. Rom. 1.5; 11.13; Gal. 1.16). This shift in emphasis gives expression to Paul's notion of his own unique and all but exclusive apostleship to the Gentiles which was not the subject, in intention or in word, of the agreement between the Jerusalem and Antioch churches. Secondly, it is remarkable that Paul, in defence of his personalized notion of his own apostleship, uses the concept in connection with Peter but not himself in Gal. 2.8. Betz suggests that Paul is citing the actual words of the agreement, with the implication that Peter was recognized as an apostle, but not Paul (1979: 98).[2] If Betz is correct, however, in arguing that Paul is using, at least in part, the actual wording of the agreement, which is possible,

---

1. See discussion in Chapter 4 section 3 above.
2. Cf. Longenecker 1990: 56; McLean 1991: 71, who argue that Paul's citation of the agreement is not verbatim.

the implication would seem to be somewhat different. In parallel phrases, such as this, ἀποστολή need be used only in the first and would be assumed in the second, just as τὸ εὐαγγέλιον is not repeated in the previous set of parallel phrases (cf. McLean 1991: 70). What is significant in Gal. 2.8 is not that ἀποστολή is used explicitly of Peter, but only implicitly of Paul, but that the concept ἀποστολή is used in preference to the personalized form ἀπόστολος. The work of apostleship, in which several members of the two churches were engaged, was at issue in the original agreement and not the personal status of the various missionaries. The personalized concept of apostolic office has become important for Paul on account of his having ceased to be engaged in the apostolate of the Antiochene church, and forfeited the authority which derived from that commission. For apostles of churches whose authority is reinforced by the commissioning community, personal status is not so important. But for Paul, who had no commissioning church after the Antioch incident, his authority needed to be sufficient in itself if it was to be effective.

James, Peter and John were reputed to be the στῦλοι, the pillars of an unnamed figurative edifice, which Barrett identifies as the Church as the New Temple (1953: 12). Betz, however, regards this as unproven (1979: 99). Paul does not say whether James, Peter and John were the pillars of the Church as a whole or only of the Jerusalem church, but there can be no doubt that Paul does not regard this status as impinging on his own apostolic authority. Whatever the case, these three men were known as the most eminent figures in the Church, and certainly in the Jerusalem church. The use of δοκοῦντες may have sarcastic and pejorative connotations (Barrett 1953: 2), or it may simply emphasize the pre-eminence of James, Peter and John (cf. Betz 1979: 99). Paul has demonstrated remarkable dexterity in ambiguity throughout this section of the letter, and this would seem to be yet another instance. As Barrett points out, Paul could not affirm or deny the standing of the στῦλοι without compromising his own position. So equivocation about the authority of the Jerusalem church and its leadership is essential to Paul's maintaining his own apostolic claim. Paul cannot avoid acknowledging the authority of James, Peter, and John, if he is to claim their acknowledgment of his own, but he is at the same time anxious not to attribute to them any jurisdiction over him or his work.

Paul includes Barnabas in the discussion once again when he records James, Peter, and John as having given the two from Antioch δεξιὰς...κοινωνίας (Gal. 2.9). This sign of the conclusion of an agreement emphasizes that Barnabas and Paul had reached accord with the Jerusalem apostles on the matter they came to discuss; the implication being that what was agreed was effectively an affirmation of the claims to authority Paul makes in Galatians. According to Betz, the handshake implies equality between Barnabas and Paul, or those they represent, on the one hand, and the Jerusalem apostles on the other (1979: 100). While this is clearly the impression Paul would like to convey (cf. Sampley 1980: 26), κοινωνία does not necessarily imply equality between the two parties (Hauck 1939: 802), but connotes unity rather than equality. James, Peter and John had recognized the gospel of the Antiochene church, despite the fact that it differed from their own teaching and the practice of the Jerusalem church, and also that there was fundamental unity between the two churches despite their differences. Paul's presentation shifts the emphasis from unity to equality, and from the Antiochene church to himself and his claim to apostolic authority equal to Peter's.

Paul briefly paraphrases the practical implication of the agreement: ἡμεῖς εἰς τὰ ἔθνη αὐτοὶ δὲ εἰς τὴν περιτομήν (Gal. 2.9). In Chapter 4 above, I argued that the agreement originally consisted in the mutual recognition of diverse interpretations of the Christian gospel by the two churches of Jerusalem and Antioch, and not in the division of missionary fields along racial or geographical lines.[1] This does not exclude the possibility, however, that Paul wishes to impose such an interpretation on the agreement in order to substantiate his claim to jurisdiction in Galatia and to exclude rival authorities, including Jerusalem, from involvement in those churches (cf. Holmberg 1978: 30).[2] This point would be strengthened if the discussion of Gal. 2.8

1. Cf. Georgi 1965: 22; Bornkamm 1971: 39-40; Schütz 1975: 156; Dunn 1977: 253; Holmberg 1978: 30-31; Gaston 1984: 65.

2. An explicit attack on the authority of the Antiochene church in Galatia would have been both unnecessary and unconvincing. The crisis which Paul had precipitated in his confrontation with Peter at Antioch would have preoccupied that community for some time, with the probable consequence that oversight of other churches effectively lapsed for a time, almost certainly until the promulgation of the Apostolic Decree. This authority vacuum in Antioch and the churches established under its auspices enabled those whom Paul opposes to intervene in the life of the

above is correct, and the introduction of ἔθνος to the agreement by Paul serves to reinforce his own conception of apostleship to the Gentiles at the time the letter was written. While the existence of territorially or ethnically defined missionary areas seems historically impossible,[1] Paul's claim to jurisdiction in Galatia depends on his exclusion of other authorities from those churches if it is to be effective.

Paul is perhaps less defensive and ambiguous, and possibly less anachronistic, if just as subjective and selective, in recounting his confrontation with Peter at Antioch in Gal. 2.11-14. It is significant that Antioch is mentioned for the first time in the narrative in Gal. 2.11 (cf. Gal. 1.21), but Paul's account of events there clearly implies his continuing association with that church until this incident. We must assume that Paul had to include this incident in his account, despite its ignominious consequences for him, since it had become known in Galatia, or, alternatively, that Paul presents his own account of the episode in order to pre-empt its being used against him in Galatia by those whom he opposes.

Perhaps the most significant aspect of this episode for Paul's assertion of his apostolic authority is the very clear inference that he did not regard Peter and Barnabas as beyond his reproach, even if James and the Jerusalem church were behind their action. The implication is that, if Paul did not hesitate to confront Peter, at least implicitly taking issue with James and the Jerusalem church in so doing, he would show no restraint in dealing with those whom he opposes in Galatia (cf. Sampley 1980: 39). However, it is the demonstration by Paul of his independence of the authority of Peter, and by implication of James and the Jerusalem church, and his repudiation of that authority when it contravened the gospel, that is of primary importance in Paul's defence of his own apostolic authority. Also, Paul's assertion of authority over and against the church of Antioch which had followed Peter demonstrates a claim to authority which did not derive from a commission from that community. Paul seeks to demonstrate freedom from their jurisdiction, even if that very episode which resulted in his independence resulted also in his alienation and isolation in the Antiochene church and beyond, and in separation

Galatian churches. See discussion below.

1. See discussion in Chapter 4 section 3b above.

from those structures on which had been based the authority he had previously exercised.

To summarize, therefore, in Galatians 1–2 Paul reinterprets his conversion experience and past dealings with the Jerusalem church, in order to legitimate his claim to authority over the Galatian churches. In particular he excludes the Antiochene church from this account. He asserts a conception of Christian apostleship in which authority derives directly from God, and is accordingly independent of the Jerusalem, and, by implication, Antioch and any other, churches, and predates his dealings with other Christian leaders. In terms of this self-conception, Paul claims complete independence of all terrestrial authority, particularly that of the Jerusalem church and its principal leaders, Peter and James, and, implicitly, also of Barnabas and the Antiochene church. This assertion of independent authority is necessitated by Paul's isolation within early Christianity in the aftermath of the Antioch incident. Paul accordingly portrays himself as independent of, but recognized by, the leadership of the Jerusalem church. The reality would seem, however, to be one of severed relations, in which Paul, estranged from the recognized authorities in the Church, is forced to create not merely his own structures with which to continue his work of Christian mission, but also his own theological rationale, with the personalized conception of apostleship, which forms the basis of his claim to authority.

4. *Paul's Antagonists in Galatia*

We have considered Paul's self-understanding as expressed in Galatians, as this reflects in part his relationship with the Jerusalem church at the time of writing. We need now to consider those whose teaching in the Galatian churches Paul opposes, and whose activities occasioned the writing of the letter, in order to establish, as far as possible, whether there was any link between these and the Jerusalem or Antioch churches and, if there was, on what basis they were operating. We are not concerned to reconstruct the theology of these people, except in so far as it enables us to address more clearly the question of their connection with Jerusalem and Antioch.

It was axiomatic for Baur's scheme of early Christianity that Paul's opponents in Galatia were the emissaries of the Jerusalem church, operating under the auspices of Peter and James (1875: 256). While most subsequent scholars have followed Baur in locating the origin of Paul's opponents in Jerusalem, they have tended to be rather more reluctant to identify Peter and James as their principals. A fairly typical position is that of Lightfoot who suggests that Paul's opponents were acting without the authority of Peter and James (1890: 29). Holl, on the contrary, suggests that they were acting on their commission from the leadership of the Jerusalem church (1921: 57). Burton argues that Paul's opponents represented a Judaistic faction in the Jerusalem church who were able to bring pressure to bear on the leadership (1921: lvi).

It would perhaps enable us to clarify the issue if we were to consider the situation of the Galatian churches at the time. These communities had been established by Barnabas and Paul, working in the apostolate of the Antiochene church. The churches of Galatia would therefore have fallen under the oversight of that at Antioch and shared, at least in part and by extension, in the κοινωνία between the Jerusalem and Antioch churches. The Antioch incident, and Paul's subsequent departure from Antioch, would not have changed this. Any activity on the part of representatives of the Jerusalem church in the Galatian churches must therefore be understood in terms of this κοινωνία . To describe those advocating circumcision as Paul's opponents is therefore something of a misnomer (cf. Martyn 1985: 312), irrespective of their connection with the Jerusalem church. If they came from Jerusalem, they were operating within a recognized relationship, to which Paul was incidental. From this point of view, Lietzmann's suggestion that Barnabas was opposing Paul in Galatia, on the ultimate authority of James (1923: 38; cf. Dunn 1983: 39), would be plausible. However, one would expect Paul to attack Barnabas far more explicitly were this the case. Furthermore, the demand for circumcision in Galatia (Gal. 5.2-3) was contrary to the agreement of the Jerusalem conference. This, and not a supposed intrusion into Paul's missionary domain, would have constituted a breach in the Jerusalem agreement.[1] As the question of circumcision of Gentile Christians had been the central issue of the conference, the decision could not have been unilaterally reversed by the senior partner in terms of the κοινωνία that bound the churches of Jerusalem and Antioch. There is no evidence that the church at Antioch came to

1.   See discussion in Chapter 4 section 3a above.

accept compulsory circumcision of Gentile Christians; nor, it must be noted, was this demanded by the delegation from James whose intervention had precipitated the Antioch incident.[1]

It would seem, therefore, that we have three alternatives for identifying the Judaists in Galatia. Either they were authorized delegates of the Jerusalem church, wilfully violating its κοινωνία with the Antiochene church, or they were representatives of a faction in the Jerusalem or Antioch church, but which did not represent the leadership of either community, or they were unconnected with the Jerusalem or Antioch churches. All three possibilities are supported in recent scholarship.

The first possibility is supported most recently by the work of Barrett and Watson.[2] While this reconstruction could account for the tension between Paul and the Jerusalem church apparent in Galatians, this is also explained adequately by the recent events in Antioch. A direct correlation between these events and the situation in Galatia is a requirement of this position. Neither the evidence of Gal. 2.11-14, nor the resolution of the Antiochene crisis through the Apostolic Decree support such a reconstruction (cf. Howard 1990: 14). Furthermore, the Jerusalem conference and Apostolic Decree had approved the Antiochene custom of waiving circumcision, but affirmed the universality of the moral, and to a more limited extent, the dietary laws (cf. Borgen 1988). Those whom Paul opposes in Galatians, however, demanded circumcision, apparently to the exclusion of virtually all other legal requirements (Gal. 5.3; cf. 4.10), and with no attention to dietary questions or rules of table fellowship, and neglect of the antinomian tendencies among at least some in the Galatian churches (Gal. 5.13-26; cf. Barclay 1988: 71). Barclay is undoubtedly correct in arguing that Paul did not necessarily respond to all his antagonists' arguments (1988: 38), and we should therefore exercise caution in seeking to account for any possible omissions. Nevertheless, there does seem to be a fundamental discrepancy between the position taken by the leadership of the Jerusalem church in the earlier controversies and the position of Paul's antagonists reflected in Galatians (cf. Dunn 1990: 258). Identifying those with whom Paul takes issue in Galatians as emissaries of the Jerusalem

1. See discussion in Chapter 5 above.
2. Barrett 1985: 6, 22; Watson 1986: 59-61.

church would therefore seem to raise more questions than it answers, and we therefore need to consider seriously the other possibilities.

The second position is that which has enjoyed widest support in recent scholarship.[1] That there was a faction in the Jerusalem church which sought the imposition of the Mosaic law on Gentile Christians, and that they were active in the Antiochene church as well as Jerusalem, is clear from Acts 15.1-2, 5 and Gal. 2.3-5.[2] This group were overruled at the Jerusalem conference, but pressure from them may have been instrumental in James's subsequent despatch of emissaries to Antioch (Gal. 2.12). However, James's delegation did not convey the demands of the Judaistic faction, even if agitation from them precipitated the action. The resolution of this second crisis with the Apostolic Decree, would have been a second defeat for the Judaists. It is conceivable that they would have taken matters into their own hands, either in response to the Apostolic Decree or by taking advantage of the crisis and confusion in the Antiochene church which would have resulted from the confrontation between Peter and Paul. Churches established under Antiochene auspices, but remote from Antioch and constant direction from the leadership of that community, would have been a weak point in any authority vacuum. Especially if they had been only recently established (cf. Gal. 1.6), they would have been susceptible to outside influence. Paul's emphasis on Jerusalem (Gal. 1.13–2.14; 4.25-31) without ever stating that the leadership of that church were behind the (however superficial) Judaizing activities in Galatia may lend weight to this view. If circumcision had been the specific issue on which the Judaistic faction had been defeated, this could perhaps account for their emphasis on circumcision in Galatia. Before reaching any conclusions, however, we must consider the third option.

The third position has enjoyed somewhat less, but nevertheless significant, support.[3] Scholars who support this position seek to account for the lack of specific evidence of a link between the Judaists

1.   Burton 1921: lvi; Schoeps 1961: 66; Koester 1971: 144-45; Richardson 1969: 94; Eckert 1971: 233; Jewett 1971: 204; Gunther 1973: 298; Betz 1979: 7; Longenecker 1990: xcv.

2.   See discussion in Chapter 4 section 1 above.

3.   Munck 1959: 129-32; Schmithals 1965b: 9-10; Brinsmead 1982: 104; Martyn 1985; Gaston 1984: 64; Barclay 1988: 42-44; Howard 1990: xiv-xix.

in Galatia and the Jerusalem church and for their apparently selective imposition of the Mosaic law in the Galatian churches. The latter problem, however, could possibly be resolved through a less rigid and monolithic notion of Judaism and nomistic Jewish Christianity (cf. Martyn 1985: 308-11). Much also depends on arguments as to whether they accused Paul of being unduly dependent upon the Jerusalem church[1] or of defying the authority of that community.[2] Only persons unconnected with the Jerusalem church could have accused Paul of being unduly subservient to that community or have regarded his dealings with its leaders as diminishing his authority, and presumably only emissaries or independent members of the Jerusalem or Antioch churches would have accused Paul of defying the authority of the former community.

Kümmel argues that, while those whom Paul opposes in Galatians are clearly Judaistic Christians, their connection with Jerusalem and the Christian community there is unclear (1975: 300). The degree of uncertainty inherent in this question is not to be underestimated, especially as it is far from clear that Paul knew precisely whom he was opposing (cf. Gal. 1.6-9; 4.20; 5.10).[3] However, the convoluted manner in which Paul defines his relationship with the Jerusalem church (cf. Dunn 1982) indicates that an unequivocal repudiation of the authority of that community would not have served his purpose in Galatians. This suggests that there was some connection between Paul's antagonists and the Jerusalem church.

It was not the Apostolic Decree whose imposition in Galatia Paul was opposing. The Jerusalem church would have expected the Antiochene church to enforce the Apostolic Decree in churches established under its auspices (cf. Dunn 1990: 258-59), but the position reflected in Galatians is contrary to its provisions.[4] It would therefore seem unlikely that Paul was dealing with accredited delegates of the Jerusalem or Antioch churches. The most plausible solution to the question would therefore seem to be that Paul was dealing with a nomistic faction which had made its presence felt in the Jerusalem and

1. Munck, Schmithals, Brinsmead.
2. This position is shared also by those who argue the first two positions identified above.
3. See discussion by Martyn 1985: 313-14.
4. See the excursus on the Apostolic Decree at the end of Part II.

Antiochene churches and which he had previously outmanoeuvred at the Jerusalem conference. Subsequent developments in Antioch had isolated Paul and provided the opportunity for the nomistic faction to assert itself again. Impressionable new churches would have been more amenable to their teaching than established communities that had already grappled with the issues (cf. Barclay 1988: 58-59), and success there would have further strengthened their position in the Jerusalem and Antioch churches. Paul is therefore careful to claim the acquiescence and support of Peter and James for his teaching and authority, despite the antagonism between them at the time of writing.

I would suggest, therefore, that there was no direct connection between those whose influence in the Galatian churches Paul opposes and the leadership of the Jerusalem and Antioch churches. Rather, it would seem that Paul was confronting a resurgence of the faction that had sought the imposition of circumcision on Gentile Christians in Antioch and so precipitated the Jerusalem conference at which they were overruled. They were able to exploit the absence of Peter from Jerusalem to increase pressure on James whose intervention in Antioch may have attempted to appease them. They were further able to exploit the disarray in the Antiochene church which resulted from James's delegation and the ensuing confrontation between Peter and Paul. Even though unable to gain dominance in Antioch as a consequence, they would seem to have exploited the lapse in oversight from Antioch to assert their authority in the Galatian, and perhaps other, churches established by the apostolate of the Antioch church.

The Antioch incident did not result in intervention by the Jerusalem church in the lives of communities outside Palestine. Not only is it doubtful whether the beleaguered community (cf. 1 Thess. 2.14-16) were in a position to do so, but any such intervention to undermine Paul would presumably have been concentrated where he was operating after the Antioch incident, rather than in the communities established under Antiochene auspices, where pressure could be, and was, applied effectively in terms of the κοινωνία between the two churches. Those advocating nomism in the churches of Galatia, I have argued, were a faction in the Jerusalem and Antiochene churches exploiting the power vacuum to assert their own position. Paul intervenes and reaffirms the Antiochene gospel which he had originally preached in Galatia and, despite the antagonism between them, cites Peter and James as recognizing the validity both of his teaching and of his apostolic authority. Far from identifying those he opposes with the Jerusalem leadership, Paul seeks to drive a wedge between them.

In summary, therefore, while Galatians reveals a degree of hostility between Paul and the leadership of the Jerusalem and Antioch churches in the aftermath of his confrontation with Peter at Antioch, there is no evidence that his intervention in the Galatian crisis involved the prosecution of that antagonism. On the contrary, Paul claims, however reluctantly, unity with the Jerusalem leadership in opposing the nomists in Galatia, while maintaining his own independence of their jurisdiction.

5. *Paul's Preaching in Corinth*

While 1 Corinthians dates from the period subsequent to that presently under discussion, Paul states that in 1 Cor. 15.1, 3 he is recapitulating his original preaching in Corinth which took place during the period currently under consideration. While the letter as a whole, and the situation it reflects, will be considered in Chapter 7 below, it is nevertheless appropriate that the situation reflected in Paul's mission preaching in Corinth be considered at this point.

There are two integrally related, but not identical, issues which require discussion before conclusions can be drawn as to Paul's statements about Peter and James, and those associated with them, in his initial preaching in Corinth. The first is the precise parameters of the kerygmatic tradition which Paul had received and which he transmitted to the Corinthians and the source from which he had received it. The second is the degree to which Paul's recapitulation of that tradition in 1 Cor. 15.1-8 is identical to the form in which he had originally transmitted it to the Corinthians. This is important, since a significant visit by Paul to the church at Antioch took place between the mission to Corinth and the writing of 1 Corinthians which could substantially have altered Paul's attitude to Peter and James, if not his relationship with them.[1]

Scholars are divided as to the parameters of the primitive tradition Paul cites in 1 Cor. 15.1-8. This text consists of the kerygma itself (1 Cor. 15.3b-4), and the list of witnesses to the resurrection (1 Cor. 15.5-8). It is the latter that is of concern for our present purpose. It is

1. See discussion in the Introduction section 5 and Chapter 7.

self-evident that Paul could not have received the tradition of his own resurrection Christophany from anybody else (cf. Gal. 1.16), and the tradition he inherited must therefore end at 1 Cor. 15.7. It is therefore the section of the text 1 Cor. 15.5-7 with which we are concerned.

Talbert (1987: 96) does not discuss the question of the parameters of the tradition Paul inherited, but asserts that the entire passage 1 Cor. 15.3-8 is a repetition of the gospel which Paul had preached in Corinth. Allo and Gaston similarly define the parameters of the tradition Paul transmitted to the Corinthians as 1 Cor. 15.3b-7 (Allo 1956: 391; Gaston 1984: 66). If this is correct, then Paul cited not only Peter, but also James, as authoritative witnesses to the resurrection.

Robertson and Plummer argue that, while 1 Cor. 15.3b-5 was definitely part of the tradition Paul had inherited and transmitted to the Corinthians, the following two verses are a matter of probability rather than certainty (1914: 335). Their principal reason, that ὅτι does not occur after 1 Cor. 15.5, cannot in itself determine the outcome to the question, for the list of witnesses could conceivably form a single clause in the credal formula.

Schmithals (1971b: 74) and Jeremias (1966: 101) identify 1 Cor. 15.3b-5 as the kerygmatic formula Paul inherited, and the latter argues that there was a Semitic original behind the Greek version Paul quotes (1966: 102). Conzelmann defines the parameters of the tradition similarly, but denies that there was a Semitic original (1969: 299). He argues that Paul added the supplementary information himself (1969: 303).

Héring argues that the rhythm of the kerygmatic formula is lost at 1 Cor. 15.5, and that the tradition therefore probably includes only 1 Cor. 15.3b-4; the list of witnesses being Paul's proof of the gospel statements cited in the formula (1962: 158). Barrett, however, points out that 1 Cor. 15.5 is Paul's only use of δώδεκα to designate the immediate disciples of Jesus, which indicates that it is not his own term (1968: 341-42). He argues that the citation of witnesses serves to demonstrate that the resurrection of Jesus is essential to all Christian preaching (1968: 341). There is no indication that the question of the resurrection had previously been controversial in Corinth, which could indicate that Paul had had no previous occasion to cite authoritative witnesses to substantiate his teaching. 1 Cor. 1.12 demonstrates that Peter was known in Corinth before the writing of 1 Corinthians.

He would, however, not have been known there before Paul's mission. The indications, therefore, would seem to be that Peter became known by reputation to the Corinthians during Paul's mission, and almost certainly in the context of his mission preaching, particularly concerning the resurrection and other traditions. This view is reinforced by the occurrence of δώδεκα, which indicates the quotation of a tradition, with which the name of Peter (here Κηφᾶς) was undoubtedly associated, and became part of the tradition of the Corinthian church.

Wilckens argues that 1 Cor. 15.3-7 contains not a single tradition, but Paul's conflation of traditions (1963: 73). He separates the kerygmatic formula in 1 Cor. 15.3b-4 from the list of authoritative witnesses to that tradition in 1 Cor. 15.5-7 (1963: 75, 80). Fuller extends Wilckens's thesis, identifying three credal traditions in 1 Cor. 15.3b-4 (1971: 14), which Paul received at Damascus (1971: 28). In 1 Cor. 15.5-8 Fuller identifies four independent resurrection traditions, the last of which is Paul's own, and the first three he received on his visit to Jerusalem recorded in Gal. 1.18-19, his informants being Peter, James, and one of the five hundred witnesses (1971: 27-28). These appearances are not part of the primitive Christian kerygma, and it is Paul who initiates the practice of citing authoritative witnesses as evidence of the resurrection (1971: 28-29).

It seems clear that Peter became known in Corinth as a consequence of Paul's mission. A faction in the Corinthian church subsequently professed allegiance of some kind to Peter before the writing of 1 Corinthians (cf. 1 Cor. 1.12). No faction is mentioned as having pledged its loyalty to James. One would expect such a faction to have emerged, had James been known as an authoritative figure in a community which was formed in a polytheistic environment which attached great importance to antiquity in religious matters[1] and was given to factionalism. As the brother of the cult deity[2] as well as being a prominent figure within the Church, James's theological leanings, far apart as they evidently were from the more factionally inclined of the Corinthian Christians, would not have prevented his becoming the acknowledged object of loyalty for a group in the Corinthian church,

---

1.   For discussion of this issue, see Georgi 1986: 158-64.
2.   I use this term in a functionalist sense, and not to imply any particular Christology.

especially as Paul would not have drawn attention to his differences with James. We must conclude, therefore, that the appearance of Jesus to James, and James's place in the Jerusalem church and beyond, were not integral to Paul's preaching in Corinth. It would seem, however, that the unique standing of Peter in the Church was apparent from, or at least implicit in, Paul's preaching in Corinth. The fact that there was someone of greater eminence than Paul in the broader Christian community, known by name to the Corinthian Christians, came to provide the factionally inclined in that church with an object of loyalty to rival Paul (cf. Gunther 1973: 301).

It seems therefore that, irrespective of the origins of the traditions included in 1 Cor. 15.3b-8, it was those articles quoted in 1 Cor. 15.3b-5 which were integral to Paul's preaching on his mission to Corinth. The appearance of Jesus to Peter and the twelve seems to have been an essential corollary to the resurrection itself. There can be no doubt that Paul mentioned his own experience of the risen Christ as well as Peter's, and probably more frequently, and certainly more vividly, but nevertheless Peter's vision of the risen Christ seems to have been an integral and confirmatory corollary to primitive Christian belief in the resurrection of Jesus, and one which Paul could not avoid in his preaching. Even if Paul's inability to exclude Peter from the tradition he transmitted to the Corinthians was on account of the presence of Silvanus (2 Cor. 1.19), and somewhat unwilling, the fact remains that Peter's name was an unavoidable part of Paul's preaching in Corinth.

Paul's citation of Peter's vision of the risen Christ implies affirmation, however unwilling, of Peter's authority in the Church, and, I would suggest, contributed significantly to the emergence of a faction pledging loyalty to Peter in the Corinthian church, or at least provided an object of loyalty for such a group. The implicit acknowledgement of Peter's authority on a cardinal article of Christian faith does not, however, imply that Paul acknowledged Peter's oversight over his work or over the churches he had established. Nor does it imply that Peter and Paul's relationship at the time of the mission to Corinth was sound. Peter is an almost impersonal factor in Paul's preaching. He is the primary witness to the resurrection, as well as being the principal custodian of Christian traditions generally, but Peter's fundamental significance in all Christian communities does not depend upon his relationship with Paul and other Christian missionaries. Paul preaches the Christian gospel, and Peter, as well as preaching the same gospel, is himself integral to that preaching. Their personal estrangement does not alter the fact that, in terms of the gospel, Peter and Paul had a relationship, even if it was severed for all practical purposes.

To conclude, therefore, it is clear from Paul's writings of the period subsequent to the Antioch incident, and his account of his preaching during that time, that, for all his professed independence of the churches of Jerusalem and Antioch and their leaders, he was unable to avoid mentioning them, even if with a degree of irony, if not explicit repudiation. In 1 Thessalonians Paul cites the Judaean churches as a type of Christian perseverance through persecution, but the Thessalonians excel them. In Galatians Paul explicitly repudiates the authority of the Jerusalem leadership over himself and his work, but claims unity with them against the group whom he opposes. Paul nevertheless asserts his independence of all human authority and his own claim to jurisdiction over the Galatian churches. In his preaching in Corinth, Paul cites Peter and the twelve as the primary witnesses to the resurrection of Christ and implicitly acknowledges their custodianship over the traditions of the Christian gospel.

These texts reflect ambiguity in Paul's relationship with the Jerusalem church. While operating independently of, and even in isolation from, the Jerusalem and Antioch churches and their leaders, Paul nevertheless is conscious of preaching the same Christian gospel and therefore of being part of a larger Christian community with them. However strained their personal relationships, Paul remains conscious of a greater Christian unity and identity, and is therefore obliged to acknowledge their part in the gospel, through Peter's primary vision of the resurrection and custodianship over Christian tradition (1 Cor. 15.5; cf. Gal. 1.18), and through experience of persecution (1 Thess. 2.14-15), and to define his own vocational self-understanding in a manner that takes into account the undisputed pre-eminence of Peter and his associates in the Church (Gal. 1.1, 11–2.10).

The ambiguity of estrangement and hostility, and of unavoidable acknowledgement of unity and authority, that characterizes Paul's statements about the Jerusalem church and its leadership in his writing and preaching of this period, contrasts sharply with what we have been able to establish of his relationships during the period prior to the incident at Antioch. We need to consider now how Paul's relationship with the Jerusalem and Antioch churches developed during the subsequent period, as a consequence of his visit to Antioch.

Chapter 7

THE RETURN TO ANTIOCH, AND ITS SIGNIFICANCE

Acts 18.22 records a visit by Paul to Antioch shortly after his mission in Corinth, but provides no account of what transpired there. The significance of this visit can therefore be deduced only on the basis of Paul's writings after the event, and developments to which these letters may allude. I shall seek to demonstrate in this chapter a distinct shift in Paul's attitude to the Jerusalem church and its leadership, which, I shall argue, is attributable largely to developments during his visit to Antioch.

While nothing is recorded of the visit, other than the brief reference in Acts 18.22, there are a number of indicators of potential significance. It would appear that Silvanus discontinued his partnership with Paul during or after the visit to Antioch, and resumed his membership of the church there. He is not mentioned in the Acts narrative after 18.5, and there is no allusion in Paul's letters to the partnership having continued after this time. I argued above that Silvanus had supported Paul in the conflict with Peter and Barnabas and subsequently joined his work of independent mission. The issue of table fellowship between Jewish and Gentile Christians in Antioch was resolved during the interval through the promulgation of the Apostolic Decree. Paul and Silvanus would therefore have returned to find table fellowship restored in Antioch. This would appear to have enabled Silvanus to resume his membership of the church, and Paul to enter a new relationship with that community, which, I shall argue below, he saw as a means to restoring relations with the Jerusalem church.

The importance of the visit, so far as ecclesiastical relationships were concerned, is difficult to establish. If Peter was still in Antioch, which is possible, then Paul could conceivably have effected some degree of reconciliation not only with him, but through him also with

James and the Jerusalem church. It is more certain that Paul was reconciled with Barnabas and the Antiochene church, even if Barnabas himself was absent from Antioch for all or part of Paul's visit. The former association and partnership between Paul and Barnabas was, however, not resumed. It would have been incompatible with their disparate commitments, and, furthermore, the success of Paul's independent missionary work and the concept of apostleship he had developed would have militated against his resuming a potentially tense working relationship with Barnabas and the Antiochene church. In addition, Paul's quite possibly effective assertion of his personal apostolic authority over the Galatian churches which had been established under Antiochene auspices, may have limited the potential for trust and confidence between him and the Antiochene church.

The period between Paul's visit to Antioch and his final visit to Jerusalem saw the composition of the entire extant Corinthian correspondence and Romans. Some scholars would place other letters, disputed or otherwise, in this period, but, as they do not impinge upon this investigation, we need not consider them here. A possible exception is Philippians which will be considered in an excursus at the end of Part III.

1. *The Evidence of 1 Corinthians*

In addition to 1 Cor. 15.5-8, discussed in the previous chapter, Paul mentions Peter in 1 Cor. 1.12, and the apostles and brothers of Jesus, and Peter especially, in 1 Cor. 9.5. It is also sometimes argued that 1 Cor. 3.10-11 alludes to the same Petrine tradition as Mt. 16.18. We need to reconstruct, so far as is possible, the relationship between Paul and the Jerusalem church and its leaders as reflected in these texts.

Paul alludes in 1 Cor. 1.12 to a faction in the Corinthian church which professed allegiance to Peter. Paul himself and Apollos, both of whom had worked in Corinth, are also mentioned as objects of factional loyalty. This raises the question whether Peter too had been to Corinth and become known in person to the church there. I argued in Chapter 6 above that Peter first became known to the Corinthian Christians through Paul's missionary preaching, in which his resurrection Christophany was integral to the gospel. A visit by Peter to Corinth would therefore not have been a prerequisite to his becoming known there by reputation and enjoying considerable prestige on account of his pre-eminence in the Christian tradition. This in itself could account for Peter's having become the object of some degree of allegiance on the part of some in the Corinthian church.[1]

Peter's reputation in Corinth, therefore, would not have required his presence there, and we need to consider whether there is in fact any evidence of his having visited Corinth. The most recent major argument in favour of such a visit, is that of C.K. Barrett (1982: 28-39). On the basis of 1 Cor. 9.5 Barrett suggests that Peter had visited Corinth, accompanied by his wife (1982: 32). The fact that Peter undertook missionary work, accompanied by his wife, and that Paul mentions it in the particular context of 1 Corinthians 9[2] is not evidence that Peter had in fact visited Corinth. Barrett, who elsewhere argues that there was a 'concerted anti-Pauline movement' in early Christianity (1985: 22), argues that Peter established a nomistic following in the Corinthian church (1982: 31). Dahl, however, has asserted that there is no indication of a Judaistic faction in Corinth, and reflects a degree of scholarly consensus in doing so (1967: 314; cf. Watson 1986: 81-83). Any factional allegiance to Peter based on personal acquaintance therefore would not have been nomistic, but, as there is little evidence to support the Baur tradition of Peter the Judaizer, the absence of a Judaistic tendency in Corinth does not in itself exclude the possibility that the faction professing loyalty to Peter had resulted from his ministry there.

Barrett argues that 1 Cor. 1.13 indicates a link between baptism and the divisions in the Corinthian congregation (1982: 29),[3] and that the group which professed allegiance to Peter consisted of people he had baptized (1982: 31). Paul, however, is using baptism to illustrate the essential unity of the Church which transcended all loyalties to human leaders and figures. Criticism of Corinthian factionalism on the basis of baptism would not have been possible had the rite itself become the cause of factions. It would seem more plausible that Paul used baptism thus, precisely because it was commonly understood to symbolize a higher loyalty than that to any church leader or figure and therefore to require a unity in the community which transcended divisions based

1. Cf. Dahl 1967: 322-25; Gunther 1973: 301.
2. For discussion of the place of 1 Cor. 9 in the letter, see Conzelmann 1969: 179.
3. Cf. Conzelmann 1969: 33; Dunn 1970: 117-19; Wedderburn 1987: 248.

on lesser loyalties. While Paul clearly saw the danger that a cultic relationship could be construed between baptizer and baptisand (1 Cor. 1.14-15), it is also apparent that such an interpretation had not arisen in Corinth, and Paul is thankful not to have occasioned it. If Peter had initiated cultic relationships in Corinth, Paul would have had to argue his point more forcefully and to direct more of his subsequent argument against Peter and his followers in Corinth (cf. Conzelmann 1969: 33-34). Rather, Paul is illustrating his argument with a hypothetical misinterpretation of Christian baptism. He can use this line of argument precisely because the situation had not yet arisen in Corinth, and Paul could point out an implication of the factionalism which he expected would caution those involved. Peter's presence in Corinth therefore cannot be substantiated on the basis of Paul's use of baptism to argue against factionalism.

Barrett suggests further that 1 Cor. 5.9-13 reflects the incident at Antioch, and Paul's criteria for acceptable company at table (1982: 33).[1] Even if this is so, it does not imply that Peter had been to Corinth. Similarly, Barrett argues that Paul's response to the question of eating meat which had been used in pagan worship in 1 Cor. 8.1–11.1 reflects the Antioch incident (1982: 33). While we need not doubt that Jewish sensitivities may have played a role in this issue in Corinth, the fundamental question was not one of table fellowship or dietary observance, but one of participation, directly or indirectly, in pagan worship (1 Cor. 8.1, 4-8).[2] The influence of Jewish monotheism may be detected in opposition to eating idol meat in the Corinthian church, but this does not require a concerted Judaistic movement, or even a Judaistic tendency, and still less the presence of Peter in Corinth. It is quite clear from 1 Cor. 8.10-13 and 10.14, 20-23 that Paul was opposed in principle to the consumption of idol meat, even if in the conditions prevailing in Corinth at the time he was constrained to tolerate it (1 Cor. 8.9; 10.25-27).[3] It would seem impossible,

1. Cf. Manson 1962: 197; Conzelmann 1969: 33.
2. Cf. Hurd 1965: 115-49, 225-26; Theissen 1982: 121-43; Meeks 1983a: 69-70, 97-100; Willis 1985; Segal 1990: 237. See also Wilson 1983: 84-94, and Countryman 1988: 70-77, who argue that the Apostolic Decree was specifically directed against Christians' participation in pagan cults.
3. Cf. Hurd 1965: 119; Willis 1985: 212; Countryman 1988: 101-104.

therefore, to distinguish between the followers of Paul and the followers of Peter on this question.

Barrett's thesis, therefore, is based upon the assumption both that Peter represented a Judaistic tendency within early Christianity and that such a position was represented in the Corinthian church by the time 1 Corinthians was written. There is no evidence in 1 Corinthians of any Judaistic tendency in the Corinthian church nor that Peter represented such a position. It is simply not possible in 1 Corinthians to distinguish between Paul's followers and Peter's. The situation reflected in 2 Corinthians was caused by a subsequent intrusion into the life of the Corinthian church, which will be discussed in the following chapter, and Paul's opponents in 2 Corinthians cannot simply be equated with any factional tendency in 1 Corinthians.[1]

While Paul's authority was clearly brought into question in Corinth, this challenge cannot be attributed to a Petrine tendency in the church, and still less identified with any activity by Peter himself in Corinth. It is quite clear that Paul is more concerned with the influence of Apollos, and with asserting his priority, and greater authority, over Apollos, than he is with Peter in 1 Cor. 3.6-9 (Conzelmann 1969: 33-35). Peter's followers are indistinguishable in doctrine from Paul's, which is precisely what one would expect if the Corinthians knew of Peter only through Paul's preaching. The Peter known in Corinth was the primary witness to the resurrection of Christ and custodian over the traditions of the Christian gospel, and not the leader of a school whose teaching differed substantially from Paul's. The factional dissent in Corinth was occasioned by dissatisfaction with Paul's leadership on the part of some of the Corinthian Christians, and was accompanied and perhaps justified by the assertion of loyalty to whomever the faction perceived to be the highest authority in the Church. For those loyal to him it was Paul the founder of the Corinthian church. For others it was Apollos the eloquent exponent of Christian wisdom, or Peter the unknown and perhaps mysterious recipient of the first

1. Cf. Barrett 1982: 35, and Hengel 1979: 98, who argue that a Petrine Judaistic mission is behind opposition to Paul throughout the Corinthian correspondence. Cf. also Watson 1986: 82, who argues that Apollos is the figure behind opposition to Paul during the same period.

vision of the risen Christ and primary custodian over the Christian traditions.[1]

In summary, therefore, Peter acquired fame and status in Corinth during Paul's mission through being cited as the primary witness to Christ's resurrection. On this account, I have argued that, when factions emerged in the Corinthian church, and some of the Christians became disaffected with Paul, Peter, as a Christian leader, unknown to the community except through Paul's preaching, but perceived to possess greater authority than Paul, naturally became the object of professed allegiance on the part of some Corinthian Christians. Paul's criticism in 1 Cor. 1.12 is of the faction rather than of Peter himself and indicates no hostility towards the person, or even the figure, of Peter. The implications of this for Paul's relationship with Peter at the time of writing will be considered more fully below when other relevant texts have been discussed, but for the present it is worth noting that Paul gives no indication of being threatened in any way by Peter, or even by his standing in the Corinthian church.

Another text on the basis of which some scholars argue that Peter had visited Corinth is 1 Cor. 3.10-11. It is asserted that the word θεμέλιος reflects the same tradition as that in which Peter is described as πέτρα (Mt. 16.18).[2] Manson and Barrett assert further that Peter is the unnamed person building on Paul's foundation in 1 Cor. 3.10. This would seem most unlikely, however, as Paul's imagery in 1 Cor. 3.10 is parallel to that in 1 Cor. 3.6 where it is Apollos who waters the seed which Paul has sown (cf. Conzelmann 1969: 74-76). There is no indication in 1 Cor. 3.10-15 that building on Paul's foundation is in itself a 'reprehensible practice' (Manson 1962: 194), provided that the person concerned builds according to Paul's intentions.[3] Paul's statements in 2 Cor. 10.12-18 and Rom. 15.15-24, cited by Manson, cannot simply be equated with this text or justify his interpretation of it. In 2 Cor. 10.12-18 Paul is dealing with opponents who deliberately seek to subvert his work in Corinth, which he does not suggest is the case in 1 Cor. 3.10-11. He simply cautions that those

1. Cf. the positions of Dahl 1967: 322-23; Brown 1973: 33; Gunther 1973: 301; Vielhauer 1975: 351; Holmberg 1978: 45; Meeks 1983a: 118; Smith 1985: 192.
2. Manson 1962: 194; Cullmann 1953: 147; Barrett 1982: 32; Vielhauer 1975: 348.
3. Cf. Watson 1986: 81-84 on the role of Apollos in Corinth.

who follow up his work should conform to the foundations he had laid. In the light of the parallelism between 1 Cor. 3.6 and 1 Cor. 3.10, it would seem clear that the latter text alludes primarily to Apollos, but perhaps also, if less pointedly, to Timothy (cf. 1 Cor. 16.10) and other of Paul's colleagues. There is no evidence at all that it alludes to Peter. Rom. 15.20 does not imply Paul's condemnation of all who build on the foundations laid by others, but merely expresses Paul's own preference for the initial work. The fact that he took it upon himself to write Romans in itself implies that this was not absolute, as is also clear from Rom. 1.13.[1] There is therefore no reason to believe that Paul thought following up the work initiated by another was in itself reprehensible, and still less to read any allusion to Peter into 1 Cor. 3.10-15 on that basis.

In short, there is no evidence that Peter had in any way been involved in the life of the Corinthian church at the time 1 Corinthians was written,[2] except in that his vision of the risen Christ was integral to Paul's preaching. The image and prestige of Peter seems to have evoked the allegiance of some members of the Corinthian church, but there is no evidence of Peter's personal involvement in this. We must therefore consider Paul's statements about Peter as of one not personally involved in the situation in Corinth.

Peter, the apostles, and the brothers of Jesus are mentioned in 1 Cor. 9.5-6. The immediate issue under discussion in 1 Corinthians 9 is that of financial support for Christian workers and the related matter of their being accompanied on their journeys by their spouses. Paul and Barnabas accept no pay for their apostolic work and are not accompanied by wives on their travels (1 Cor. 9.6) which, I have suggested, was the custom of the church of Antioch and its missionaries.[3] Peter, the apostles, and the brothers of Jesus, however, do accept payment and are accompanied by their wives on their travels, which was presumably the practice of the Jerusalem church (cf. Theissen 1982: 27-67). The question of apostolic rights is discussed in 1 Corinthians in the context of the issue of consumption of meat which

1.   Watson 1986: 103-105; Wedderburn 1988: 98. Cf. Kettunen 1979: 138; Shaw 1983: 138-40.

2.   Cf. the arguments of Robertson and Plummer 1914: 12; Allo 1925: 9; Héring 1962: 5; Cullmann 1953: 56.

3.   See discussion in Chapter 3 above.

had been offered to pagan deities and participation in the civic cult. Paul and Barnabas's foregoing their rights as apostles is an example to the Corinthians of flexibility, of renunciation of the privileges of their status, and self-sacrifice for the sake of the gospel and the Corinthian Christians. There is no implied criticism of those who do receive financial support from the churches in which they work and are accompanied in their travels by their spouses, for this is an apostolic ἐξουσία (1 Cor. 9.4, 6). Even if there is an implication that Paul and Barnabas display outstanding virtue in waiving their rights, and are therefore somewhat morally superior, the passage would be meaningless without Paul's unequivocal acknowledgement of the inalienable rights of Christian workers, which Peter, the brothers of Jesus, and unspecified other apostles exercise.[1]

A significant aspect of Paul's argument in 1 Corinthians 9 is that he cites Barnabas as an ally and colleague, more akin to himself than to Peter in his personal conduct in his apostolic work. I suggested in Chapter 3 that this was attributable to their both conforming to the custom of the Antiochene church in these matters. Barnabas is accordingly mentioned with unequivocal approval, which is to be expected when the practice in question is one they share, and which Barnabas may have been instrumental in formulating. While the conduct of Peter, the brothers of Jesus, and the other apostles is far from reprehensible, there is a clear implication that Barnabas and Paul exceed the requirements of their apostolic vocation, and accordingly excel those apostles who are accompanied by their spouses and receive payment for their work. Nevertheless, there is no hint of hostility towards either Peter or Barnabas in this text.

1.   Schmithals argues that Paul's ability to compare himself with the other apostles, when they differ in the matters of support and being accompanied by spouses, implies that in other respects they are similar (1971b: 59). This stands to reason, since Paul defined apostleship in terms of his own vocational self-conception, and could therefore recognize others as Christian apostles only in so far as they conformed to himself. Paul is less self-conscious in his usage of ἀπόστολος in 1 Cor. than in Gal., but the criteria of apostleship remain those on which Paul's self-identity was founded. The arguments of Munck (1949: 114) and Schmithals (1971b: 80) that Peter is excluded from the category of apostle in 1 Cor. 9 are therefore unlikely, and Barrett rightly asserts that οἱ λοιποὶ ἀπόστολοι (1 Cor. 9.5) includes Peter (1968: 204). See discussion in Chapter 6 section 3 and in the Appendix.

A further reference to Peter, James, and the other apostles, occurs in Paul's treatment of Corinthian distortions or misunderstandings of his doctrine on the resurrection. He prefaces this with a summary of the gospel which he had inherited from the primitive Christian community and passed on to the Corinthians (1 Cor. 15.3b-4). This is followed by a list of post-resurrection appearances of Christ, including those cited in Paul's original preaching (1 Cor. 15.5-8). Whatever the precise history of the tradition or traditions contained in this text, we are concerned here with the text as it stands in 1 Corinthians.[1] Paul is concerned to substantiate his doctrine of the resurrection by demonstrating its universality in Christian teaching.[2]

Paul refers to two individuals, Peter and James, and follows their names with reference to τοῖς δώδεκα and τοῖς ἀποστόλοις πᾶσιν respectively (1 Cor. 15.5, 7). The precise identity of these two groups is difficult to establish, especially as later church tradition has tended to identify them (Mt. 10.2; Lk. 6.13; 22.14; Rev. 21.14; cf. Acts 1.26). In Chapter 6 I argued that the appearance to Peter and the twelve was part of Paul's original preaching in Corinth, and that the expression accordingly was one he had inherited, directly or indirectly, from the primitive community. The appearance to James was not included in Paul's original preaching in Corinth, even though Paul almost certainly knew the tradition from the time of his first visit to Jerusalem after his conversion (Gal. 1.19; cf. Fuller, 1971: 28). Who the apostles are in 1 Cor. 15.7, and how they relate to the twelve and to James, must now be considered.

Brown points out that James and Paul were not followers of Jesus, but were converted through resurrection appearances (cf. Acts 1.12), and accordingly suggests that the sequence: Peter, the δώδεκα, the five hundred, represents the disciples of Jesus, while the sequence: James, the ἀπόστολοι, Paul, represents those who converted to Christianity after the resurrection of Jesus (1973: 34). The plausibility of this distinction depends on how rigidly it is applied and on a somewhat unlikely supposition that none of the apostles was a follower of Jesus. Whether ἀπόστολος is part of the tradition, and refers to all who are engaged in the Christian apostolate, or Paul imposes his own,

---

1. For discussion of the traditions behind the text, see Chapter 6 section 5 above.
2. Allo 1956: 389; Barrett 1968: 341.

narrower, definition of apostleship, the two sequences cannot be regarded as mutually exclusive. Schmithals's attempts to exclude Peter from recognition by Paul as an apostle, both in this text and elsewhere (1971b: 79), are somewhat forced and unconvincing. Furthermore, in defining his own self-conception, Paul was forced in part to model himself on those who were recognized as authorities in the Church. That Peter was not merely one such figure, but the epitome of Christian authority as primary witness to the resurrection is clear from Paul's comparison of himself with Peter in Galatians 1–2. This is independently attested by the ubiquity of the figure of Peter in the early Christian literature.[1] If apostleship includes Peter, as clearly it must, this implies that the two sequences overlap, at least in part.

Rengstorf identifies the twelve as 'the innermost circle of the disciples of Jesus' (1935: 325; cf. Orr and Walther 1976: 321). To this position Barrett adds that the twelve were of little significance in the life of the Church after the earliest period (1968: 342). The inclusion of Judas Iscariot in the Synoptic lists (Mt. 10.4; Mk 3.19; Lk. 6.14), the references to ἕνδεκα during the period subsequent to the crucifixion (Mt. 28.16; Mk 16.14; Lk. 24.9, 33), and the election of Matthias to replace Judas (Acts 1.11-26), indicate strongly that the twelve existed as a recognizable entity in the ministry of Jesus[2] and that Paul inherited the designation, which he does not use elsewhere in his extant writings, from the primitive community.

The apostles are more difficult to identify, not least because later tradition has identified them with the twelve. They were, however, clearly not coterminous with the twelve in the earliest days of the Church, although Peter at least clearly belonged to both groups. Unlike the twelve, the apostles are defined by function rather than by number (cf. Schmithals 1971b: 68). This raises the question of definition, and of whose criteria are being applied. Paul mentions himself with some awkwardness after τοῖς ἀποστόλοις πᾶσιν, with the phrase ὡσπερεὶ τῷ ἐκτρώματι (1 Cor. 15.8), which clearly implies that this appearance was something of an anticlimax after the previous one, rather than the climax to the entire sequence. The juxtaposition of the apparition to all the apostles and the one to Paul

---

1. For discussion of Peter's role in early Christianity, see Cullmann 1956; Brown 1973; Smith 1985.
2. For the contrary position, see Conzelmann 1969: 303.

indicates that it is those acknowledged as apostles in terms of Paul's own self-conception, and not all who share in the work of the Christian apostolate, to whom Paul refers in 1 Cor. 15.7. Fuller argues that the framework in which the traditions are arranged in 1 Cor. 15.5-7 is of Paul's making, and that he arranged traditions received from different sources (1971: 28). It is not implausible that Paul created the category of appearance τοῖς ἀποστόλοις πᾶσιν and inserted it in the sequence immediately before the appearance to himself, to conform with his definition of apostleship. Schütz argues that Paul could not have created the category of appearance to all the apostles, because its usage in 1 Cor. 15.7 excludes himself (1975: 96-97). This view, however, does not appreciate the connection between the appearance to all the apostles and that to Paul. 1 Cor. 15.7b-8 could be paraphrased to read 'he appeared to all the apostles, of whom I was the last'. Paul uses the expression τοῖς ἀποστόλοις πᾶσιν not to exclude himself, but to include himself among the apostles despite his lack of the credentials of authority which other early Christian leaders possessed. The view that Paul is referring in 1 Cor. 15.7 to a category of appearance, axiomatic to his definition of apostleship, rather than to a particular appearance, is strengthened by the fact that ἐφάπαξ is not repeated (cf. 1 Cor. 15.6). Paul regards his own apostolic vocation as having been the last (1 Cor. 15.8), and accordingly, I would suggest, includes reference to Christ's appearance to all the apostles, not because these were necessarily historically distinct occasions from those previously mentioned, but because they are a criterion of apostleship (cf. 1 Cor. 9.1; Gal. 1.16). Paul cannot therefore be referring to all Christian missionaries, all who participate in the apostolate of the Church, an ever-increasing number of whom must have been converted after him (cf. 1 Thess. 2.7). The vision of the risen Christ, with its vocational overtones, is a criterion of the apostleship under discussion (Rengstorf 1933: 431; Conzelmann 1969: 305), and one which Paul exploits fully in asserting his authority (Gal. 1.16; cf. 1 Cor. 9.1). The apostles referred to in 1 Cor. 15.7 are those who conform to the criteria of Paul's personalized notion of apostleship. This forms an interesting contrast to Acts 1.24 where a criterion for election to the twelve is participation in the earthly ministry of Jesus. This was a criterion of authority which Paul could not assert, and his awkwardness in explaining his own vocation in 1 Cor. 15.8 indicates that this was a problem for him (cf. Rowland

1982: 376). Paul's inability to claim what clearly was a significant criterion of authority in the early Church means that he has not only to emphasize those criteria he could assert, as he does with the vision of the risen Christ in Gal. 1.16, but also to claim the overriding grace of God which negates any shortcomings in his credentials for Christian leadership (1 Cor. 15.9; cf. Gal. 1.15).

While Paul is concerned primarily with demonstrating the authority with which the resurrection of Christ is preached, 1 Cor. 15.1-8 nevertheless is important for discerning his relationship with those others whose authority he cites in support of his doctrine of the resurrection. The fact that Paul cites these authority figures, including by name two with whom he had previously been involved in controversy, indicates that they pose less of a threat to him in Corinth than does the doctrinal waywardness of some of the Corinthian Christians. This despite the existence of a clique of adherents to Peter in the Corinthian church (1 Cor. 1.12). This indicates that relations between Paul and Peter, and between Paul and James and the Jerusalem church, to the extent that they were actively pursued, were not hostile, even if Paul's placing James after Peter, the twelve, and the five hundred, is a deliberate measure to relativize James's importance. Paul is sufficiently secure in his own authority in the Corinthian church to be able, without prejudice to his own position, to cite leading Jerusalem Christians as authoritative witnesses to the resurrection and to acknowledge that his own vision was somewhat different to the other resurrection appearances. The fact that the priority of Peter's vision seems to have given rise to a faction in the Corinthian church which pledged allegiance to him, and at least implicitly acknowledged Peter as having greater authority than Paul, does not alter Paul's confidence in his own position. That Paul was mistaken in this assurance may be testified by the subsequent history of his dealings with the Corinthian church, to be discussed in the following chapter, but this was a matter of his relationship with the Corinthian Christians themselves, and not with Peter or James.

While it would seem that Paul's relationship with those whose authority he cites was at least sufficiently sound or sufficiently remote for them to pose no apparent threat to his authority in Corinth, there are nevertheless indications that Paul's authority had been brought into question, at least partly through comparison with other Christian leaders. It may be significant that Apollos is not mentioned in

1 Corinthians 15, and his authority not cited.[1] While this is far from being evidence that Paul is arguing against Apollos's teaching, it does confirm the impression that Apollos, and not Peter, is the one whose following in Corinth threatens to undermine Paul's authority.

In conclusion, therefore, 1 Corinthians reflects a situation where Paul is confident of his own authority in Corinth, despite the difficulties, and does not feel threatened by the admirers of Peter. There is no hint of hostility towards Peter or James and they are cited to support Paul's doctrine of the resurrection. There are, however, indications that Paul's relationship with Barnabas was sounder than that with Peter or James, in that Paul cites Barnabas as his colleague whose conduct of his apostleship and private life is similar to his own, and, by implication, morally superior to that of Peter, the brothers of Christ, and other apostles who exercise their apostolic ἐξουσία in the churches in which they work.

2. *The Evidence of Romans*

The Roman church was one with which Paul had had no contact prior to writing his letter, other than his acquaintance with some of its members, such as Aquila and Priscilla (Acts 18.2, 18; Rom. 16.3). His letter to the Christians in Rome was written from Corinth, shortly before Paul's journey to Jerusalem to deliver the collection; after which journey he hoped to visit Rome (Rom. 15.23-29). Paul's statements about the Jerusalem church and the collection reveal a certain amount of information about his relationship with that community and its leadership, which is to be considered here.

When he wrote 1 Cor. 16.2, Paul was uncertain as to whether or not he would make the journey to Jerusalem for the delivery of the collection. When he wrote Romans, however, he was committed to undertaking the delivery in person, despite considerable apprehension, whether of the Roman authorities or of the Temple hierarchy (Rom. 15.31). The complex issues surrounding the collection will be

---

1. Cf. the account of Apollos's background in Acts 18.24-26. According to this text Apollos knew the way of the Lord, but nevertheless required instruction as he knew only the baptism of John. No resurrection appearance is mentioned, and Apollos's ignorance of Christian baptism could conceivably indicate that he did not know the resurrection traditions.

considered below, and, for the present, it is sufficient to note that it was not necessarily, and certainly not only, the Jerusalem Christians whom Paul feared. Nevertheless, Paul was anxious as to the acceptability of his act of διακονία to τοῖς ἁγίοις (Rom. 15.31), who are undoubtedly the Jerusalem Christians.[1] Whatever the reasons for this, the fact that Paul did not know, and could merely surmise somewhat pessimistically, how he would be received by the Jerusalem church indicates a prolonged lack of contact between them. The probability is that there had been no direct communication since the incident at Antioch and that Paul feared the animosity generated through that episode, together with increasing social, political, and religious tensions in Judaea, would overshadow the renewal of contact when he arrived in Jerusalem.

The Jerusalem church had, so far as can be established, no reason to expect the arrival of Paul with the collection, except on the basis of rumour and hearsay. The agreement in terms of which the collection was conceived belonged to the κοινωνία between the Jerusalem and Antioch churches, to which Paul had been party as a representative of the Antiochene community.[2] Paul was no longer a member of the Antiochene church and therefore no longer party to that κοινωνία, or to the undertaking made in terms of it by the Antiochene church. The acceptability of the collection would therefore depend on Paul's own relationship with the Jerusalem church and the prevailing attitude there to the gospel he preached (Dunn 1988: 879), as well as on factors external to that relationship, such as the political situation in Judaea[3] which could impinge on it. If, however, ascendant Jewish nationalism meant that the Jerusalem church would compromise its safety by accepting a gift from Gentile Christians, it is nevertheless significant that there was neither the confidence in their relationship, nor the contact between them, for the leadership of the Jerusalem church to communicate to Paul that the delivery of the collection would be inopportune at that time.

The indications, therefore, are that such relations as may have existed at the time Romans was written, between Paul and the Jerusalem church, were under considerable strain, both on account of

1. See discussion in Chapter 4 section 3c above.
2. For discussion, see Chapter 4 section 2 above.
3. For discussion, see Brandon 1957: 88-100; Reicke 1984.

lack of communication between them, and on account of the conflict that had ensued in the last contact at Antioch. This is not to say that there was hostility between Paul and the Jerusalem church, something of which there is no indication in Paul's letters subsequent to Galatians.[1] Nevertheless there was a history of distrust and conflict in the relationship, and Paul could not determine how the passing of time, and lack of contact, would affect matters.

Despite his apprehension, Paul was nevertheless determined to deliver the collection to Jerusalem in person, before visiting Rome. This raises the question of the significance of Jerusalem and the Jerusalem church for Paul, as reflected in Romans 15, particularly in v. 19: ἀπὸ Ἰερουσαλὴμ καὶ κύκλῳ μέχρι τοῦ Ἰλλυρικοῦ πεπληρωκέναι τὸ εὐαγγέλιον τοῦ Χριστοῦ. While a number of scholars interpret this reference to Jerusalem in terms simply of its geographical position at the eastern extremity of Paul's preaching,[2] a view which must raise questions about the reference to Arabia in Gal. 1.17, the majority ascribe some theological significance to Jerusalem and the church there.[3] Jerusalem was located at the historical and geographical centre of Jewish life and was the focus of the eschatological expectations founded on the Jewish salvation-historical tradition. That this was also true of early Christianity is evident from the location there of the predominantly Galilaean primitive Christian community, led by the primary witness to the resurrection, Peter. The eschatological, theological, and traditional significance of Jerusalem and the authority vested in the Christian community there by virtue of this, determined the nature of the κοινωνία between the Jerusalem and Antiochene churches. Paul, despite having excluded himself from that κοινωνία, and any active relationship with the Jerusalem church, nevertheless recognized the salvation-historical significance of Jerusalem and located the start of his work of Christian apostleship there, theologically if not historically or geographically.

In summary, Romans 15 indicates that Paul was not in contact with

---

1. For discussion of 2 Cor. and Phil., see Chapter 8 and the excursus below.
2. Käsemann 1974: 294-95; Cranfield 1979: 760-61; Ziesler 1988: 343. Cf. also Schlier 1977: 432; Achtemeier 1987: 61. See discussion in Chapter 2.
3. Holl 1921: 63-65; Schweizer 1959: 97; Schlier 1977: 438; Holmberg 1978: 50; Dunn 1988: 863; Stuhlmacher 1989: 148. Cf. also Michel 1955: 460; Cranfield 1979: 761.

the Jerusalem church at the time Romans was written. However, he intended shortly to renew contact when delivering the collection. The collection was the material repayment of a spiritual debt, which implies recognition of the primacy of the Jerusalem church as well as of the salvation-historical significance of Jerusalem. Paul is not constrained to defend his apostleship in Romans and therefore has no need to demonstrate or argue his independence of Jerusalem (cf. Wedderburn 1988: 27). Paul's material independence is a corollary of the absence of communication, however, but his theological bond with Jerusalem as salvation-historical place and focus of eschatological expectation is undiminished thereby.

To conclude, therefore, Paul's writings of the period commonly described as the 'third missionary journey' reveal an absence of any effective relationship with the Jerusalem church and its leaders. There is no evidence of any contact between them. Paul is secure in his own position, apart from internal difficulties in Corinth, and perhaps also in Philippi, and seems unthreatened by the authority he recognizes in the Jerusalem church and its leaders. This contrasts sharply with the defensiveness evident in Galatians. Paul displays no animosity towards the Jerusalem church and its leaders, although he is apprehensive of his reception in Jerusalem when he delivers the collection, thus renewing contact with the church there for the first time since the Antioch incident. We need to turn our attention now to the collection in order to understand more fully its significance for Paul's relationship with the Jerusalem church.

3. *The Collection*

The collection for the church at Jerusalem belongs to the final period in Paul's missionary activity, that traditionally described as the 'third missionary journey'. In this section we are concerned with it primarily for the ways in which the concept of the collection enlightens our understanding of Paul's attitude to, and relationship with, the Jerusalem church.

In Chapter 4 we discussed the Jerusalem conference, at which the relationship of κοινωνία between the Jerusalem and Antioch churches was confirmed through an agreement to respect the two communities' diverse interpretations of the gospel, in particular the Antiochenes' waiving certain Jewish legal observances for Gentile Christians, and specifically circumcision. In terms of this κοινωνία, the Antiochenes were asked τῶν πτωχῶν μνημονεύωμεν (Gal. 2.10). I argued that this cannot simply be reduced to the collection but had wider implications. μνημονεύω implies obligation, and the financial aspect of it is not merely voluntary charity, as has been shown above. Furthermore, it is not the material poverty of the πτωχοί that creates the obligation of the Antiochene Christians, but the position of the Jerusalem church at the fountainhead of the Gospel, and the relationship of κοινωνία between the two communities.

The collection Paul undertook during his last years of freedom is not identical to that agreed between the Jerusalem and Antioch churches at the Jerusalem conference.[1] Paul had long severed his ties with the Antioch church and no longer shared in the κοινωνία between the Jerusalem and Antioch churches. The obligation had not been upon Paul as an individual Christian missionary, but as one of the apostles operating under the auspices of the church at Antioch, and would therefore no longer have involved him after his departure from Antioch. Paul nowhere in his writings concerning the collection refers to it as a contractual obligation he had entered with the Jerusalem church, but explains it at most as a moral obligation (Rom. 15.27). The historical discontinuity between the Jerusalem conference and Paul's collection project, which explains the different basis upon which the two collections were raised, is indicated by the aorist form of ἐσπούδασα in Gal. 2.10, as Wedderburn suggested (1988: 39). He argues that the aorist indicates that Paul was no longer as enthusiastic about remembering the poor at the time of writing Galatians as he had been at the time of the conference. I would argue further that, not only would Paul no longer have been as enthusiastic about the collection as he was at the time of the conference, and as he came to be by the time he wrote 2 Corinthians 8, 2 Corinthians 9 and Romans, but he was not committed to such a project at all at the time he wrote Galatians.

It was after Galatians had been written, and after the visit to

1. This point has been argued along somewhat similar lines by Wedderburn (1988: 37-41). Wedderburn, while recognizing the discontinuity between the Jerusalem conference and Paul's collection project, does not recognize the root cause of that disruption, viz. Paul's departure from Antioch and the church which had entered the agreement through him.

Antioch recorded in Acts 18.22, that Paul began to organize the collection.[1] Whatever the significance of Paul's visit to Antioch, there is no indication whatever that he resumed working under Antiochene auspices and thereby became subject once again to the agreement between Jerusalem and Antioch. While I would argue that this visit was significant, its importance does not lie in any resumption of Paul's previous involvement in the life of the Antiochene church. Suhl suggests that the purpose of the visit was the organization of the collection (1975: 136). It would seem more likely, however, that Paul's intention in visiting Antioch was to restore a sound relationship with that church (Haenchen 1971: 548; cf. Conzelmann 1987: 156), and that the decision to raise the collection was the consequence rather than the cause of the visit to Antioch. Even if the idea predated the visit, it is unlikely that Paul would have committed himself and his churches to the project before assessing the situation, so far as he could, while at Antioch. If Paul sought to establish a relationship of κοινωνία (cf. Rom. 15.26) between his churches and the community at Jerusalem, on the same or similar basis to that between the Jerusalem and Antioch churches, the collection may have been conceived with that end in mind. The willingness of the Jerusalem church to enter such a relationship, however, would have been far from certain. Paul must have become aware of the Apostolic Decree when he visited Antioch, but there is no indication of his having applied it in his churches subsequently, which the Jerusalem leadership would certainly have expected. They would also have required Paul to accept some measure of subordination, an unlikely eventuality after several years' independent work, during which he had developed a very clear concept of independent apostleship accountable only to God, and had achieved very considerable missionary success. Willingness on the part of the Jerusalem church to enter a relationship of κοινωνία with Paul and his churches would have been particularly unlikely when Paul evidently initiated his collection unilaterally, and expected it to form the basis of κοινωνία rather than being a mutually recognized act in terms of it (cf. Rom. 15.26-27; 2 Cor. 8.4; 9.13). While Paul does explain the collection as reciprocation of a spiritual debt (Rom. 15.27; cf. 2 Cor. 8.14; 9.12-14), the reality is that there was no

1.   Cf. Georgi 1965: 33; Hyldahl 1986: 70-74; Watson 1986: 59; Wedderburn 1988: 30.

direct, pre-existing, relationship between his churches and that at Jerusalem but only the tenuous and unilateral link through himself. This may account in part for Paul's fears, once the collection had been raised, for its acceptability to the Jerusalem church (Rom. 15.31). We shall return to this point below.

Jerusalem is not mentioned as the destination of the funds under discussion in 2 Corinthians 8. It is apparent, however, from the involvement of Titus and others, that a particular fund-raising project is at issue, and not Christian giving, or any related concept, in general. The beneficiaries are described as τοὺς ἁγίους (2 Cor. 8.4),[1] a term which Paul applies to all Christians but which, in his extant writings, he uses either of his addressees or of the Jerusalem church, but never of any other third party. It is also clear that this is a project which involves churches other than Corinth and requires some degree of coordination; a function which Paul delegates to others, but for which he claims the ultimate responsibility (2 Cor. 8.20). Prior knowledge of this project on the part of the Corinthian church is presupposed (cf. 1 Cor. 16.1-4), and there can be little doubt that it is the collection for the Jerusalem church that is at issue.

Paul informs the Corinthians he is sending Titus to Corinth, undoubtedly to attend to the full range of issues confronting the Christian community there, as is indicated by the words σπουδὴν ὑπὲρ ὑμῶν (2 Cor. 8.16), but particularly to supervise the completion of the collection. Titus had evidently won the confidence of the Corinthian Christians, and secured their loyalty to Paul, and was therefore the obvious person to undertake this somewhat sensitive function. Titus is to be accompanied by two unnamed agents. The first of these is identified only as τὸν ἀδελφὸν οὗ ὁ ἔπαινος ἐν τῷ εὐαγγελίῳ διὰ πασῶν τῶν ἐκκλησιῶν (2 Cor. 8.18), and the second mentioned in similarly oblique terms in 2 Cor. 8.22, but is significantly described as τὸν ἀδελφὸν ἡμῶν in contrast to the other (cf. Furnish 1984: 424). Betz argues that the use of ἀδελφός is in deliberate avoidance of ἀπόστολος (1985: 81), in which case Paul is probably anxious that the authority of these persons should not be misunderstood or abused. The reason for Paul's not identifying these persons by name is uncertain, but Martin points out that this is not the only such occurrence (1986: 275; cf. Phil. 4.2). Paul clearly knew

1.   Cf. Rom. 15.25-26; 1 Cor. 16.4; 2 Cor. 9.12.

precisely whom he intended to send with Titus, and the fact that they were not his own nominees (2 Cor. 8.19, 23) would presumably have eliminated any uncertainty he could have entertained on the subject. Georgi and Nickle suggest that the names were subsequently excised from the text on account of the disfavour into which these persons fell.[1] This is possible, but unsupported by any textual evidence (cf. Martin 1986: 275). It would seem more likely, therefore, that Paul wishes to enhance Titus's standing and authority, and in not naming the other two he does not impart his authority onto them, so that they could not function on their own if they arrived in Corinth without Titus (Betz 1985: 73). The brothers could function on Paul's authority in Corinth only if Titus was there too.

More important than the names of the anonymous brothers, however, are the churches they represent (2 Cor. 8.23), particularly as this is where Paul's relationship with the Jerusalem and Antioch churches comes into contention. Nickle argues that the two are Judas Barsabbas and Silas (Acts 15.22), and that they represent the Judaean churches (1966: 18-22). There is no evidence to support this view (Furnish 1984: 434), and furthermore it presupposes a continuity between the Jerusalem council and Paul's collection project which, as argued above, is not merely unattested but implausible on account of the unforeseen change in Paul's standing in the Antiochene church. Furnish suggests that the brothers are the representatives of the Macedonian churches (1984: 435), and this is undoubtedly more plausible. Betz argues that the brothers are ecclesiastical-political allies of Paul (1985: 73), about whom Paul, on Betz's arguments cited above, must have been somewhat wary. The two brothers must be considered separately.

The purpose of the appointment of the first brother, to whom Paul significantly does not apply the possessive ἡμῶν, if not explicitly of the second, was to protect Paul and his colleagues from any suspicion of dishonesty or impropriety in handling the collection money (2 Cor. 8.20-21). He is well-known among the churches (2 Cor. 8.18),[2] which indicates that he is not simply a leader of a local congregation (Furnish 1984: 434). Nevertheless he is being introduced to the Corinthians, apparently for the first time. It is not clear in which

1.   Georgi 1965: 24; Nickle 1966: 20.
2.   Cf. Hainz 1972: 149; Martin 1986: 274.

churches the brother is famous, even if Corinth is not one of them. Presumably it is, or at least includes, those which appointed him to assist in the collection (2 Cor. 8.19). Paul's unease about the potential activities of this person when not under Titus's supervision would seem to indicate that he comes from outside those churches under Paul's jurisdiction. Paul's visit to Antioch in Acts 18.22 may hold the key to this problem. If Paul's decision to raise the collection was a consequence of this visit, as argued above, then it is possible that the decision was taken in consultation with the leaders of the Antiochene church who were undertaking the collection agreed to at the Jerusalem conference. If the Antiochene collection was intended for the sabbatical year 54–55 CE [1] then it would not have been completed by the time of Paul's visit to Antioch (c. 52 CE). If Paul's collection was to be raised in conjunction with that of the Antioch church, then it is possible that that community would have seconded one of its members to assist in the coordination of the project. It is probable that any such person would have supported Peter and Barnabas against Paul at the Antioch incident and been committed to the implementation of the Apostolic Decree, which could account for Paul's wariness of his activity in his churches, and especially in Corinth. 2 Corinthians 8 was written very soon after the resolution of the crisis in the Corinthian church,[2] and Paul would on that account have been especially anxious about outside involvement in that community. I would suggest, therefore, that this brother whom Paul does not acknowledge as his own and whom he did not appoint was prominent in the churches of Syria and Cilicia, and perhaps more widely in Asia Minor, that his work was based at Antioch, and that he was nominated by the Antiochene church to assist in the coordination of Paul's collection project.

The second anonymous brother, whom Paul describes as ἡμῶν, and in whose praise he is lavish where he had merely mentioned as fact the fame of the other, is, like the first, an ἀπόστολος ἐκκλησιῶν (2 Cor. 8.23), but it appears that he enjoys Paul's personal confidence to a greater extent than does the first, even if Paul does not want him acting in Corinth without Titus. He appears from 2 Cor. 8.22 to have been known to Paul for some time and to be familiar, however

---

1. For discussion of the date of the collection, see Jeremias 1928: 98-103; Suhl 1975: 135.

2. See discussion in the Introduction sections 4a and 5.

indirectly, with the situation in Corinth. This, and the lower status indicated by his being mentioned after the other brother, suggests that he was a more local figure, and probably came from one of the churches Paul had established in Greece or western Asia Minor (cf. Furnish 1984: 436), who had been chosen to assist in the coordination of the collection project, but in a capacity broader than that of representing his own community in the delivery to Jerusalem (cf. Acts 20.4).

Whatever the standing of the anonymous brothers, Paul emphasizes that it is Titus who is his κοινωνός and συνεργός (2 Cor. 8.23). Titus is closer to Paul (Martin 1986: 277), and also to the Corinthians, and is the one from whom the Corinthian Christians are to take directions, rather from the others, and the possibility cannot be excluded that they are deliberately unnamed in order to undermine their capacity to assert authority in the Corinthian church and to intervene in its life in matters other than the collection. If the senior of the two anonymous brothers came from Antioch, Paul would have been particularly anxious to ensure that he acted only within his terms of reference.

There is no evidence to suggest, and good reason to doubt, that either or both of the anonymous brothers came from Jerusalem, or was associated with that community in any way. There is no indication therefore that the Jerusalem church was in any way involved in Paul's collection project, and Paul's relationship with that church and its leaders remained effectively in abeyance, and would not be re-activated until Paul actually arrived in Jerusalem and offered the collection to the church.

In his final extant correspondence with the Corinthian church, and any other Achaian Christians,[1] Paul elaborates the theological significance he attributes to the collection as it impinges on his and the Corinthian and other Pauline Christians' relationship with the Jerusalem church. The collection is not merely provision for the needs of the ἅγιοι but is also the cause of thanksgiving to God (2 Cor. 9.12). The actions of the Corinthian Christians will cause the Jerusalem Christians to thank God and to pray for the Corinthian Christians διὰ τὴν ὑπερβάλλουσαν χάριν τοῦ θεοῦ ἐφ' ὑμῖν (2 Cor. 9.14). This is a more confident expectation than Paul later expressed in writing to the Roman Christians. The apparent discrepancy, however, is

1.   See the Introduction sections 4a and 5 for discussion.

explained by the recent history of Paul's relationship with the Corinthian Christians, which would have constrained him from telling them of the possible futility of the collection project. In his letter to the Corinthians, Paul implies that he expects that the collection will cause the Jerusalem church to accept the Gentile Christians and their gift without hesitation or inhibition. The implication of this is that a relationship would be formed between the Christians of Jerusalem and the Pauline churches. As Paul's own relationship with the Jerusalem church had been strained and all but severed, he could not himself provide the basis for any relationship, κοινωνία or otherwise, between the communities he had established and that at Jerusalem. However, if Paul was rejoining the collection project of the Antiochene church, in whose inception he had played a role, he could conceivably claim for his churches a relationship on the same basis as that in terms of which the collection had originally been agreed. I would suggest that it is the consummation of such a κοινωνία with the Jerusalem church which Paul seeks through the collection, and this he anticipates in 2 Corinthians 9.

In this chapter I have sought to establish the nature of Paul's relationships with the Jerusalem and Antioch churches and their leaders during the period after his visit to Antioch recorded in Acts 18.22. The significance of this event can be reconstructed only on the basis of the shift in Paul's attitude to these churches, as reflected in his writings of the subsequent period.

Nothing is recorded of the visit to Antioch, other than that it took place. It appears, however, to have been of considerable significance. Not only does it seem to have effected a degree of reconciliation between Paul and Barnabas and the Antiochene church, but possibly also between Paul and Peter, and by extension perhaps the Jerusalem church, though this is less certain, and, in either event, it did not result in an active relationship between Paul and the church in Jerusalem. This reconciliation did not lead to the resumption of Paul's partnership with Barnabas and involvement in the life and work of the Antiochene church. This would have been impractical in view of Paul's commitments in Greece and western Asia Minor and the success of his independent work. Paul's partnership with Silvanus seems to have ended with this visit to Antioch, but there is no reason to suppose that this was due to conflict between them.

An important aspect of Paul's visit to Antioch seems to have been his rejoining the collection project which had been agreed between the churches of Jerusalem and Antioch at the time of the Jerusalem conference. It seems likely that the Antioch church seconded one of its more prominent members to assist Paul in the collection among his churches. By resuming the commitment he had made on behalf of the Antiochene church, Paul hoped to claim for his own churches the relationship of κοινωνία that the Antiochene church enjoyed with the Jerusalem church.

In Paul's writings subsequent to his visit to Antioch, there is little evidence of tension between him and the Jerusalem and Antioch churches and such leaders in those communities as Peter, James, and Barnabas. This supports the view that this visit effected a degree of reconciliation. While there is no indication of direct contact between Paul and the Jerusalem church, there is a clearly discernible diminution in animosity on Paul's part, to the extent that he is not defensive of his apostolic claims and does not perceive himself to be threatened by professions of loyalty to Peter in Corinth. There are clearer signs of reconciliation between Paul and the Antiochene church, and some indication of collaboration in the collection project. We can conclude therefore that the visit to Antioch was of considerable significance for the final years of Paul's missionary work, to which we must now direct our attention.

Chapter 8

PAUL'S FINAL YEARS OF FREEDOM

In this chapter we are concerned with the concluding years of Paul's missionary career. In the previous chapter I argued that Paul's return to Antioch some time after his altercation there with Peter resulted in his resumption of his commitment to the collection for the Jerusalem church. This had been agreed between the churches of Jerusalem and Antioch at the Jerusalem conference, as an obligation upon the Antiochene church in terms of its κοινωνία with the Jerusalem church. In joining what was essentially a project of the Antiochene church, and taking upon himself but one aspect of their obligation to remember the poor, Paul intended to claim for his churches the same relationship of κοινωνία with the Jerusalem church as that which the Antiochene Christians enjoyed.

The crisis in Corinth is significant for two reasons. Firstly, the widely held view that Paul's opponents in Corinth were Judaistic delegates of the Jerusalem church raises the possibility of a new dimension to Paul's relationship with that community during his final missionary years. Secondly, the crisis delayed the completion of the collection project in Greece, so that Paul was unable to join in the delivery of the collection from Antioch to Jerusalem. To clarify this point, it is worth recapitulating the chronological reconstruction I argued in the Introduction.

The collection for the Jerusalem church, which had been undertaken by the Antiochene church as a corollary to the agreement of the Jerusalem conference, was scheduled for delivery in 55 CE. At the time of writing 1 Corinthians (c. 53 CE) Paul had not committed himself to participation in the delivery. If the delegates from the churches of the Pauline mission accompanied those of the Antiochene, the implicit claim to κοινωνία with the Jerusalem church on the same basis as the Antiochene would have been sufficient for Paul's purpose, and his absence might have facilitated the process. However, during 54 CE Paul became aware of the activities of external agents in the Corinthian church, and much of that and the following year was accordingly spent in seeking resolution to the crisis. It was only by the end of the sailing season of 55 CE that Titus could complete the collection in Corinth. When the collection was taken to Jerusalem in 56 CE, therefore, Paul's presence with the delegates of the churches was essential if any claim to a continuing relationship between the church of Jerusalem and those churches established by Paul was to be pursued. The outcome of this project is unknown and would in any event be rendered irrelevant by the outbreak of the Jewish War ten years later. What is certain is that the delivery of the collection resulted, directly or indirectly, in Paul's arrest in Jerusalem and the effective termination of his missionary career.

1. *Paul's Opponents in Corinth*

The identity of Paul's opponents is a contentious issue and one which has enjoyed considerable attention in scholarship. Our concern here is not so much the theology of Paul's opponents as their links, if any, with the Jerusalem and Antioch churches. If they were the authorized delegates of either community, their presence in Corinth represents an intrusion in Paul's churches unattested during any earlier period. The situation in Corinth may have been paralleled in Philippi and could therefore be representative of a wider phenomenon. [1]

It is not possible here to discuss in full the complexities surrounding the early history of the church in Corinth. The factious atmosphere in the community at the time 1 Corinthians was written was noted in the previous chapter, and it is not unlikely that this correlated in some way with the personalities, inclinations, and ambitions of the leaders of the various house churches.[2] That these activities were another aspect of the same phenomenon which occasioned Paul's anxiety at the influence of Apollos in the Corinthian church (1 Cor. 1.12-13; 3.4-9, 22; 4.6)[3] must be regarded as probable. Whether or not opposition to

---

1. For discussion of Philippi, see the excursus below.
2. See discussion by Theissen 1982: 69-143; Meeks 1983a: 56-63; Marshall 1987: 345.
3. Cf. Robertson and Plummer 1914: 16; Holmberg 1978: 67-69; Watson 1986:

Paul during the period in which the component letters of
2 Corinthians were written stemmed directly from the factional tendencies reflected in 1 Corinthians, there is no evidence of the involvement of the Jerusalem church, or other external Christian influences,
in the life of the Corinthian church during the earlier period.

Attempts to identify the opponents of Paul in 2 Corinthians 10–13
may be divided into three groups. The first are those who follow Baur
in identifying Paul's antagonists as the delegates, however subordinate
or otherwise, of the Jerusalem church, and, to a greater or lesser
extent Judaistic.[1] The second group are those who identify Paul's
opponents as gnostics.[2] Thirdly come those scholars who identify
Paul's opponents as non-nomistic, Palestinian or diaspora Jewish
Christians, independent of the Jerusalem church.[3]

The more radical gnostic hypotheses are now widely discredited,
but those which refer rather to a proto-gnostic tendency within a
broader Hellenistic Jewish tradition, as do Kümmel and Wilson, still
merit consideration and may for the present purpose be included with
the third group of scholars. It is widely recognized that the Mosaic
law was not an issue in 2 Corinthians 10–13.[4] While this excludes the
group identified in Chapter 6 above as those whose influence in the
Galatian churches Paul is opposing, it does not exclude the possibility
that Paul's opponents in Corinth were delegates of the Jerusalem
church.

Paul's opponents came from within the Jewish tradition, as verses
such as 2 Cor. 11.22 make abundantly clear.[5] Their precise location

81-84; Sellin 1987: 3015. For contrary views, see Munck 1959: 167; Schmithals
1965a: 105; Barrett 1982: 1-39; Hurd 1965: 214; Conzelmann 1969: 34.

1. Käsemann 1942; Schoeps 1961: 78-81; Barrett 1982: 1-39; Barrett 1971;
Barrett 1973; Oostendorp 1967; Gunther 1973; Holmberg 1978: 45-46; Thrall 1980;
Lüdemann 1983; Barnett 1984.

2. Lütgert 1908; Bultmann 1933; Bultmann 1947; Bultmann 1985; Schmithals
1971a; Schmithals 1965a; Schmithals 1965b; Marxsen 1968: 83; Kümmel 1975: 209;
Wilson 1982.

3. Lake 1911: 219-35; Bornkamm 1961: 169-72; Georgi 1986; Theissen 1982:
27-77; Black 1984; Furnish 1984: 52-55; Watson 1986: 81-82; Sellin 1987: 3023;
Sumney 1990.

4. Lake 1911: 222; Käsemann 1942: 20; Georgi 1986: 248; Black 1984: 86;
Furnish 1984: 52-53; Watson 1986: 81-87.

5. Cf. von Rad *et al.* 1939; Georgi 1986: 41-60; Schulz and Quell 1964: 545.

within the diversity of that tradition, however, is more difficult to establish, especially as a radical dichotomy between Palestinian and Hellenistic Judaism is no longer tenable. We need therefore to concentrate upon such evidence as may indicate a connection with Jerusalem and the Jerusalem church, bearing in mind that an eschatological orientation towards Jerusalem does not imply any connection with the Jerusalem church, nor does membership of that community in itself constitute authority from the Jerusalem church to intervene in the Corinthian church.

The expression ὑπερλίαν ἀπόστολοι in 2 Cor. 11.5 and 2 Cor. 12.11 is a potentially significant indicator, if it can be established whether Paul applies it to his opponents in Corinth, or to the leadership of the Jerusalem church, and, in the latter case, whether or not it has sarcastic overtones. Much therefore depends on whether the ὑπερλίαν ἀπόστολοι are to be identified with the ψευδαπόστολοι of 2 Cor. 11.13. Käsemann argues that the ὑπερλίαν ἀπόστολοι are the Jerusalem apostles, while the ψευδαπόστολοι are Paul's opponents in Corinth (1942: 20-24). This view is opposed by Bultmann (1947: 25-30) and Georgi (1986: 32), but supported by Barrett (1971: 246). Thrall argues that Paul did not know whether any of the Jerusalem apostles were among his rivals in Corinth and accordingly allowed for the possibility in his argument (1980: 48). Given that, on whatever historical reconstruction, Paul had already encountered his opponents, with humiliating consequences (2 Cor. 2.1) by the time 2 Corinthians 10–13 was written,[1] he could have been in no doubt as to who they were and on what basis they legitimated their intervention in the Corinthian church. McClelland argues that ὑπερλίαν ἀπόστολοι was a self-designation of pneumatic Christians in Corinth, against whom Paul is writing, and does not refer to intruders at all (1982: 84-85). It is, however, most unlikely that any member of the Christian community in Corinth would have used his Jewish pedigree as a basis on which to attack Paul's authority (cf. 2 Cor. 11.22), and more unlikely that Paul, elsewhere so defensive of his own apostleship (cf. Gal. 1–2; 1 Cor. 9; 15.7-11), should give even the most tacit assent to such self-attribution among the Corinthian Christians. If his opponents did not have a reasonable claim to Christian apostleship, in terms of Paul's particular conception thereof, he would certainly have

---

1. See the Introduction section 5 for discussion of chronology.

refuted their claim altogether in 2 Cor. 11.5 and 2 Cor. 12.11 rather than merely asserting his own equality with them.

It seems certain, therefore, that Paul's rivals came from outside Corinth, and that their claim to Christian apostleship was to at least some degree incontrovertible, even though Paul does state his determination to undermine their claim to equality with himself (2 Cor. 11.12). Furthermore, the close association of the ὑπερλίαν ἀπόστολοι with another Jesus, a different Spirit, and a different gospel (2 Cor. 11.4), clearly indicates that they are the same as the ψευδαπόστολοι of 2 Cor. 11.13, whom Paul describes as deceitful workers (2 Cor. 11.13), and, by implication, servants of Satan (2 Cor. 11.14-15). Therefore, despite being unable to refute entirely their claims to Christian apostleship, Paul nevertheless repudiates unequivocally the authenticity of the gospel they preach (cf. Thrall 1980: 52).

While Paul associates his opponents with ἄλλον Ἰησοῦν, ἢ πνεῦμα ἕτερον, and ἢ εὐαγγέλιον ἕτερον (2 Cor. 11.4), there is no evidence of any doctrinal basis to his allegations.[1] Whereas in Galatians Paul's arguments are reasoned and theological, if at times rash, in 2 Corinthians 10–13 they have little or no theological grounding. This, and the emphasis on Paul's person and apostleship, strongly suggests that the conflict was one of authority rather than theology (cf. Lincoln 1979: 207). It was a question not so much of the content of the Christian gospel as of the relationship of the preacher of that gospel to the community created through his preaching (cf. 2 Cor. 12.12).

This lack of doctrinal differences between Paul and his opponents does not prove that they had no direct connection with the Jerusalem church, but it may point in that direction. It was noted in previous chapters that, while the Jerusalem church cannot be considered Judaistic in the rigid and absolute sense first articulated by the Tübingen school, there nevertheless were differences between the gospels of the Jerusalem and Antiochene churches. This does not imply that either church was theologically monolithic, however, and we have had occasion in this study to note theological controversy within both. Paul had been for many years involved in the life and apostolate of the Antiochene church, and it is therefore probable that he would have had closer theological affinities with Christians with roots in the Jewish Diaspora than with Christians of Palestinian Jewish

1. Cf. Barrett 1971: 242; Murphy-O'Connor 1990.

origin; the dichotomy, however, must not be overemphasized. There is little if any information available about relationships between churches outside Palestine and the Jerusalem church, other than that between Jerusalem and Antioch. It is quite probable that other churches, unconstrained by such relationships as bound the Antiochene church, would have exercised greater freedom from the Jerusalem church, as Paul himself came to do after the Antioch incident. Theories which locate the origins of Paul's opponents in the Diaspora therefore merit particular consideration. Georgi has described the writer of Luke–Acts as a 'kindred author' to Paul's opponents (1986: 319). Friedrich has suggested a link with the group associated with Stephen in the early days of the Jerusalem church (1963). Hyldahl (1977) and Watson (1986: 81-84) have argued that Apollos and his associates could plausibly be identified with Paul's opponents in Corinth. It is notable that at least the first two of these three hypotheses involve an eschatological orientation towards Jerusalem without any apparent subordination to the Jerusalem church, and certainly without nomistic inclinations. Extreme caution is therefore needed in positing a direct relationship with the Jerusalem church on the basis of a theological orientation towards that city.

Paul's rivals, therefore, would seem to have represented, very broadly, the same spectrum of early Christianity as himself. They may nevertheless have been as forthright in their condemnation of Paul as he was of them (cf. Green 1985: 58), or they may have held a less narrow and individualistic conception of apostleship than Paul, in which case they may have been more accommodating than he was. This is not to deny the clear evidence that Paul's opponents seriously and wilfully undermined his authority in Corinth, but they may not have shared Paul's exclusive and territorial notion of apostleship, in terms of which he asserted his jurisdiction (cf. Rom. 1.5; 11.13; 1 Cor. 3.6, 12; 9.2; Gal.1.6; 2.8-9), and therefore have regarded their activities in Corinth as entirely valid and consistent with their own apostolic self-conception.

The practical question of language may give some indication as to the origins of Paul's rivals. Allusions to their rhetorical competence (2 Cor. 10.1, 10; 11.16) indicate that they were fluent in Greek and suggests an origin in the Diaspora rather than in Palestine. Thrall's suggestion that they used interpreters (1980: 47) is unconvincing, since, if this were the case, Paul could have exploited his fluency in

Greek, however crude by the standards of rhetorical performance, against the need of his opponents to use interpreters. Therefore, not only is there no evidence of any connection between Paul's opponents and the Jerusalem church, but their fluency in Greek and familiarity with Hellenistic rhetorical conventions indicates that their origins were in the Jewish Diaspora rather than Palestine.

Käsemann argues that only persons emanating from Jerusalem could have exerted such authority in Corinth to undermine Paul's position there (1942: 26; cf. Holmberg 1978: 45-46). This assumption defies the evidence of 1 Corinthians which indicates that the influence of Apollos was at least a potential threat to Paul's authority, and far more so than that of Peter (cf. 1 Cor. 3.6-9).[1] Furthermore, any disaffection with Paul would have facilitated the intrusion of rival authority figures in the church. If Paul's authority was further discredited through his demonstration of weakness against the intruders (2 Cor. 10.1-2; 13.2-3; 2.1), their ascendancy in Corinth would have been expedited. In Weberian terms, we are dealing with a charismatic movement against Paul in the Corinthian church, in which the demonstration of power was the crucial factor (cf. 2 Cor. 10.4-5, 9-11; 11.6-7, 16-18, 29-30; 12.10-12; 13.2-3, 10). The fact that Paul's authority in Corinth was successfully challenged, at least for a time, therefore does not require that his opponents emanated from Jerusalem, or that their activities were authorised by that community, but only that they should have presented themselves to the community as more convincing bearers of divine power, and therefore as wielding authority which exceeded Paul's.

Barrett argues that Paul alludes in 2 Cor. 10.13-16 to the agreement he and Barnabas had entered into with Peter and James in Jerusalem (1971: 238), with the implication that his rivals were violating it by their presence in Corinth. This interpretation is disputed by Furnish who argues that Paul accuses his opponents of exceeding their own commission and failing to recognize their own limitations (1984: 480, 481). I argued above (Chapter 4 section 3b) that the agreement between the churches of Jerusalem and Antioch did not include the demarcation of missionary territories along geographical or ethnic lines, but the mutual recognition of the validity of the gospel as preached by the two parties. Paul was, furthermore, a party to this

---

1. See discussion in Chapter 7 section 1.

agreement not in his own right, but as a representative of the Antiochene church. Paul's subsequent appropriation of the Jerusalem conference in order to legitimate his own apostolic claims, as discussed in Chapter 6 above, modified the wording of the agreement to reflect his conception of his own apostolic vocation, with its specific orientation towards mission to the Gentiles (Gal. 2.8-9; cf. Rom. 1.5; 11.13; Gal. 1.16). It was Paul's claim to jurisdiction in Galatia that occasioned his geographical interpretation of the agreement. If this claim is reflected in 2 Cor. 10.13-16 it represents a unilateral reinterpretation of the original agreement and would be meaningful only in terms of Paul's self-conception and where his authority was unquestioned. The Jerusalem agreement does not impinge upon the situation in Corinth, and we should therefore prefer Furnish's interpretation of 2 Cor. 10.13-16 and see Paul's claim to jurisdiction in Corinth in terms of his having founded the church there (cf. 1 Cor. 3.6, 12; 9.2). Paul 'does not appeal to an exclusive right to come to Corinth as a missionary, but to the historical fact that it was granted to him to do this' (Beyer 1939: 599).

Barrett argues that the use of commendatory letters by Paul's rivals is evidence of their having been commissioned by the Jerusalem church (1973: 40-41; cf. Holmberg 1978: 45-46). This, however, is refuted by Georgi and Furnish, and Watson has argued that Apollos could have been the recipient of a commendatory letter from the Ephesian church.[1] Furthermore, 2 Cor. 3.1-3 implies that the Corinthian Christians themselves could have issued letters. The Jerusalem church were not the only possible authors of such letters, and, furthermore, a letter of introduction does not necessarily imply the authorization of specific activities in the community to which the letter is addressed.

The nature of the rival apostles' relationship with the Jerusalem church is crucial to understanding the nature of their apostleship. There is no evidence that they were ἀπόστολοι/*šlḥym* in the sense of being emissaries of the church in Jerusalem, or of any other church, such as Paul had been when working from Antioch. Rather, as Paul himself had become since the Antioch incident, they were independent charismatic figures whose apostolic authority was conceived as being

---

1.   Georgi 1986: 244-45; Furnish 1984: 193; Watson 1986: 83-84. Cf. Acts 18.27.

derived directly from God, and whose relationship with the Jerusalem church may well have been as tenuous, ambivalent, ambiguous, and fraught as Paul's own. A phenomenological similarity to Paul may be discerned, but also a different conception of their vocation. While Paul, in principle if not in practice, worked only in churches he himself had established after his break with the Antiochene church,[1] his opponents in Corinth evidently did not so restrict the scope of their activities. Their activity in Corinth towards the end of Paul's missionary career, however, does not constitute intervention by the Jerusalem church in Paul's work, and does not impinge at all upon Paul's relationship with that community. The impression of a relationship in abeyance between Paul and the Jerusalem church is unaffected by the crisis in Corinth.

2. *The Delivery of the Collection*

When he wrote 1 Cor. 16.2 Paul was not committed to participating in the delivery of the collection to Jerusalem. When he wrote Rom. 15.30-31, however, the journey to Jerusalem was a definite, and apparently imminent, intention. A number of reasons for Paul's final decision to go to Jerusalem are possible, but confidence that his reception there would be favourable is not one of them.

Paul's apprehension was not caused entirely by uncertainty as to his and the collection's reception by the Christian church in Jerusalem (Schmithals 1965a: 80). In Rom. 15.31 he makes it clear that his fears are of the ἀπειθούντων, rather than of the Jerusalem Christians. The collection had wider social and political implications and accordingly a broader range of perils than intra-Christian concerns. If the collection was perceived by the Temple hierarchy to have diverted funds that would otherwise have reached the Temple, in the form of Temple Tax[2] or voluntary contributions, or by the Roman authorities to have misused their protection of funds being conveyed to Jerusalem for the purposes of the Temple,[3] then Paul's grounds for anxiety would have had nothing to do with his reception by the church in

---

1. For discussion of exceptions, see Chapter 6 section 3 (Galatia) and Chapter 7 section 2 (Rome) above.
2. For comparison of the collection with Temple Tax, see Nickle 1966: 87-98.
3. Cf. Knox 1925: 298; Nickle 1966: 88.

Jerusalem, except in so far as they reacted in response to the external pressures resulting from such perceptions. The Christian community in Jerusalem would have risked implicating itself in infringements of both Jewish and Roman law, had it accepted the collection money in such circumstances. In the deteriorating political situation in Judaea at the time,[1] the risks to a marginalized group which had previously incurred the wrath of the religio-political authorities (1 Thess. 2.14-16; cf. Acts 6.8–7.1; 8.1-4; 12.1-3) would have been considerable and may have constrained the Jerusalem church from responding favourably to Paul's overtures.

A further possible cause of anxiety for Paul would have been that the collection could have been perceived as a demonstration of his success in the Gentile mission. This would have offended Jewish particularism, and the Jerusalem church may have been constrained by militant public sentiment not to associate with Gentile Christians.[2]

I have argued in Chapters 6 and 7 above that Paul's relationship with the Jerusalem church had effectively been in abeyance since the Antioch incident, and he could therefore not be certain of his own standing with that community, or of his reception, and that of the collection, when he arrived. Had Paul been able to complete the collection in time to join the delivery from Antioch, as he had originally intended, his personal standing would not have been so important. Not only would it not have been necessary for Paul to make the journey himself (cf. 1 Cor. 16.2), but his personal identity, and any negative connotations associated therewith in the Jerusalem church, would have been subsumed in the collective identity of the Antiochene church with which the Jerusalem church had a relationship of κοινωνία.

The crisis in Corinth, however, delayed delivery of the collection from Paul's churches for at least a year. The Antiochene church would therefore already have conveyed their collection to Jerusalem. Paul and the representatives of at least some of his churches[3] could not therefore simply join in the Antiochene collection and claim for themselves the κοινωνία which existed between the Jerusalem and Antioch churches. There would be no implicit recognition of κοινωνία, and

1.   Cf. Stern 1974: 359-72; Jagersma 1985: 131-35.
2.   Cf. Holmberg 1978: 42; Urbach 1981: 292.
3.   Cf. 1 Cor. 16.1 and Rom. 15.26, which may indicate that the churches of Asia Minor, particularly Galatia, may have conveyed their contribution separately.

therefore an implicit assertion of κοινωνία would not suffice. The delegates of Paul's churches would have to deliver their collection on their own, and an explicit claim to κοινωνία between Paul's churches and the Jerusalem church would therefore have to be made. The collection, envisaged as an expression of, and an act within, a κοινωνία that already existed, became instead the basis for a claim to a distinct κοινωνία. Paul could not be certain that such a claim would be accepted, for it would require of the Jerusalem church an expression of solidarity with Gentile Christians at a time of heightening Jewish nationalism. Furthermore, the collection was, in effect if not in intention, a demonstration of Paul's missionary success, and therefore of the validity of his apostleship, and independence of the jurisdiction of the Jerusalem church. Whatever primacy he recognized in the Jerusalem church (Rom. 15.27), Paul was travelling to Jerusalem not in submission but in self-vindication.

Paul's arrival in Jerusalem is recorded in Acts 21.17. The collection is not mentioned in the subsequent contact with the Jerusalem church. This is in itself no evidence that the collection was rejected, since its dubious legality and contemporary irrelevance could both have led Luke to pass it over in silence. In the Introduction, however, I argued that Acts 11.27-30 relates the delivery of the collection from Antioch, earlier in the Acts narrative so as to be included with other Antioch-related material. Luke, however, includes Paul in this delivery, which may represent a conflation of what became two separate deliveries, and serve to conceal the reasons for Paul's arrest. While affirming that Paul delivered a collection to the Jerusalem church, acting in collaboration with the Antiochene church, Luke avoids connecting this act with Paul's arrest and the termination of his missionary career. Acts 21.24, however, may indicate that part of the collection money was purposely spent on Temple rituals, and Holmberg suggests that this implied Paul's acquiescence in, or at least submission to, the interpretation the Jerusalem church placed on the collection, as an act of subordination by the churches Paul had established, and by Paul himself, to the jurisdiction of the Jerusalem church and its leaders (1978: 43). In the circumstances prevailing in Judaea at the time, however, the Jerusalem church may have felt too vulnerable to enter a relationship of κοινωνία with Paul and his churches (cf. Rom. 15.31). The consequences of the delivery of the collection, as envisaged by either side, are unrecorded, and, even if realized temporarily, would have been brought to an end by the outbreak of the Jewish War in 66 CE. That Paul was arrested in Jerusalem (Acts 21.33) cannot be doubted, whatever the precise circumstances (cf. Schmithals 1965a: 83). That this arrest permanently ended Paul's freedom is also beyond serious doubt. It is therefore appropriate that this study ends with Paul's final arrest in Jerusalem and the consequent termination of his work of Christian mission.

Excursus

THE EVIDENCE OF PHILIPPIANS

In the Introduction (section 4a), I noted that the date of Philippians is a matter of considerable dispute in contemporary scholarship, there being three principal theories as to its provenance. If Philippians was written from Caesarea or Rome during the late 50's or early 60's CE, then it post-dates the period with which we are concerned, even if it conveys information relevant to an earlier period. If, however, Philippians was written from Ephesus in c. 55 CE, as is widely and plausibly argued, then it would be contemporary with the component letters of 2 Corinthians, and directly relevant to the period under consideration.

An assessment of the information contained in Philippians is further complicated by the question of its integrity. There is a significant majority of scholarly opinion in favour of the integrity of the letter.[1] Gnilka divides canonical Philippians into two components (1976: 5-10), and others divide it into three.[2] It is not necessary for the present purpose to discuss the arguments for and against these hypotheses in detail. Those scholars who assert the integrity of the letter recognize a division at Phil. 3.1-2, and those who postulate a redactional canonical letter identify a component including the section Phil. 3.1b/2–4.1/3. While Beare observes that, if this section does represent a separate letter, its original destination is uncertain (1959: 24), the majority of scholars who favour a redactional hypothesis do not date this component significantly later than the other sections of the canonical letter. We can therefore assume a date for the hypothetical fragment within a year of any of the other components of the canonical letter, and regard Philippi as its probable destination.[3]

The date of Philippians depends largely on its place of origin. While Martin points out that Paul was not necessarily literally a prisoner at the time of writing (1976: 21), the majority of scholars date the letter to Paul's known incarcerations, either in Rome (cf. Acts 28.16, 30) or in Caesarea (cf. Acts 23.33–27.1), or to a hypothetical imprisonment in Ephesus. Paul's imprisonment in Rome, favoured by Lightfoot,

---

1.   Lightfoot 1868: 67; Vincent 1897: xxxii; Plummer 1919: xii; Bonnard 1950: 9; Furnish 1963: 88; Kümmel 1975: 333; Houlden 1970: 40; Jewett 1970: 51-54; Hawthorne 1983: xxxii; Alexander 1989.

2.   Beare 1959: 4; Bornkamm 1962; Marxsen 1968: 62; Collange 1979; Vielhauer 1975a: 162.

3.   With the exception of 2 Cor. 6.14–7.1, the destination of the components of the composite canonical letters is not seriously disputed.

Vincent, Plummer, Beare, and Houlden,[1] would have commenced, at the earliest, in 58 or 59 CE, after his arrest in Jerusalem, which concludes the period under consideration. Paul's Caesarean captivity, to which Robinson (1976: 60-61) and Hawthorne (1983: xxxix) date Philippians, likewise dates from after Paul's arrest in Jerusalem, and would, according to the calculations in the Introduction, have been during the years c. 56-59 CE.

Paul's hypothetical imprisonment at Ephesus at some time during the period c. 53-55 CE (cf. 1 Cor. 15.32; 2 Cor. 1.8-10) is advanced as the date and occasion of Philippians by Duncan, Bonnard, Knox, Bornkamm, Marxsen, Fuller, Collange, Vielhauer, and Watson.[2] Gnilka suggests that the component letter including Phil. 3.1b–4.1 was written from Corinth (1976: 24, 25), in which case it would be contemporary with Romans. There is substantially less evidence to support such a hypothesis, however, and questions arise as to the compatibility between the circumstances reflected in Philippians and Romans. As this particular question does not concern the issue of the relevance of the former letter to this study, we need consider it no further.

Two major objections to the Ephesian hypothesis are raised by Hawthorne, which merit brief consideration. Hawthorne regards it as a 'fatal flaw' in the hypothesis that Paul's Ephesian imprisonment is reconstructed entirely by conjecture (1983: xxxix). That such a conjecture is sound, and a strong case can be presented in its favour, is evidenced by the strength of scholarly opinion which supports the hypothesis (cf. Watson 1986: 73). Hawthorne objects further that the absence of any mention of the collection project excludes the possibility that Philippians was written from Ephesus during that period (1983: xxxix). This is a more serious problem. While Knox and Collange's dating of Paul's imprisonment in Ephesus to before the collection[3] seems implausible, Martin has pointed out that Timothy's projected visit to Philippi (Phil. 2.19) may have been in connection with the collection (1976: 87). While Paul's despatch of emissaries to Corinth evidently did not obviate the need for letters (cf. 2 Cor. 8; 2 Cor. 9), the particular problems in Corinth, not reflected in Philippi (cf. Phil. 4.15), may have necessitated written communication. Furthermore, Timothy may have conveyed to Philippi a letter from Paul concerning the collection. I would tentatively raise a further possibility, that, if Sampley has correctly understood the nature of Paul's relationship with the Philippian church (1980: 51-72), which partly financed his missionary activities (Phil. 4.15-18; cf. 2 Cor. 11.9), then this may have affected their involvement in the collection project (but cf. 2 Cor. 8.1-5; 9.1-3). The absence of reference to the collection in Philippians is therefore no obstacle to dating the letter to the years 54-55 CE.

While the question of the date and place of writing of Philippians is far from

1. Lightfoot 1868: 1-28; Vincent 1897: xxii; Plummer 1919: xiii; Beare 1959: 23; Houlden 1970: 42.
2. Duncan 1929; Bonnard 1950: 10; Knox 1954: 87; Bornkamm 1962: 199; Marxsen 1968: 65; Fuller 1966: 34; Collange 1979: 15-17; Vielhauer 1975a: 168-69; Watson 1986: 73. Knox and Collange date this imprisonment to an earlier period in Paul's life than the other scholars cited.
3. Knox 1954: 87; Collange 1979: 15.

resolved, it has been shown that the plausibility of Paul's hypothetical imprisonment in Ephesus, and the dating of the letter to that incarceration, is sufficiently strong to merit considering the information relevant to this book contained therein. This concerns principally the identity of those against whom Paul is writing in Philippians 3.

Paul makes no mention of Jerusalem or the Jerusalem church in Philippians, either as the explicit objects of his wrath, or in support of his position against that which he is opposing (cf. Holmberg 1978: 48). While a number of scholars have identified those against whom Paul is writing in Phil. 3.2-16 as non-Christian Jews,[1] a clear majority regard them as Christians. The majority of scholars identify Paul's opponents as Judaistic Christians, while a number allude also to antinomian tendencies which Paul opposes in Philippi.[2] Phil. 3.19 is explicable within the context of an attack on Judaizing Christianity (cf. Dunn 1988: 903-905), however, as will become apparent in the discussion below, and the antinomian interpretation is not necessary and certainly cannot point towards the Jerusalem church as the origin of those whom Paul opposes. That Paul is opposing Judaizing Christians is argued by Duncan, Georgi, Collange, Gnilka, and Watson.[3] Schmithals, Koester, and Marxsen point to gnosticising tendencies in Paul's Jewish Christian opponents,[4] but, as argued in Chapter 8 above in connection with Paul's opponents in Corinth, these features are better understood within the broader diversity of thought in Hellenistic Judaism, a direction in which Koester himself points.

Identifying Paul's opponents is complicated by the fact that they are a potential rather than an active threat to the Philippian church (Phil. 1.2).[5] Paul may be referring to a specific group of Judaistic Christian missionaries about whom he had heard from prison, or he may be referring to the general danger of the tendency within early Christianity most likely to mislead the Philippians, or to undermine his work generally. In either case, Paul's information may not have been complete or accurate.

It is quite clear that those whom Paul is opposing are Judaists who might seek to persuade the Philippian Christians to undergo circumcision (Phil. 3.2-5). Paul describes them as τοὺς ἐχθροὺς τοῦ σταυροῦ τοῦ Χριστοῦ (Phil. 3.18). This does not necessarily mean that they oppose Christian teaching (cf. Houlden 1970: 103-105), but rather that they oppose Paul's particular theology of the cross of Christ and its implications for the Mosaic law (cf. Gal. 2.15-21; 5.2-7).[6] This position, as I have argued in Chapters 4 and 5 above, was represented in the Jerusalem church not by the leadership, but by a faction which had sought to impose Mosaic obligations on the Gentile Christians in Antioch, and so precipitated the Jerusalem conference, at which they were overruled. I argued in Chapter 6 that this group subsequently exploited the crisis in the Antiochene church following Paul's confrontation with

1. Lightfoot 1868: 71; Klijn 1964; Houlden 1970: 103-105; Hawthorne 1983: xlvii.
2. Vincent 1897: xxxiii; Plummer 1919: xv; Beare 1959: 132; Martin 1976: 33.
3. Duncan 1929: 275-77; Georgi 1986: 341; Collange 1979: 15-16; Gnilka 1976: 212-14; Watson 1986: 74-76.
4. Schmithals 1957: 313-14; Koester 1962: 321-24; Marxsen 1968: 63.
5. Cf. Plummer 1919: xv; Watson 1986: 77.
6. Cf. Koester 1962: 325; Murphy-O'Connor 1990.

Peter, and exerted influence in the Galatian, and perhaps other, churches, which led to Paul's intervention in Galatia. Georgi (1986: 341) and Watson (1986: 80) have pointed to the similarities between the positions opposed in Galatia and Philippi, and the latter has identified Paul's opponents in Philippi as the people from James.

Paul's opponents in Philippians 3 are clearly Judaistic Christians, and therefore cannot be identified with the group against whose intrusion in Corinth Paul was struggling at the same time, if the Ephesian hypothesis is accepted.[1] Rather, I would suggest, Paul, in prison and uncertain that he will be freed, writes to a church with which he had a particularly close relationship (cf. Phil. 4.1, 15) and expresses his fears about those whom he sees as the gravest threat to his teaching. The vigour and stridency of Paul's expression is to be attributed to the candidness with which he writes to the Philippian community, and perhaps the frustration of being incarcerated (but cf. Phil. 1.12), and not to the likelihood that the Philippians would succumb to the influence of those against whom Paul writes. The threat is hypothetical (cf. Phil. 3.2), but provides Paul with an opportunity to express his frustration and anger to a sympathetic readership. Whereas Paul's opponents in Corinth threaten his authority in the community, but not his doctrine, those whom he had opposed in Galatia, and who might seek to exploit Paul's imprisonment and even his possible death, threatened the gospel to whose apostleship Paul had dedicated his life. The Judaistic faction in the Jerusalem church, and others who adhered to similar views, are therefore, I would suggest, the most likely targets of Paul's attack in Philippians 3. They are not to be identified with the leadership of the Jerusalem church, or the community as a whole, and do not alter our reconstruction of Paul's relationship with the Jerusalem church during the period subsequent to his departure from Antioch.

In further substantiation of this position I would argue that, if elements representing the Jerusalem church and carrying the authority of its leadership were threatening to undermine Paul's authority in churches he had founded, then Paul would have regarded the collection as a futile project and have abandoned it. Certainly he would not have risked his life in Jerusalem if he saw his work in Greece threatened by the Jerusalem church, and his presence in those churches all the more essential. Paul could not hope to buy off the hostility of the Jerusalem church with the collection, and, moreover, if there was such hostility towards Paul among the leadership of the Jerusalem church, the Antiochene church would not have jeopardized its κοινωνία with Jerusalem by allowing Paul to rejoin the collection project. Therefore, while there is good reason to believe that Philippians was written from Ephesus in c. 54 CE, and while it is clear that Paul is attacking Judaistic Christians in the letter, there is no evidence that these represented the Jerusalem church, even if they came from there. Our reading of Philippians therefore does not alter our reconstruction of Paul's relationship with the Jerusalem church.

---

1.   Cf. Collange 1979: 14-15, who argues that these are the opponents of 2 Cor. 10–13, whom Paul had not yet encountered in person.

CONCLUSION

This study has revealed a dynamic and developing dimension to Paul's Christian career, in which fluctuating relationships with other Christians are integral to the evolution of his Christian identity and apostolic vocation. Previous scholarship has been hampered by too static and too idealized an understanding of Paul. This can be attributed substantially to a scholarly tradition whose theological agenda has been determined by Paul's impact upon the Protestant reformation, and whose historiographical methodology has derived from dialectic philosophy. Scholarship has therefore not been sufficiently critical in its reading of Paul's letters, particularly in reconstructing the history behind the events alluded to in the autobiographical section Gal. 1.11–2.14. Not only have Paul's anachronistic assertions been accepted without adequate scrutiny, but statements made late in his career have been read back anachronistically and uncritically into the earlier stages, so that the evolution of Paul's apostolic self-conception has not been fully appreciated, and nor have the historical circumstances that gave rise to its development.

A major weakness with previous treatments of Paul, and in particular his relationship with the church of Jerusalem has been its lack of appreciation of the importance of the church of Antioch. I have therefore paid particular attention to the role of the Antiochene church through the successive stages of Paul's ministry, and have argued that, against this background, the development of his apostolic self-conception can be more fully understood. The Antioch church was a community that Paul joined some years after his conversion and was his base for the most settled period in his Christian life. He derived his dyadic identity from this community and began his apostolic work as an emissary of the Antiochene church. It is significant that he was associated with a community which clearly played an important part in evolving the theological trajectory with which Paul later came almost exclusively to be associated.

Paul's apostolic formation took place in Antioch and in the apostolate of the Antiochene church. Later separation from the church of Antioch meant that the ideological superstructure of Paul's apostleship required redefinition, but nevertheless the Antiochene pattern of apostolic work continued to shape Paul's own. The significance of the Antiochene Christian community in Paul's life is therefore crucial to understanding not only the period of his association with that church, but also the subsequent period, when he operated independently. The apostolic self-conception that Paul developed compensated for his separation from the Antiochene church. Apostleship and apostolic authority derived directly from, and accountable only to, God was Paul's psychological and theological response to his loss of dyadic identity and apostolic commission, which had derived previously from the Antiochene church.

The period in Paul's life between his conversion and his joining the church of Antioch was an unsettled time during which he was unable to become fully integrated into any Christian community and was twice a fugitive. His conversion had not involved, nor did it bring him immediately into the fellowship of, a Christian congregation. His subsequent journeying, and sojourning, in Arabia, Damascus, Jerusalem and Tarsus, appear to have been of short duration, and to have provided no stability to Paul's life. The unsettled nature of Paul's existence during the years following his conversion indicates strongly that the subsequent period, his association with the church of Antioch, was of crucial and formative importance for him and his work.

Paul's prolonged association with the church of Antioch forms a distinct contrast to the unsettled period which preceded it. The relative stability which this represents, even if a substantial part of Paul's time and energy were devoted to the outreach of the Antiochene church in Syria and Asia Minor, is significant to a degree that has hitherto not been recognized in New Testament scholarship. Paul's integration into the life of the church in Antioch meant that his dyadic identity, the basis of his social orientation and self-perception, was derived from that community. Paul's work of Christian mission was an aspect and extension of his membership of the Antioch church, and his vocation to apostleship originated in his commission from this community. The reconstruction I have proposed brings a significantly different perspective to bear upon the events of this period, from that which has enjoyed a degree of consensus in modern New Testament scholarship.

Not only was the apostolic work in which Paul was involved a commission delegated by the Antiochene church, but it was as a delegate of that community that Paul participated in the Jerusalem conference. The conference was occasioned by controversy in the Christian community at Antioch concerning matters of Jewish observance in a church composed largely of Gentiles. The Christian community in Antioch sought resolution to the crisis through conferring with the leaders of the church of Jerusalem, in the context of the κοινωνία between the two churches. Paul was involved in the deliberations not in his personal capacity but as a delegate of the Antiochene church. His personal status and theological opinions were not at issue.

The Jerusalem conference affirmed the gospel of uncircumcision preached and lived by the Antiochene church, while the Jerusalem church maintained its gospel of circumcision. This accommodation strengthened the κοινωνία between the churches of Jerusalem and Antioch, and the predominance of the former in that relationship. Paul's participation in this κοινωνία ended, however, as an indirect consequence of the conference, when the tension between the independence of the Antiochene church and the predominance of the Jerusalem church brought him into conflict with Peter and Barnabas in Antioch. While the κοινωνία between the churches of Jerusalem and Antioch endured the strain, and was arguably strengthened thereby and through the Apostolic Decree, Paul was as a consequence excluded from the fellowship of the Antiochene church and its κοινωνία with the Jerusalem church.

Membership of the Antioch church had brought stability to Paul through social integration and orientation, and dyadic embeddedness and identity, as well as providing his commission as an apostle. The comprehensive significance of this community during their period of association indicates the degree of significance of their separation. Previous scholars, not having appreciated fully the importance of Paul's association with the church of Antioch, have accordingly not appreciated the significance of his separation from that church. Since all Paul's extant writings date from the period subsequent to his departure from Antioch, it is particularly important that the cataclysmic transformation in his circumstances be recognized.

Paul's independence was occasioned by his position having become untenable in the Antiochene church. Far from being the ideal circumstances in which to operate as a Christian apostle, Paul's independence, or rather, isolation, was an unforeseen and unsought result of his unsuccessful confrontation with Peter and Barnabas. His response to this was to develop a theocentric self-identity, which would compensate for his loss of dyadic identity and apostolic role. Paul's assertion of a personalized conception of apostleship and apostolic authority, derived directly from, and accountable only to, God, and of a self-identity which was integrally bound up with the gospel he preached and his vocation to preach it, is to be understood not as the direct and immediate consequence of his conversion experience, but as his response to isolation and social dislocation in the aftermath of the Antioch incident.

Paul's separation from the church at Antioch effectively separated him from the church at Jerusalem also. His membership of the Antiochene church had included him in the κοινωνία between the two churches, but he, and therefore the churches he founded during his period of independent apostleship, had no personal or direct relationship with the Jerusalem church. Paul sought, however, to create a relationship between his churches and that at Jerusalem, analogous to that between the churches of Jerusalem and Antioch. In order to accomplish this Paul sought reconciliation with the church of Antioch and, in order to claim for himself and his churches a part in the κοινωνία between that community and the church of Jerusalem, joined in the collection of the Antiochene church for that of Jerusalem. The crisis in the Corinthian church, however, delayed the completion of Paul's part in this project and required that the collection from his churches be delivered separately. This fundamentally altered the basis on which the offering was made.

Instead of being a transaction within a κοινωνία that already existed between the churches of Jerusalem and Antioch, and in which Paul tacitly claimed a part, the collection became the basis of a claim to κοινωνία between Paul and his churches on the one hand, and the church of Jerusalem on the other. The estrangement between Paul and the leaders of the Jerusalem church made such an overt, direct, and unilateral, claim to κοινωνία hazardous. This accounts in part for Paul's pessimism as to the acceptability of the collection to the Jerusalem church, reflected in Romans. While the response of the Jerusalem church to Paul's overtures is not recorded, there can be no doubt that the delivery of the collection was the occasion of Paul's arrest in Jerusalem, which effectively terminated his missionary career.

Paul's relationship with the Jerusalem church was not static. It passed through successive stages, and the direction of its development was not uniform. Paul's Christian career began without contact with the Jerusalem church, and his subsequent sojourn in Jerusalem established no lasting relationship with that community. It was participation in the κοινωνία between the Antioch church and that of Jerusalem that realized Paul's only stable relationship with the Jerusalem church, and this ended in his confrontation with Peter at Antioch after the Jerusalem conference. Paul's independent missionary career was conducted without contact with the Jerusalem church and its leadership and ended when he sought to forge a relationship between his churches and the church at Jerusalem.

Appendix

THE NATURE OF PRIMITIVE CHRISTIAN APOSTLESHIP

In the course of this study I have alluded to a number of issues which, though
secondary to my discussion, have impinged upon it. My approach to these issues has
not always been in conformity with such scholarly consensus as there may be, and
this has particularly been the case with the question of apostleship. I therefore conclude with this appendix which provides some account of this, and indicates where I
believe further research is needed.

Too often and too uncritically earlier scholarship has identified Paul as the
uniquely endowed and commissioned apostle to the Gentiles from the moment of his
conversion. The theological agenda of critical scholarship, with its dichotomy
between Paul and the Judaizing Christianity commonly associated with Peter, and
emphasis on the Pauline doctrine of justification by faith, have exacerbated rather
than rectified this view, and I have argued that it needs radical revision. We need to
see Paul's statements about his apostleship in Galatians and elsewhere as reflecting
his self-conception at the time that letter was written, and not as recording accurately
the historical reality of the previous decades, or of his Christian career as a whole.

Paul's egocentric and individualistic portrayal of his own apostleship stems not
from his Damascus road experience, but from the isolation which resulted from the
Antioch incident. The self-sufficient and independent concept of apostleship provides
compensation at the theological level for Paul's loss of dyadic identity and apostolic
commission, previously derived from the church at Antioch. Paul defined himself in
terms of those who exercised effective authority in the Church, so far as he was able
to conform to their credentials, and was accordingly able to recognize others as
apostles only in so far as they conformed to his own criteria.

Paul's apostolic conception replaced a more fluid and less personal notion of
apostleship, which was defined in terms of function rather than status and authority,
and was an activity of the Christian communities, carried out by delegated members.
The primitive notion of apostolic work, in which the status of the individual was not
important, was replaced by Paul with a concept of apostolic office in which the status
of the individual was all important. We are concerned not with two types or levels of
apostleship, but with two fundamentally different notions of apostleship.

Since the time of Lightfoot, it has been recognized that the equation of the apostles
and the twelve in the Synoptic Gospels, Acts and Revelation, is not historically
tenable (cf. 1890: 97). Subsequent scholarship has generally recognized the apostles

228 Paul, Antioch and Jerusalem

as a wider group than the twelve, but, largely on account of presupposing Paul's implicit definition of apostleship in Galatians and elsewhere as universally applicable, has understood neither the circumstances which gave rise to Paul's articulation of his distinctive conception of apostleship, nor the essentially straightforward nature of primitive Christian apostleship, clear in function but fluid in membership.[1]

Munck has recognized the cause of the confusion in scholarship and notes that 'the apostolic idea has been mainly taken from Paul, and. . . been transferred to the earlier apostles before Paul, and. . . Paul has then been allowed to embrace this and take it over from the others' (1949: 100-101).[2] If the concept of apostleship derived from Paul is recognized as applying only to him, and only during a limited period of his life, then the task of reconstructing the nature of primitive Christian apostleship, which Paul exercised as an emissary of the Antiochene church but later fundamentally remodelled on himself, becomes feasible. I would argue, therefore, that scholarship needs to identify the concept of apostleship articulated by Paul, locate it in its specific historical context, and to consider other primitive notions of Christian apostleship reflected in the New Testament, including Paul's earlier apostolic work, without presupposing Paul's specific conception in other forms of apostleship. This would enable a broader understanding of early Christian apostleship, which takes into account the specific circumstances in which apostleship was exercised.

1.   Cf. Linton 1932: 81-82; Rengstorf 1933; Manson 1948; Mosbech 1948; Ehrhardt 1958: 1-2; Hanson 1961; Klein 1961; Schmithals 1971b; Roloff 1965; Barrett 1968: 343; Barrett, 1970; Barrett 1983; Schnackenburg 1970: 300-301; Kirk 1975: 260.
2.   Cf. Mosbech 1948: 198; Schmithals 1971b: 81, 264.

BIBLIOGRAPHY

Abbott-Smith, G.
    1922   *A Manual Greek Lexicon of the New Testament* (Edinburgh: T. & T. Clark).
Abrams, P.
    1982   *Historical Sociology* (Shepton Mallet: Open Books).
Achtemeier, P.J.
    1987   *The Quest for Unity in the New Testament Church* (Philadelphia: Fortress Press).
Agnew, F.H.
    1976   'On the Origin of the Term *Apostolos*', *CBQ* 38: 49-53.
    1986   'The Origin of the NT Apostle-Concept: A Review of Research', *JBL* 105: 75-96.
Agouridou, S.
    1971   Εἰσαγωγὴ εἰς τὴν Καινὴν Διαθήκην (Athens: Gregory).
Aland, K., and B. Aland
    1988   *Griechisch-deutsches Wörterbuch zu den Schriften des Neuen Testaments und der frühchristlichen Literatur* (Berlin: de Gruyter).
Alexander, L.C.A.
    1989   'Hellenistic Letter-Forms and the Structure of Philippians', *JSNT* 37: 87-101.
Allen, V.
    1964   'Uncertainty of Outcome and Post-Decision Dissonance Reduction', in Festinger 1964: 34-44.
Allo, E.-B.
    1925   *Saint Paul première épître aux Corinthiens* (Paris: Librairie Lecoffre).
    1956   *Saint Paul seconde épître aux Corinthiens* (Paris: Librairie Lecoffre).
Althaus, P.
    1966   *Der Brief an die Römer* (Göttingen: Vandenhoeck & Ruprecht).
Ambrozic, A.M.
    1972   'Indissolubility of Marriage in the New Testament: Law or Ideal', *Studia Canonica* 17: 269-88.
Applebaum, S.
    1974a   'The Legal Status of the Jewish Communities in the Diaspora', in *The Jewish People in the First Century*, I (ed. S. Safrai and M. Stern; Assen: Van Gorcum) 420-63.
    1974b   'The Organization of the Jewish Communities in the Diaspora', in *The Jewish People in the First Century*, I (ed. S. Safrai and M. Stern; Assen: Van Gorcum) 464-503.

Arendt, H.
  1958   'What Was Authority?', in *Authority* (ed. C.J. Friedrich; Cambridge, MA: Harvard University Press) 81-112.
Aus, R.D.
  1979   'Paul's Travel Plans to Spain and the "Full Number of the Gentiles" of Rom. xi: 25', *NovT* 21: 223-62.
Baird, W.
  1985   'Visions, Revelation, and Ministry: Reflections on 2 Cor. 12.1-5 and Gal. 1.11-17', *JBL* 104: 651-62.
Banks, R.
  1980   *Paul's Idea of Community* (Exeter: Paternoster Press).
Barclay, J.M.G.
  1988   *Obeying the Truth* (Edinburgh: T. & T. Clark).
Barnett, P.W.
  1984   'Opposition in Corinth', *JSNT* 22: 3-17.
Barrett, C.K.
  1953   'Paul and the "Pillar" Apostles', in *Studia Paulina* (ed. J.N. Sevenster and W.C. van Unnik; Haarlem: Bohn) 1-19.
  1957   *A Commentary on the Epistle to the Romans* (London: A. & C. Black).
  1966   *The Holy Spirit and the Gospel Tradition* (London: SPCK).
  1968   *A Commentary on the First Epistle to the Corinthians* (London: A. & C. Black).
  1969   'Titus', in *Neotestamentica et Semitica* (ed. E.E. Ellis and M. Wilcox; Edinburgh: T. & T. Clark) 1-14.
  1970   *The Signs of an Apostle* (London: Epworth Press).
  1971   'Paul's Opponents in II Corinthians', *NTS* 17: 233-54.
  1973   *A Commentary on the Second Epistle to the Corinthians* (London: A. & C. Black).
  1978   'Shaliah and Apostle', in *Donum Gentilicium* (ed. E Bammel et al.; Oxford: Clarendon Press) 88-102.
  1982   *Essays on Paul* (London: SPCK).
  1983   *Church, Ministry, and Sacraments in the New Testament* (Exeter: Paternoster Press).
  1985   *Freedom and Obligation* (London: SPCK).
Barton, S.C.
  1982   'Paul and the Cross: A Sociological Approach', *Theology* 85: 13-19.
  1984   'Paul and the Resurrection: A Sociological Approach', *Religion* 14: 67-75.
  1986   'Paul's Sense of Place: An Anthropological Approach to Community Formation in Corinth', *NTS* 32: 225-46.
Bates, W.H.
  1965   'The Integrity of II Corinthians', *NTS* 12: 56-69.
Batey, R.
  1965   'Paul's Interaction with the Corinthians', *JBL* 84: 139-46.
Bauckham, R.J.
  1979   'Barnabas in Galatians', *JSNT* 2: 61-70.

Bauer, W.F.
1971   *Orthodoxy and Heresy in Earliest Christianity* (trans. R.A. Kraft *et al.*; Philadelphia: Fortress Press).
Bauer, W.F., W.F. Arndt and F.W. Gingrich
1957   *A Greek-English Lexicon of the New Testament* (Cambridge: Cambridge University Press).
Baumgarten, J.
1975   *Paulus und die Apokalyptik* (Neukirchen–Vluyn: Neukirchener Verlag).
Baur, F.C.
1875, 1876   *Paul: The Apostle of Christ* (2 vols.; ed. E. Zeller; trans. A. Menzies; London: Williams & Norgate).
1878   *The Church History of the First Three Centuries* (trans. A. Menzies; London: Williams & Norgate).
Beare, F.W.
1959   *The Epistle to the Philippians* (London: A. & C. Black).
Becker, J.
1976   *Der Brief an die Galater* (NTD, 8; Göttingen: Vandenhoeck & Ruprecht).
Beckford, J.A.
1978   'Accounting for Conversion', *BJSoc* 29: 249-62.
1982   'The Restoration of "Power" to the Sociology of Religion', *SocAn* 44: 11-31.
Behm, J.
1933   'ἀνατίθημι', in *TDNT*, I: 353-54.
Beker, J.C.
1980   *Paul the Apostle* (Edinburgh: T. & T. Clark).
Berger, K.
1977   'Almosen für Israel', *NTS* 3: 180-204.
Berger, P.L.
1967   *The Social Reality of Religion* (London: Faber & Faber).
Berger, P.L., and T. Luckmann
1966   *The Social Construction of Reality* (London: Penguin).
Bertram, G.
1973   'φρήν, ἄφρων', in *TDNT*, IX: 220-35.
Best, E.
1972   *A Commentary on the First and Second Epistles to the Thessalonians* (London: A. & C. Black).
1985   *Paul and his Converts* (Edinburgh: T. & T. Clark).
1986   'Paul's Apostolic Authority?', *JSNT* 27: 3-25.
Best, T.F.
1983   'The Sociological Study of the New Testament: Promise and Peril of a New Discipline', *SJT* 36: 181-94.
Betz, H.D.
1972   *Der Apostel Paulus und die sokratische Tradition* (Tübingen: Mohr).
1975   'The Literary Composition and Function of Paul's Letter to the Galatians', *NTS* 21: 353-79.
1979   *Galatians* (Philadelphia: Fortress Press).
1985   *2 Corinthians 8 and 9* (Philadelphia: Fortress Press).

Beyer, H.W.
1935a   'διακονός', in *TDNT*, II: 88-93.
1935b   'εὐλογία', in *TDNT*, II: 754-63.
1939   'κανών', in *TDNT*, III: 596-602.
Bierstedt, R.
1954   'The Problem of Authority', in *Freedom and Control in Modern Society*
(ed. M. Berger *et al.*; New York: Octagon) 67-81.
Black, D.A.
1984   *Paul, Apostle of Weakness* (New York: Peter Lang).
Blank, J.
1968   *Paulus und Jesus* (Munich: Kösel).
Blass, F.W., A. Debrunner and R.W. Funk
1961   *A Greek Grammar of the New Testament and Other Early Christian
Literature* (Cambridge: Cambridge University Press).
Blau, P.M.
1968   'Weber's Theory of Bureaucracy', in *Max Weber* (ed. D.H. Wrong;
Englewood Cliffs, NJ: Prentice-Hall) 141-45.
Bocheński, J.M.
1974   *Was ist Autorität?* (Freiburg: Herder).
Bonnard, P.
1950   *L'épître de Saint Paul aux Philippiens* (Neuchâtel: Delachaux & Niestlé).
Borgen, P.J.
1983a   *Paul Preaches Circumcision and Pleases Men and Other Essays on
Christian Origins* (trans. L. Cope; Trondheim: Tapir) 43-58.
1983b   'God's Agent in the Fourth Gospel', in *Logos was the True Light and
Other Essays on the Gospel of John* (Trondheim: Tapir).
1988   'Catalogues of Vices, the Apostolic Decree, and the Jerusalem Meeting', in
The Social World of Formative Christianity and Judaism (ed. J Neusner *et
al.*; Philadelphia: Fortress Press) 126-41.
Bornkamm, G.
1961   'The History of the Origin of the So-called Second Letter to the
Corinthians', *NTS* 8: 258-64.
1962   'Der Philipperbrief als paulinische Briefsammlung', in *Neotestamentica et
Patristica* (ed. W.C. van Unnik *et al.*; Leiden: Brill) 195-205.
1966   'The Missionary Stance of Paul in I Corinthians 9 and in Acts', in *Studies
in Luke–Acts* (ed. L.E. Keck and J.L. Martyn; Nashville: Abingdon Press)
194-207.
1971   *Paul* (trans. D.M.G. Stalker; London: Hodder and Stoughton).
Bott, E.
1957   *Family and Social Network* (London: Tavistock).
Böttger, P.C.
1991   'Paulus und Petrus in Antiochien: Zum Verständnis von Galater 2.11-21',
NTS 37: 77-100.
Bowker, J.W.
1971   ' "Merkabah" Visions and the Visions of Paul', *JSS* 16: 157-73.
Brandon, S.G.F.
1957   *The Fall of Jerusalem and the Christian Church* (London: SPCK).

Brinsmead, B.H.
　1982　*Galatians—Dialogical Response to Opponents* (Chico, CA: Scholars Press).
Brockhaus, U.
　1972　*Charisma und Amt* (Wuppertal: Brockhaus).
Brown, R.E., *et al.*
　1973　*Peter in the New Testament* (London: Geoffrey Chapman).
Brown, R.E., and J.P. Meier
　1983　*Antioch and Rome* (New York: Paulist Press).
Brownlee, W.H.
　1982　'The Wicked Priest, the Man of Lies, and the Righteous Teacher—The Problem of Identity', *JQR* 73: 1-37.
Bruce, F.F.
　1968　'Paul and Jerusalem', *TynBul* 19: 3-25.
　1982a　*The Epistle of Paul to the Galatians* (Exeter: Paternoster Press).
　1982b　*New Testament History* (London: Pickering & Inglis).
　1982c　*1 and 2 Thessalonians* (Waco, TX: Word Books).
　1985　*The Pauline Circle* (Grand Rapids: Eerdmans).
　1986　'The Apostolic Decree of Acts 15', in *Studien zum Text und zur Ethik des Neuen Testaments* (ed. W. Schrage; Berlin: de Gruyter) 115-24.
Brunner, E.
　1959　*The Letter to the Romans* (trans. H.A. Kennedy; London: Lutterworth).
Büchsel, F.
　1935　'δωρεάν', in *TDNT*, II: 167.
Buck, C.H.
　1950　'The Collection for the Saints', *HTR* 43: 1-29.
Buckland, W.W.
　1939　*A Manual of Roman Private Law* (Cambridge: Cambridge University Press).
Buckland, W.W., and A.D. McNair
　1952　*Roman Law and Common Law* (Cambridge: Cambridge University Press).
Bultmann, R.K.
　1933　'γινώσκω, γνῶσις', in *TDNT*, I: 689-714.
　1947　'Exegetische Probleme des zweiten Korintherbriefes', in *Exegetica* (ed. E. Dinckler; Tübingen: Mohr) 298-322.
　1953　'New Testament and Mythology', in *Kerygma and Myth* (trans. R.H. Fuller; London: SPCK) 1-44.
　1956　*Primitive Christianity in its Contemporary Setting* (trans. R.H. Fuller; London: Thames & Hudson).
　1961　'Is Exegesis without Presuppositions Possible?', in *Existence and Faith* (ed. and trans. S.M. Ogden; London: Hodder & Stoughton) 289-96.
　1985　*The Second Letter to the Corinthians* (ed. E. Dinkler; trans. R.A. Harrisville; Minneapolis, MN: Augsburg).
Bultmann, R.K., and D. Lührmann
　1973　'φαίνω', in *TDNT*, IX: 1-2.
Burchard, C.
　1970　*Der dreizehnte Zeuge* (Göttingen: Vandenhoeck & Ruprecht).

Burke, U.P.
    1980   *Sociology and History* (London: George Allen & Unwin).
Burridge, K.O.L.
    1980   *New Heaven, New Earth* (Oxford: Basil Blackwell).
Burton, E.D.W.
    1921   *The Epistle to the Galatians* (Edinburgh: T. & T. Clark).
Caird, G.B.
    1955   *The Apostolic Age* (London: Gerald Duckworth).
    1963   *The Gospel of St Luke* (Harmondsworth: Penguin).
Callan, T.
    1986   'Competition and Boasting: Toward a Psychological Portrait of Paul', *ST*
                40: 137-56.
Campenhausen, H.F. von
    1947   'Der urchristliche Apostelbegriff', *ST* 1: 96-130.
    1969   *Ecclesiastical Authority and Spiritual Power in the Church of the First
                Three Centuries* (trans. J.A. Baker; London: A. & C. Black).
Canon, L.K.
    1964   'Self-Confidence and Selective Exposure to Information', in Festinger
                1964: 83-96.
Catchpole, D.R.
    1977   'Paul, James and the Apostolic Decree', *NTS* 23: 428-44.
Chadwick, H.
    1982   *History and Thought of the Early Church* (London: Variorum).
Chapple, A.L.
    1984   *Local Leadership in the Pauline Churches: Theological and Social Factors
                in its Development: A Study Based on I Thessalonians, I Corinthians and
                Philippians* (unpublished PhD thesis, University of Durham).
Charlesworth, J.H. (ed.)
    1983   *The Old Testament Pseudepigrapha*, I (London: Darton, Longman &
                Todd).
Chidester, D.S.
    1984   'The Challenge to Christian Ritual Studies', *ATR* 66: 23-34.
    1986   'Religious and Political Power' (unpublished paper).
Childs, B.S.
    1984   *The New Testament as Canon: An Introduction* (London: SCM Press).
Chow, J.K.M.
    1989   *Patronage and Power: Studies on Social Networks in Corinth* (unpublished
                PhD thesis, University of Durham).
Cohen, S.J.D.
    1989   'Crossing the Boundary and Becoming a Jew', *HTR* 82: 13-34.
Cohn-Sherbok, D.
    1983   'Some Reflections on James Dunn's: "The Incident at Antioch (Gal. 2.
                11-18)" ', *JSNT* 18: 68-74.
Collange, J.-F.
    1979   *The Epistle of Saint Paul to the Philippians* (trans. A.W. Heathcote;
                London: Epworth Press).

Collingwood, R.G.
 1924   *Speculum Mentis* (Oxford: Clarendon Press).
 1930   *The Philosophy of History* (History Association Leaflet).
 1946   *The Idea of History* (Oxford: Oxford University Press).
Collins, A.Y.
 1979   'The Early Christian Apocalypses', *Semeia* 14: 61-122.
Collins, J.J.
 1979   'The Jewish Apocalypses', *Semeia* 14: 21-60.
 1983   *Between Athens and Jerusalem* (New York: Crossroad).
 1984   *The Apocalyptic Imagination* (New York: Crossroad).
 1985   'A Symbol of Otherness: Circumcision and Salvation in the First
           Century', in *'To See Ourselves As Others See Us'* (ed. J. Neusner and
           E.S. Frerichs; Chico, CA: Scholars Press) 163-86.
Collins, R.F.
 1984   *Studies on the First Letter to the Thessalonians* (Leuven: Leuven
           University Press).
Conn, W.W., *et al.*
 1978   *Conversion* (New York: Alba House).
Conzelmann, H.G.
 1969   *Der erste Brief an die Korinther* (Göttingen: Vandenhoeck & Ruprecht).
 1973   *History of Primitive Christianity.* (trans. J.E. Steely; Nashville: Abingdon
           Press).
 1987   *Acts of the Apostles* (ed. E.J. Epp and C.R. Matthews; trans. J. Limburg
           et al.; Philadelphia: Fortress Press).
Conzelmann, H.G., and W. Zimmerli
 1973   'χάρις', in *TDNT*, IX: 372-402.
Coser, L.A.
 1956   *The Functions of Social Conflict* (London: Routledge & Kegan Paul).
Countryman, L.W.
 1988   *Dirt, Greed and Sex* (London: SCM Press).
Cranfield, C.E.B.
 1975, 1979 *The Epistle to the Romans* (2 vols.; Edinburgh: T. & T. Clark).
Culianu, I.P.
 1983   *Psychanodia. I. A Survey of the Evidence concerning the Ascension of the
           Soul and its Relevance* (Leiden: Brill).
Cullmann, O.
 1953   *Peter* (trans. F.V. Filson; London: SCM Press).
Dahl, N.A.
 1967   'Paul and the Church at Corinth according to 1 Corinthians 1-4', in
           Christian History and Interpretation (ed. W.R. Farmer *et al.*; Cambridge:
           Cambridge University Press) 313-36.
Dahl, R.A.
 1968   'Power', in *International Encyclopedia of the Social Sciences*, XII (New
           York: Macmillan) 405-15.
Danby, H. (trans.)
 1933   *The Mishnah* (Oxford: Oxford University Press 1933).

Dautzenberg, G.
    1987   'Der zweite Korintherbrief als Briefsammlung: Zur Frage der literarischen
              Einheitlichkeit und des theologischen Gefüges von 2 Kor 1-8', in *ANRW*,
              25.4 (ed. W. Haase; Berlin: de Gruyter) 3045-66.
Davidson, J.R.
    1964   'Cognitive Familiarity and Dissonance Reduction', in Festinger 1964:
              45-60.
Davidson, J.R., and S.B. Kiesler
    1964   'Cognitive Behavior before and after Decisions', in Festinger 1964:
              10-20.
Dean-Otting, M.
    1984   *Heavenly Journeys* (Frankfurt: Lang).
Delling, G.
    1959a   'πλεονεξία', in *TDNT*, V: 266-74.
    1959b   'πλῆθος', in *TDNT*, VI: 274-79.
    1964   'σκόλοψ', in *TDNT*, VII: 409-13.
    1969a   'ἐπιταγή', in *TDNT*, VIII: 36-37.
    1969b   'ὑπερβολή', in *TDNT*, VII: 520-22.
Dewey, A.J.
    1985   'A Matter of Honor: A Socio-Historical Analysis of 2 Corinthians 10',
              HTR 78: 209-18.
Dibelius, M.F.
    1925   *An die Thessalonicher I, II; An die Philipper* (Tübingen: Mohr).
    1956   *Studies in the Acts of the Apostles* (trans. H. Greeven; London: SCM
              Press).
Dietzfelbinger, C.
    1985   *Die Berufung des Paulus als Ursprung seiner Theologie* (Neukirchen–
              Vluyn: Neukirchener Verlag).
Diffenderfer, M.R.
    1986   *Conditions of Membership in the People of God: A Study Based on Acts
              15 and Other Relevant Passages in Acts* (unpublished PhD thesis,
              University of Durham).
Dill, S.
    1904   *Roman Society from Nero to Marcus Aurelius* (London: Macmillan).
Dilthey, W.
    1976   *Selected Writings* (ed. H.P. Rickman; Cambridge: Cambridge University
              Press).
    1988   *Introduction to the Human Sciences* (trans. R.J. Betanzos; London:
              Harvester Wheatsheaf).
Dinckler, E.
    1953   *Signum Crucis* (Tübingen: Mohr).
Dobschütz, E. von
    1909   *The Apostolic Age* (trans. F.L. Pogson; London: Green).
Donaldson, T.L.
    1989   'Zealot and Convert: The Origin of Paul's Christ-Torah Antithesis', *CBQ*
              31: 655-82.

Douglas, M.
    1966   *Purity and Danger* (London: Routledge & Kegan Paul).
Duncan, G.S.
    1929   *St Paul's Ephesian Ministry* (London: Hodder & Stoughton).
    1934   *The Epistle of Paul to the Galatians* (London: Hodder & Stoughton).
Dunn, J.D.G.
    1970   *Baptism in the Holy Spirit* (London: SCM Press).
    1975   *Jesus and the Spirit* (London: SCM Press).
    1977   *Unity and Diversity in the New Testament* (London: SCM Press).
    1982   'The Relationship between Paul and Jerusalem according to Galatians 1 and 2', *NTS* 28: 461-78.
    1983   'The Incident at Antioch', *JSNT* 18: 3-57.
    1985   'Once More—Gal.1.18: ἱστορῆσαι Κηφᾶν in Reply to Otfried Hofius', *ZNW* 76: 138-39.
    1988   *Romans* (2 vols.; Waco, TX: Word Books).
    1990   *Jesus, Paul, and the Law* (Louisville: Westminster Press).
Dupont, J.
    1970   'The Conversion of Paul, and its Influence on his Understanding of Salvation by Faith', in *Apostolic History and the Gospel* (ed. W.W. Gasque and R.P. Martin; trans. R.P. Martin; Exeter: Paternoster Press) 176-94.
Durkheim, E.
    1938   *The Rules of Sociological Method* (ed. G.E.G. Catlin, S.A. Solovay and J.H. Müller; New York: Free Press).
    1976   *The Elementary Forms of Religious Life* (trans. J.W. Swain; London: Allen & Unwin).
Eckert, J.
    1971   *Die urchristlichen Verkündigung im Streit zwischen Paulus und seinen Gegnern nach dem Galaterbrief* (Regensburg: Pustet).
Ehrhardt, A.A.T.
    1953   *The Apostolic Succession* (London: Lutterworth).
    1958   *The Apostolic Ministry* (Edinburgh: Oliver & Boyd).
Ehrman, B.D.
    1990   'Cephas and Peter', *JBL* 109: 463-74.
Eliade, M.
    1958   *Rites and Symbols of Initiation* (New York: Harper & Row).
Elliott, J.H.
    1979   *A Home for the Homeless* (London: SCM Press).
Epstein, I.
    1959   *Judaism* (Harmondsworth: Penguin).
Epstein, I. (ed. and trans.)
    1938   *The Babylonian Talmud* (London: Soncino).
Esler, P.F.
    1987   *Community and Gospel in Luke–Acts* (Cambridge: Cambridge University Press).

Etzioni, A.
    1975   *A Comparative Analysis of Complex Organizations* (New York: Free
                Press).
Evans-Pritchard, E.E.
    1951   *Social Anthropology* (London: Routledge & Kegan Paul).
    1962   *Essays in Social Anthropology* (London: Faber & Faber).
Falk, Z.W.
    1964   *Hebrew Law in Biblical Times* (Jerusalem: Wahrmann).
Fargue, M. la
    1988   'Sociohistorical Research and the Contextualization of Biblical Theology',
                in *The Social World of Formative Christianity and Judaism* (ed. J. Neusner
                et al.; Philadelphia: Fortress Press) 3-16.
Feeley-Harnik, G.
    1982   'Is Historical Anthropology Possible? The Case of the Runaway Slave', in
                Humanizing America's Iconic Book (ed. G.M. Tucker and D.A. Knight;
                Chico, CA: Scholars Press) 95-126.
Fenton, J.C.
    1963   *The Gospel of St Matthew* (Harmondsworth: Penguin).
Festinger, L.
    1957   *A Theory of Cognitive Dissonance* (Stanford: Stanford University Press).
    1964   *Conflict, Decision, and Dissonance* (London: Tavistock).
Festinger, L., H.W. Riecken and S. Schachter
    1956   *When Prophecy Fails* (New York: Harper & Row).
Festinger, L., and E. Walster
    1964   'Post-Decision Regret and Decision Reversal', in Festinger 1964: 100-111.
Filson, F.V.
    1939   'The Significance of the Early House Churches', *JBL* 58: 105-12.
    1960   *A Commentary on the Gospel according to St Matthew* (London: A. & C.
                Black).
    1964   *A New Testament History* (London: SCM Press).
Finley, M.I.
    1985   *Ancient History: Evidence and Models* (London: Chatto & Windus).
Fitzmyer, J.A.
    1968   'A Life of Paul', in *The Jerome Biblical Commentary* (ed. R.E. Brown *et
                al.*; London: Geoffrey Chapman) 215-22.
    1979   'The Office of Teaching in the Christian Church according to the New
                Testament', in *Teaching Authority and Infallibility in the Church* (ed.
                P.C. Empie *et al.*; Minneapolis, MN: Augsburg) 182-212.
    1981, 1985 *The Gospel according to Luke* (2 vols.; New York: Doubleday).
Foerster, W.
    1933   'ἄξιος', in *TDNT*, I: 379-80.
    1935   'ἔξεστιν, ἐξουσία', in *TDNT*, II: 560-61.
Forbes, C.
    1984   'Comparison, Self-Praise and Irony: Paul's Boasting and the Conventions
                of Hellenistic Rhetoric' (unpublished paper).
Frame, J.E.
    1912   *The Epistles of St Paul to the Thessalonians* (Edinburgh: T. & T. Clark).

Fredriksen, P.
    1986   'Paul and Augustine: Conversion Narratives, Orthodox Tradition, and the Retrospective Self', *JTS* 37: 3-34.

Friedrich, C.J.
    1958   'Authority, Reason, and Discretion', in *Authority* (ed. C.J. Friedrich; Cambridge, MA: Harvard University Press) 28-48.

Friedrich, G.
    1935   'εὐαγγέλιον', in *TDNT*, II: 721-36.
    1939   'κηρύσσω', in *TDNT*, III: 697-714.
    1963   'Die Gegner des Paulus im 2. Korintherbrief', in *Abraham unser Vater* (ed. O. Betz *et al.*; Leiden: Brill) 181-215.

Friedrich, J., W. Pöhlmann and P. Stuhlmacher
    1976   'Zur historischen Situation und Intention von Röm 13, 1-7', *ZTK* 73: 131-66.

Frost, F.J.
    1971   *Greek Society* (Lexington: Heath).

Fuller, R.H.
    1966   *A Critical Introduction to the New Testament* (London: Gerald Duckworth).
    1971   *The Formation of the Resurrection Narratives* (London: SPCK).

Fung, R.K.Y.
    1988   *The Epistle to the Galatians* (Grand Rapids: Eerdmans).

Furnish, V.P.
    1963   'The Place and Purpose of Philippians III', *NTS* 10: 80-87.
    1984   *II Corinthians* (New York: Doubleday).

Gager, J.G.
    1975   *Kingdom and Community* (Englewood Cliffs, NJ: Prentice-Hall).
    1981   'Some Notes on Paul's Conversion', *NTS* 27: 697-704.
    1982   'Shall we Marry our Enemies?', *Int* 36: 256-65.
    1986   'Jews, Gentiles, and Synagogues in the Book of Acts', *HTR* 79: 91-99.

Garnsey, P.D.A., and R.P. Saller
    1987   *The Roman Empire: Economy, Society and Culture* (London: Gerald Duckworth).

Gaston, L.
    1984   'Paul and Jerusalem', in *From Jesus to Paul* (ed. P. Richardson and J.C. Hurd; Waterloo: Wilfrid Laurier University Press) 61-72.
    1986   'Paul and the Law in Galatians 2–3', in *Anti-Judaism in Early Christianity*, I (ed. P. Richardson; Waterloo: Wilfrid Laurier University Press) 127-54.

Gaventa, B.R.
    1986a   *From Darkness to Light* (Philadelphia: Fortress Press).
    1986b   'Galatians 1 and 2: Autobiography as Paradigm', *NT* 28: 307-26.

Geertz, C.
    1976   ' "From the Native's Point of View": On the Nature of Anthropological Understanding', in *Meaning in Anthropology* (ed. K.H. Basso and H.A. Selby; Albuquerque: University of New Mexico Press).

Gellner, E.
    1977   'Patrons and Clients', in *Patrons and Clients* (ed. E. Gellner and
                J. Waterbury; London: Gerald Duckworth) 1-6.
Gennep, A. van
    1960   *The Rites of Passage* (trans. M.B. Vizedom and G.L. Caffee; London:
                Routledge & Kegan Paul).
Georgi, D.
    1965   *Die Geschichte der Kollekte des Paulus für Jerusalem* (Hamburg: Herbert
                Reich Evangelischer Verlag).
    1986   *The Opponents of Paul in Second Corinthians* (trans. H. Attridge *et al.*;
                Edinburgh: T. & T. Clark).
Gerhardsson, B.
    1961   *Memory and Manuscript* (trans. E.J. Sharpe; Uppsala: ASNU).
    1964   *Tradition and Transmission in Early Christianity* (trans. E.J. Sharpe; Lund:
                Gleerup).
    1979   *The Origins of the Gospel Traditions* (London: SCM Press).
Geyser, A.S.
    1953   'Paul, the Apostolic Decree and the Liberals in Corinth', in *Studia Paulina*
                (ed J.N. Sevenster and W.C. van Unnik; Haarlem: Bohn) 124-38.
Giet, S.
    1957   'Nouvelles remarques sur les voyages de Saint Paulà Jérusalem', *RevScR*
                31: 329-42.
Gilchrist, J.M.
    1988   'Paul and the Corinthians—The Sequence of Letters and Visits', *JSNT* 34:
                47-69.
Gnilka, J.
    1976   *Der Philipperbrief* (Freiburg: Herder).
Goffman, E.
    1956   *The Presentation of Self in Everyday Life* (Edinburgh: Edinburgh
                University Press).
Goguel, M.
    1964   *The Primitive Church* (trans. H.C. Snape; London: George Allen &
                Unwin).
Goppelt, L.
    1970   *Apostolic and Post-Apostolic Times* (trans. R.A. Guelich; London:
                A. & C. Black).
Gowan, D.E.
    1984   *Bridge between the Testaments* (Pittsburg: Pickwick Press).
Graves, R.
    1957   'Brain-washing in Ancient Times', in W.W. Sargant (ed.), *Battle for the
                Mind* (London: Pan Books) 166-76.
Green, H.C.B.
    1975   *The Gospel according to Matthew* (Oxford: Oxford University Press).
Green, W.S.
    1985   'Otherness within: Towards a Theory of Difference in Rabbinic Judaism',
                in *'To See Ourselves As Others See Us'* (ed. J. Neusner and
                E.S. Frerichs; Chico, CA: Scholars Press) 49-69.

Greeven, H.
1977 'Propheten, Lehrer, Vorsteher bei Paulus', in *Das kirchliche Amt im neuen Testament* (ed. K. Kertelge; Darmstadt: Wissenschaftliche Buchgesellschaft) 305-61.

Grundmann, W.
1935a 'δόκιμος', in *TDNT*, II: 255-60.
1935b 'δύναμαι, δύναμις', in *TDNT*, II: 284-317.
1939 'θαρρέω', in *TDNT*, III: 25-27.
1959 'ταπεινός', in *TDNT*, VIII: 1-26.

Gunther, J.J.
1973 *St Paul's Opponents and Their Background* (Leiden: Brill).

Haenchen, E.
1971 *The Acts of the Apostles* (trans. B. Noble *et al.*; Oxford: Basil Blackwell).

Hahn, F.
1965 *Mission in the New Testament* (trans. F. Clarke; London: SCM Press).
1974 'Der Apostolat im Urchristentum', *Kerygma und Dogma* 20: 54-77.

Hainz, J.
1972 *Ekklesia* (Regensburg: Pustet).
1982 *Koinonia* (Regensburg: Pustet).

Halperin, D.J.
1986 *The Faces of the Chariot* (Tübingen: Mohr).

Hamm, D.
1990 'Paul's Blindness and its Healing: Clues to Symbolic Intent (Acts 9.22 and 26)', *Bib* 71: 63-72.

Hanson, A.T.
1961 *The Pioneer Ministry* (London: SCM Press).

Hardwyck, J.A., and M. Braden
1962 'Prophecy Fails Again: A Report of a Failure to Replicate', *Journal of Abnormal and Social Psychology* 65: 136-41.

Harnack, C.G.A. von
1908 *The Mission and Expansion of Christianity in the First Three Centuries* (trans. J. Moffatt; London: Williams & Norgate).
1921 *Marcion: Das Evangelium vom Fremden Gott* (Leipzig: Hinrichs).

Harris, C.C.
1969 'Reform in a Normative Organisation', *SociolRev* 17: 167-86.

Harrison, A.R.W.
1968 *The Law of Athens* (Oxford: Clarendon Press).

Harvey, V.A.
1967 *The Historian and the Believer* (London: SCM Press).

Hatch, E.
1880 *The Organization of the Early Christian Churches* (London: Rivingtons).

Hauck, F.
1939 'κοινωνός, κοινωνία', in *TDNT*, III: 797-809.
1959 'περισσεύω', in *TDNT*, VI: 58-61.

Hauck, F., and E. Bammel
1959 'πτωχός', in *TDNT*, VI: 885-915.

242 *Paul, Antioch and Jerusalem*

Hawthorne, G.F.
    1983   *Philippians* (Waco, TX: Word Books).

Hedrick, C.W.
    1981   'Paul's Conversion/Call: A Comparative Analysis of the Three Reports in Acts', *JBL* 100: 415-32.

Hegel, G.W.F.
    1956   *The Philosophy of History* (trans. J. Sibree; New York: Dover).

Hengel, M.
    1973   *Judaism and Hellenism* (trans. J.S. Bowden; Philadelphia: Fortress Press).
    1979   *Acts and the History of Earliest Christianity* (trans. J.S. Bowden; London: SCM Press).
    1983   *Between Jesus and Paul* (trans. J.S. Bowden; London: SCM Press).

Héring, J.
    1962   *The First Epistle of Saint Paul to the Corinthians* (trans. A.W. Heathcote and P.J. Allcock; London: Epworth Press).
    1967   *The Second Epistle of Saint Paul to the Corinthians* (trans. A.W. Heathcote and P.J. Allcock; London: Epworth Press).

Herman, G.
    1987   *Ritualised Friendship and the Greek City* (Cambridge: Cambridge University Press).

Hexter, J.H.
    1971   *Doing History* (London: George Allen & Unwin).

Hill, D.
    1972   *The Gospel of Matthew* (London: Oliphants).

Hock, R.F.
    1980   *The Social Context of Paul's Ministry* (Philadelphia: Fortress Press).

Hofius, O.
    1984   'Gal 1 18: ἱστορῆσαι Κηφᾶν', *ZNW* 75: 73-85.

Holl, K.
    1921   'Der Kirchenbegriff des Paulus in seinem Verhältnis zu dem der Urgemeinde', in *Gesammelte Aufsätze zur Kirchengeschichte*, II (Darmstadt: Wissenschaftliche Buchgesellschaft) 44-67.

Holladay, C.R.
    1977   *Theios Aner in Hellenistic Judaism* (Missoula, MT: Scholars Press).

Holladay, C.R. (ed.)
    1983   *Fragments from Hellenistic Jewish Authors*, I (Chico, CA: Scholars Press).

Holmberg, B.
    1978   *Paul and Power* (Lund: Gleerup).
    1980   'Sociological versus Theological Analysis of the Question Concerning a Pauline Church Order', in *Die Paulinische Literatur und Theologie* (ed. S. Pedersen; Århus: Aros) 187-200.
    1990   *Sociology and the New Testament* (Minneapolis, MN: Fortress Press).

Holtz, T.
    1974   'Die Bedeutung des Apostelkonzils für Paulus', *NovT* 16: 110-48.
    1986   'Der antiochenische Zwischenfall (Galater 2.11-14)', *NTS* 32: 344-61.

Houlden, J.L.
    1970   *Paul's Letters from Prison* (Harmondsworth: Penguin).
    1983   'A Response to James D.G. Dunn', *JSNT* 18: 58-67.
Howard, G.
    1977   'Was James an Apostle? A Reflection on a New Proposal for Gal.i.19', *NovT* 19: 63-64.
    1990   *Paul: Crisis in Galatia* (Cambridge: Cambridge University Press).
Hughes, P.E.
    1962   *Paul's Second Letter to the Corinthians* (Grand Rapids: Eerdmans).
Humphreys, S.C.L.M.
    1978   *Anthropology and the Greeks* (London: Routledge & Kegan Paul).
Hurd, J.C.
    1965   *The Origin of I Corinthians* (London: SPCK).
    1967   'Pauline Chronology and Pauline Theology', in *Christian History and Interpretation* (ed. W.R. Farmer *et al.*; Cambridge: Cambridge University Press) 225-48.
    1986   'Paul Ahead of His Time: 1 Thess. 2.13-16', in *Anti-Judaism in Early Christianity*, I (ed. P. Richardson; Waterloo: Wilfrid Laurier University Press) 21-36.
Hurtado, L.H.
    1979   'The Jerusalem Collection and the Book of Galatians', *JSNT* 5: 46-62.
Hyldahl, N.
    1973   'Die Frage nach der literarische Einheit des Zweiten Korintherbriefes', *ZNW* 64: 289-306.
    1977   'Den korintiske situation—en skitse', *Dansk Teologisk Tidsskrift* 40: 18-30.
    1986   *Die Paulinische Chronologie* (Leiden: Brill).
Jagersma, H.
    1985   *A History of Israel from Alexander the Great to Bar Kochba* (trans. J.S. Bowden; Philadelphia: Fortress Press).
James, W.
    1902   *The Varieties of Religious Experience* (New York: Longman).
Jecker, J.D.
    1964   'The Cognitive Effects of Conflict and Dissonance', in Festinger 1964: 21-32.
Jeremias, J.
    1928   'Sabbathjahr und neutestamentliche Chronologie', *ZNW* 27: 98-103.
    1966   *The Eucharistic Words of Jesus* (trans. N. Perrin; London: SCM Press).
    1969   *Jerusalem in the Time of Jesus* (trans. F.H. and C.H. Cave; London: SCM Press).
Jervell, J.
    1984   *The Unknown Paul* (Minneapolis, MN: Augsburg).
Jewett, R.
    1970   'The Epistolary Thanksgiving and the Integrity of Philippians', *NovT* 12: 40-53.
    1971   'The Agitators and the Galatian Congregation', *NTS* 17: 198-212.

Paul, Antioch and Jerusalem

1978	'The Redaction of I Corinthians and the Trajectory of the Pauline School', abstract in *JAAR* 46: 571-72.
1979	*Dating Paul's Life* (London: SCM Press).
1984	'The Thessalonian Church as a Millenarian Movement' (SBL Seminar Paper).
1986	*The Thessalonian Correspondence* (Philadelphia: Fortress Press).

Johanson, B.C.

1987	*To All the Brethren* (Stockholm: Almqvist & Wiksell).

Johnson, S.E.

1972	*A Commentary on the Gospel according to St Mark* (London: A. & C. Black).

Jones, J.W.

1956	*The Law and Legal Theory of the Greeks* (Oxford: Clarendon Press).

Jouvenel, E. de

1958	'Authority: The Efficient Imperative', in *Authority* (ed. C.J. Friedrich; Cambridge, MA: Harvard University Press) 159-69.

Judge, E.A.

1960	*The Social Pattern of the Christian Groups in the First Century* (London: Tyndale Press).

Kanter, R.M.

1972	*Commitment and Community* (Cambridge, MA: Harvard University Press).

Kasch, W.

1964	'συνίστημι', in *TDNT*, VII, 896-99.

Käsemann, E.

1942	*Die Legitimität des Apostels* (Darmstadt: Wissenschaftliche Buchgesellschaft).
1964	*Essays on New Testament Themes* (trans. W.J. Montague; London: SCM Press).
1969	*New Testament Questions of Today* (trans. W.F. Bunge; London: SCM Press).

Kaser, M.

1965	*Roman Private Law* (trans. R. Dannenbring; Durban: Butterworth).

Kaye, B.N.

1979	'Acts' Portrait of Silas', *NovT* 21: 13-26.

Keck, L.E.

1965	'The Poor among the Saints in the New Testament', *ZNW* 56: 100-29.
1966	'The Poor among the Saints in Jewish Christianity and Qumran', *ZNW* 57: 54-78.
1989	'Images of Paul in the New Testament', *Int* 43: 341-51.

Kee, H.C.

1980	*Christian Origins in Sociological Perspective* (Philadelphia: Westminster Press).

Kennedy, G.A.

1984	*New Testament Interpretation through Rhetorical Criticism* (Chapel Hill: University of North Carolina Press).

Kettunen, M.
1979 *Der Abfassungszweck des Römerbriefes* (Helsinki: Suomalainen Tiedeakatemia).
Kilpatrick, G.D.
1946 *The Origins of the Gospel according to St Matthew* (Oxford: Clarendon Press).
Kim, S.
1981 *The Origin of Paul's Gospel* (Grand Rapids: Eerdmans).
Kirk, J.A.
1975 'Apostleship since Rengstorf: Towards a Synthesis', *NTS* 21: 249-64.
Kittel, G.
1942 'λογεία', in *TDNT*, IV: 282-83.
Klausner, J.
1944 *From Jesus to Paul* (trans. W.F. Stinespring; London: George Allen & Unwin).
Klein, G.
1961 *Die zwölf Apostel* (Göttingen: Vandenhoeck & Ruprecht).
1967 *Rekonstruktion und Interpretation* (Munich: Kaiser Verlag).
Kleinknecht H., F. Baumgärtel, W. Bieder, E Sjøberg and E. Schweizer
1959 'πνεῦμα', in *TDNT*, VI: 332-451.
Klijn, A.F.J.
1964 'Paul's Opponents in Philippians III', *NovT* 7: 278-84.
Knox, J.
1954 *Chapters in a Life of Paul* (London: A. & C. Black).
Knox, W.L.
1925 *St Paul and the Church of Jerusalem* (Cambridge: Cambridge University Press).
Koester, H.
1962 'The Purpose of the Polemic in a Pauline Fragment (Philippians iii)', *NTS* 8: 317-32.
1971 'ΓΝΩΜΑΙ ΔΙΑΦΟΡΟΙ: The Origin and Nature of Diversification in the History of Early Christianity', in *Trajectories through Early Christianity* (ed. J.M. Robinson and H. Koester; Philadelphia: Fortress Press) 144-57.
1982 *Introduction to the New Testament* (New York: De Gruyter).
Koptak, P.E.
1990 'Rhetorical Identification in Paul's Autobiographical Narrative: Galatians 1.13–2.14', *JSNT* 40: 91-113.
Kraabel, A.T.
1981 'The Disappearance of the "God-fearers"', *Numen* 28: 113-26.
1982 'The Roman Diaspora: Six Questionable Assumptions', *JJS* 33: 445-64.
Kraft, R.A.
1965 *The Apostolic Fathers*, III (New York: Nelson).
Krailsheimer, A.J.
1980 *Conversion* (London: SCM Press).
Krentz, E.
1975 *The Historical-Critical Method* (London: SPCK).

Kruse, C.G.
      1983   *New Testament Models for Ministry* (Nashville: Nelson).
Kuhn, T.S.
      1970   *The Structure of Scientific Revolutions* (Chicago: University of Chicago Press).
Kümmel, W.G.
      1975   *Introduction to the New Testament* (trans. H.C. Kee; London: SCM Press).
Kyrtatis, D.J.
      1987   *The Social Structure of the Early Christian Communities* (London: Verso).
Lagrange, M.-J.
      1925   *Saint Paul épître aux Galates* (Paris: Librairie Lecoffre).
Lake, K.
      1911   *The Earlier Epistles of St Paul* (London: Rivingtons).
Lake, K., and S. Lake
      1937   *An Introduction to the New Testament* (New York: Harper).
Lambrecht, J.
      1978   'The Fragment 2 Cor vi 14–vii 1: A Plea for its Authenticity', in *Miscellanea Neotestamentica* (ed. T. Baarda *et al.*; Leiden: Brill) 143-61.
Lampe, G.W.H.
      1961   *A Patristic Greek Lexicon* (Oxford: Clarendon Press).
Lang, F.
      1986   *Die Briefe an die Korinther* (Göttingen: Vandenhoeck & Ruprecht).
Lasswell, H.D., and A. Kaplan
      1952   *Power and Society* (London: Routledge & Kegan Paul).
Leaney, A.R.C.
      1958   *A Commentary on the Gospel according to St Luke* (London: A. & C. Black).
Leenhardt, F.-J.
      1961   *The Epistle to the Romans* (trans. H. Knight; London: Lutterworth).
Leeuw, G. van der
      1964   *Religion in Essence and Manifestation* (trans. J.E. Turner; London: George Allen & Unwin).
Lévi-Strauss, C.
      1963   *Structural Anthropology* (trans. C. Jacobson and B.G. Schoepf; New York: Basic Books).
Lewis, I.M.
      1989   *Ecstatic Religion* (London: Routledge).
Liddell, H.G., and R. Scott
      1940   *A Greek-English Lexicon* (Oxford: Clarendon Press).
Lietzmann, H.
      1923   *An die Galater* (Tübingen: Mohr).
      1937   *The Beginnings of the Christian Church* (trans. B.L. Woolf; London: Nicholson and Watson).
Lietzmann, H., and W.G. Kümmel
      1969   *An die Korinther I.II* (Tübingen: Mohr).

Lightfoot, J.B.
  1868   *St Paul's Epistle to the Philippians* (London: Macmillan).
  1890   *Saint Paul's Epistle to the Galatians* (London: Macmillan).
Lightfoot, J.B., and J.R. Harmer
  1891   *The Apostolic Fathers* (London: Macmillan).
Lincoln, A.T.
  1979   ' "Paul the Visionary": The Setting and Significance of the Rapture to
            Paradise in II Corinthians XII. 1-10', *NTS* 25: 204-20.
Linton, O.
  1932   *Das Problem der Urkirche in der neueren Forschung* (Uppsala: Almqvist &
            Wiksell).
  1949   'The Third Aspect: A Neglected Point of View: A Study in Gal. 1–2 and
            Acts 9 and 15', *ST* 3: 79-95.
Liver, J.
  1963   'The Half-Shekel Offering in Biblical and Post-Biblical Literature', *HTR*
            56: 173-98.
Lohfink, G.
  1965   'Eine alttestamentliche Darstellungsform für Gotteserscheinungen in der
            Damaskusberichten (Apg 9; 22; 26)', *BZ* 9: 246-57.
  1976   *The Conversion of St Paul* (trans. B.J. Malina; New York: Franciscan
            Herald Press).
Lohse, E.
  1951   *Die Ordination im Spätjudentum und im Neuen Testament* (Göttingen:
            Vandenhoeck & Ruprecht).
  1976   *The New Testament Environment* (trans. J.E. Steely; Nashville: Abingdon
            Press).
  1981   *The Formation of the New Testament* (trans. M.E. Boring; Nashville:
            Abingdon Press).
Longenecker, R.N.
  1964   *Paul, Apostle of Liberty* (Grand Rapids: Baker Book House).
  1990   *Galatians* (Waco, TX: Word Books).
Lüdemann, G.
  1983   *Paulus, der Heidenapostel. II. Antipaulinismus im frühen Christentum*
            (Göttingen: Vandenhoeck & Ruprecht).
  1984   *Paul: Apostle to the Gentiles* (trans. F.S. Jones; London: SCM Press).
  1988   'Acts of the Apostles as a Historical Source', in *The Social World of
            Formative Christianity and Judaism* (ed. J. Neusner et al.; Philadelphia:
            Fortress Press) 109-25.
  1989   *Early Christianity according to the Traditions in Acts* (trans. J.S. Bowden;
            London: SCM Press).
Lukes, S.M.
  1974   *Power: A Radical View* (London: Macmillan).
Lull, D.J.
  1980   *The Spirit in Galatia* (Chico, CA: Scholars Press).
Lütgert, W.
  1908   *Freiheitspredigt und Schwarmgeister in Korinth* (Gütersloh: Bertelsmann).

Lyons, G.
    1985   *Pauline Autobiography* (Atlanta: Scholars Press).
McClelland, S.E.
    1982   ' "Super-Apostles, Servants of Christ, Servants of Satan": A Response',
                JSNT 14: 82-87.
McEleney, N.J.
    1974   'Conversion, Circumcision and the Law', *NTS* 20: 319-40.
MacIntyre, A.
    1985   *After Virtue* (London: Gerald Duckworth).
McKelvey, R.J.
    1969   *The New Temple* (Oxford: Oxford University Press).
McLean, B.C.
    1991   'Galatians 2.7-9 and the Recognition of Paul's Apostolic Status at the
                Jerusalem Conference: A Critique of G. Luedemann's Solution', *NTS* 37:
                67-76.
MacMullen, R.
    1967   *Enemies of the Roman Order* (Cambridge, MA: Harvard University Press).
    1974   *Roman Social Relations* (New Haven: Yale University Press).
McNeile, A.H.
    1928   *The Gospel according to St Matthew* (London: Macmillan).
Malherbe, A.J.
    1983   *Social Aspects of Early Christianity* (Philadelphia: Fortress Press).
    1987   *Paul and the Thessalonians* (Philadelphia: Fortress Press).
Malina, B.J.
    1979   'The Individual and the Community—Personality in the Social World of
                Early Christianity', *BTB* 9: 126-38.
    1981   *The New Testament World* (London: SCM Press).
    1982   'The Social Sciences and Biblical Interpretation', *Int* 36: 229-42.
    1986   *Christian Origins and Cultural Anthropology* (Atlanta: John Knox).
Malinowski, B.K.
    1944   *A Scientific Theory of Culture* (ed. H. Cairns; Chapel Hill: University of
                North Carolina Press).
    1965   'The Role of Magic and Religion', in *Reader in Comparative Religion*
                (ed. W.A. Lessa and E.Z. Vogt; New York: Harper & Row) 63-71.
Mandell, S.
    1984   'Who Paid the Temple Tax When the Jews Were under Roman Rule?',
                HTR 77: 223-38.
Manson, T.W.
    1948   *The Church's Ministry* (London: Hodder & Stoughton).
    1962   *Studies in the Gospels and Epistles* (ed. M. Black; Manchester: Manchester
                University Press).
Marshall, I.H.
    1983   *1 and 2 Thessalonians* (Grand Rapids: Eerdmans).
Marshall, P.
    1987   *Enmity in Corinth: Social Conventions in Paul's Relations with the
                Corinthians* (Tübingen: Mohr).

Bibliography 249

Martin, R.P.
1976   *Philippians* (London: Oliphants).
1986   *2 Corinthians* (Waco, TX: Word Books).
Martyn, J.L.
1985   'A Law-Observant Mission to the Gentiles: The Background of Galatians', *SJT* 38: 307-24.
Marxsen, W.
1968   *Introduction to the New Testament* (trans. G. Buswell; Oxford: Basil Blackwell).
Maurer, C.
1969   'τίθημι', in *TDNT*, VIII: 152-58.
Meeks, W.A.
1978   'Toward a Social Description of Pauline Christianity' (Max Richter Conversation Paper).
1982   'The Social Context of Pauline Theology', *Int* 36: 266-77.
1983a   *The First Urban Christians* (New Haven: Yale University Press).
1983b   'Social Functions of Apocalyptic Language in Pauline Christianity', in *Apocalypticism in the Mediterranean World and the Near East* (ed. D. Hellholm; Tübingen: Mohr) 689-94.
Meeks, W.A., and R.L. Wilken
1978   *Jews and Christians in Antioch in the First Four Centuries of the Common Era* (Missoula, MT: Scholars Press).
Meier, S.A.
1988   *The Messenger in the Ancient Semitic World* (Atlanta: Scholars Press).
Mengel, B.
1982   *Studien zum Philipperbrief* (Tübingen: Mohr).
Menoud, P.H.
1953   'Revelation and Tradition: The Influence of Paul's Conversion on his Theology', *Int* 7: 131-41.
Merton, R.K.
1967   *On Theoretical Sociology* (New York: Free Press).
Metzger, B.M.
1964   *The Text of the New Testament* (Oxford: Clarendon Press).
1975   *A Textual Commentary on the Greek New Testament* (London: United Bible Societies).
Meyer, R.
1959   'περιτέμνω, περιτομή', in *TDNT*, VI: 72-84.
Michaelis, W.
1931   'Judaistische Heidenchristen', *ZNW* 30: 83-88.
1942   'μιμέομαι, μιμητής', in *TDNT*, IV: 659-74.
1959   'πρῶτος, πρῶτον', in *TDNT*, VI: 685-70.
Michel, O.
1942   'μνημονεύω', in *TDNT*, IV: 682-83.
1954   'οἰκοδομή', in *TDNT*, V: 144-47.
1955   *Der Brief an die Römer* (Göttingen: Vandenhoeck & Ruprecht).
Mitchell, J.C.
1969   'The Concept and Use of Social Networks', in *Social Networks in Urban*

Situations (ed. J.C. Mitchell; Manchester: Manchester University Press) 1-50.

Morgan, R.C., and J. Barton
1988   *Biblical Interpretation* (Oxford: Oxford University Press).

Mosbech, H.
1948   'Apostolos in the New Testament', *ST* 2: 166-200.

Mosley, D.J.
1973   *Envoys and Diplomacy in Ancient Greece* (Wiesbaden: Steiner).

Moulton, H.K. (ed.)
1977   *The Analytical Greek Lexicon Revised* (Grand Rapids: Zondervan).

Moulton, J.H., and G. Milligan
1929   *The Vocabulary of the Greek Testament* (London: Hodder & Stoughton).

Moulton, W.F., A.S. Geden and H.K. Moulton
1978   *A Concordance to the Greek Testament* (Edinburgh: T. & T. Clark).

Munck, J.
1949   'Paul, the Apostles, and the Twelve', *ST* 3: 96-110.
1959   *Paul and the Salvation of Mankind* (trans. F. Clarke; London: SCM Press).

Munck, J., W.F. Albright and C.S. Mann
1967   *The Acts of the Apostles* (New York: Doubleday).

Munro, W.
1983   *Authority in Paul and Peter* (Cambridge: Cambridge University Press).

Murphy-O'Connor, J.
1983   *St Paul's Corinth* (Wilmington, DE: Michael Glazier).
1990   'Another Jesus (2 Cor 11.4)', *RB* 97: 238-51.

Murray, R.
1985   ' "Disaffected Judaism" and Early Christianity: Some Predisposing Factors', in *'To See Ourselves As Others See Us'* (ed. J. Neusner and E.S. Frerichs; Chico, CA: Scholars Press) 263-81.

Mussner, F.
1974   *Der Galaterbrief* (Freiburg: Herder).
1976   *Petrus und Paulus—Pole der Einheit* (Freiburg: Herder).

Neusner, J.
1975   *Early Rabbinic Judaism* (Leiden: Brill).
1984a   *Ancient Judaism* (Chico, CA: Scholars Press).
1984b   *Judaism in the Beginning of Christianity* (London: SPCK).
1985   'The Experience of the City in Late Antique Judaism', in *Approaches to Ancient Judaism. V. Studies in Judaism and Its Greco-Roman Context* (ed. W.S. Green; Atlanta: Scholars Press) 37-52.

Neyrey, J.H.
1988   'Bewitched in Galatia: Paul and Cultural Anthropology', *CBQ* 50: 72-100.

Nicholas, B.
1962   *An Introduction to Roman Law* (Oxford: Clarendon Press).

Nickle, K.F.
1966   *The Collection* (London: SCM Press).
1981   *The Synoptic Gospels* (London: SCM Press).

Niebuhr, H.R.
    1964   'The Churches of the Disinherited', in *Religion, Culture and Society*
            (ed. L. Schneider; New York: John Wiley & Sons) 466-70.
Niederwimmer, K.
    1989   *Die Didache* (Göttingen: Vandenhoeck & Ruprecht).
Nock, A.D.
    1933   *Conversion* (Oxford: Oxford University Press).
O'Dea, T.F.
    1964   'Five Dilemmas in the Institutionalization of Religion', in *Religion, Culture
            and Society* (ed. L. Schneider; New York: John Wiley & Sons) 580-88.
Oepke, A.
    1954   'παρουσία, πάρειμι', in *TDNT*, V: 858-71.
Oepke, A., and J. Rohde
    1973   *Der Brief des Paulus an die Galater* (Berlin: Evangelische Verlagsanstalt).
Ogg, G.
    1968   *The Chronology of the Life of Paul* (London: Epworth Press).
Ollrog, W.-H.
    1979   *Paulus und seine Mitarbeiter* (Neukirchen–Vluyn: Neukirchener Verlag).
O'Neill, J.C.
    1972   *The Recovery of Paul's Letter to the Galatians* (London: SPCK).
Oostendorp, D.W.
    1967   *Another Jesus: A Gospel of Jewish-Christian Superiority in II Corinthians*
            (Kampen: Kok).
Orr, W.F., and J.W. Walther
    1976   *I Corinthians* (New York: Doubleday).
Osborne, R.E.
    1966   'Paul and the Wild Beasts', *JBL* 85: 225-30.
Osten-Sacken, P. von der
    1989   *Die Heiligkeit der Tora* (Munich: Kaiser Verlag).
Painter, J.
    1982   'Paul and the πνευματικοί at Corinth', in *Paul and Paulinism* (ed.
            M.D. Hooker and S.G. Wilson; London: SPCK) 237-50.
Pareto, V.
    1935   *The Mind and Society* (trans. A. Livingston; 4 vols.; London: Cape).
Parker, P.
    1967   'Once More, Acts and Galatians', *JBL* 86: 175-82.
Parsons, T.
    1954   *Essays in Sociological Theory* (New York: Free Press).
    1958   'Authority, Legitimation, and Political Action', in *Authority* (ed.
            C.J. Friedrich; Cambridge, MA: Harvard University Press) 197-221.
Peabody, R.L.
    1968   'Authority', in *International Encylopedia of the Social Sciences*, I (New
            York: Macmillan) 473-77.
Pearson, B.A.
    1971   'I Thessalonians 2.13-16: A Deutero-Pauline Interpolation', *HTR* 64:
            79-94.
    1986   'Christians and Jews in First-century Alexandria', *HTR* 79: 206-216.

Petersen, N.R.
1978   *Literary Criticism for New Testament Critics* (Philadelphia: Fortress Press).
1986   *Rediscovering Paul* (Grand Rapids: Eerdmans).
Pfeiffer, R.H.
1949   *History of New Testament Times* (Westport: Greenwood).
Pitt-Rivers, J.A.
1977   *The Fate of Shechem, or the Politics of Sex* (Cambridge: Cambridge University Press).
Plummer, A.
1915   *A Critical and Exegetical Commentary on the Second Epistle of St Paul to the Corinthians* (Edinburgh: T. & T. Clark).
1919   *A Commentary on St Paul's Epistle to the Philippians* (London: Scott).
Poland, L.M.
1985   *Literary Criticism and Biblical Hermeneutics: A Critique of Formalist Approaches* (Chico, CA: Scholars Press).
Polzin, R.M.
1977   *Biblical Structuralism* (Philadelphia: Fortress Press).
Popper, K.R.
1972   *Objective Knowledge* (Oxford: Oxford University Press).
1980   *The Logic of Scientific Discovery* (trans. K.R. Popper *et al.*; London: Hutchinson).
Price, R.M.
1980   'Punished in Paradise', *JSNT* 7: 33-40.
Procksch, O., and K.G. Kuhn
1933   'ἅγιος', in *TDNT*, I: 88-110.
Rad, G. von, K.G. Kuhn and W. Gutbrod
1939   ''Ισραήλ, 'Ιουδαῖος, 'Εβραῖος', in *TDNT*, II: 356-91.
Radcliffe-Brown, A.R.
1952   *Structure and Function in Primitive Society* (London: Cohen & West).
Räisänen, H.
1983   *Paul and the Law* (Tübingen: Mohr).
1986   *The Torah and Christ* (Helsinki: Finnish Exegetical Association).
Rajak, T.
1985a   'Jewish Rights in the Greek Cities under Roman Rule: A New Approach', in *Approaches to Ancient Judaism. V. Studies in Judaism and its Greco-Roman Context* (ed. W.S. Green; Atlanta: Scholars Press) 19-36.
1985b   'Jews and Christians as Groups in a Pagan World', in *'To See Ourselves as Others See Us'* (ed. J. Neusner and E.S. Frerichs; Chico, CA: Scholars Press) 247-62.
Rambo, L.R.
1982   'Current Research on Religious Conversion', *RevScR* 8: 146-59.
Reicke, B.I.
1953   'Der geschichtliche Hintergrund des Apostelkonzils und der Antiochia-Episode, Gal.2, 1-14', in *Studia Paulina* (ed. J.N. Sevenster and W.C. van Unnik; Haarlem: Bohn) 172-87.
1959   'προΐστημι', in *TDNT*, VI: 700-703.

1984 'Judaeo-Christianity and the Jewish Establishment, AD 33-66', in *Jesus and the Politics of his Day* (ed. E. Bammel and C.F.D. Moule; London: SCM Press) 145-52.

Reitzenstein, R.
1978 *Hellenistic Mystery-Religions* (trans. J.E. Steely; Pittsburg: Pickwick Press).

Rengstorf, K.H.
1933 'ἀποστέλλω', in *TDNT*, I: 398-406.
1934 *Apostolat und Predigtamt* (Stuttgart: Kohlhammer).
1935 'δώδεκα', in *TDNT*, II: 321-28.
1959 'προθυμία', in *TDNT*, VI: 697-700.
1964 'σημεῖον', in *TDNT*, VII: 200-61.

Reumann, J.
1979 'Teaching Office in the New Testament?', in *Teaching Authority and Infallibility in the Church* (ed. P.C. Empie et al.; Minneapolis, MN: Augsburg) 213-31.

Richardson, G.P.
1969 *Israel in the Apostolic Age* (Cambridge: Cambridge University Press).
1980 'Pauline Inconsistency: I Corinthians 9.19-23 and Galatians 2.11-14', *NTS* 26: 347-62.

Roberts, F.J.
1965 'Some Psychological Factors in Religious Conversion', *British Journal of Social and Clinical Psychology* 4: 185-87.

Robertson, A., and A. Plummer
1914 *A Critical and Exegetical Commentary on the First Epistle of St Paul to the Corinthians* (Edinburgh: T. & T. Clark).

Robinson, J.A.T.
1976 *Redating the New Testament* (London: SCM Press).

Robinson, J.M., and H. Koester
1971 *Trajectories through Early Christianity* (Philadelphia: Fortress Press).

Roetzel, C.J.
1982 *The Letters of Paul* (London: SCM Press).

Rogers, E.M., and F.F. Shoemaker
1971 *Communication of Innovations* (New York: Free Press).

Roloff, J.
1965 *Apostolat—Verkündigung—Kirche* (Gütersloh: Mohn).
1981 *Die Apostelgeschichte* (Göttingen: Vandenhoeck & Ruprecht).

Rowland, C.C.
1982 *The Open Heaven* (London: SPCK).
1985 *Christian Origins* (London: SPCK).

Saake, H.
1973 'Paulus als Ekstatiker', *NovT* 15: 153-60.

Safrai, S.
1974a 'Jewish Self-Government', in *The Jewish People in the First Century*, I (ed. S. Safrai and M. Stern; Assen: Van Gorcum) 377-419.

1974b   'Relations between the Diaspora and the Land of Israel', in Safrai and Stern (eds.), *The Jewish People in the First Century*, I: 184-215.

Sainte Croix, G.E.M. de

1981   *The Class Struggle in the Ancient Greek World* (London: Gerald Duckworth).

Saller, R.P.

1982   *Personal Patronage under the Early Empire* (Cambridge: Cambridge University Press).

Sampley, J.P.

1977   ' "Before God, I do not lie" (Gal. 1.20): Paul's Self-Defence in the Light of Roman Legal Praxis', *NTS* 23: 477-82.

1980   *Pauline Partnership in Christ* (Philadelphia: Fortress Press).

1988   'Paul, his Opponents in 2 Corinthians 10-13, and the Rhetorical Handbooks', in *The Social World of Formative Christianity and Judaism* (ed. J. Neusner et al.; Philadelphia: Fortress Press) 162-77.

Sanday, W., and A.C. Headlam

1902   *The Epistle to the Romans* (Edinburgh: T. & T. Clark).

Sanders, E.P.

1977   *Paul and Palestinian Judaism* (London: SCM Press).

1983   *Paul, the Law, and the Jewish People* (London: SCM Press).

1986   'Paul on the Law, his Opponents, and the Jewish People in Philippians 3 and 2 Corinthians 11', in *Anti-Judaism in Early Christianity*, I (ed. P. Richardson; Waterloo: Wilfrid Laurier University Press) 75-90.

Sanders, J.N.

1955   'Peter and Paul in Acts', *NTS* 2: 133-43.

Sanders, J.T.

1966   'Paul's "Autobiographical" Statements in Galatians 1–2', *JBL* 85: 335-43.

Sandmel, S.

1958   *The Genius of Paul* (Philadelphia: Fortress Press).

1969   *The First Christian Century in Judaism and Christianity* (New York: Oxford University Press).

1978   *Judaism and Christian Beginnings* (New York: Oxford University Press).

Sargant, W.W.

1957   *Battle for the Mind* (London: Pan Books).

Schäfer, P.

1984   'New Testament and Hekhalot Literature: The Journey into Heaven in Paul and in Merkavah Mysticism', *JJS* 35: 19-35.

Schlatter, A.

1934   *Paulus: Der Bote Jesus* (Stuttgart: Calwer Verlag).

Schlier, H.

1971   *Der Brief an die Galater* (Göttingen: Vandenhoeck & Ruprecht).

1977   *Der Römerbrief* (Freiburg: Herder).

Schmidt, A.

1990   'Das historische Datum des Apostelkonzils', *ZNW* 81: 122-31.

Schmidt, H.W.

1966   *Der Brief des Paulus an die Römer* (Berlin: Evangelische Verlagsanstalt).

Schmidt, K.L.
    1933   'ἀκροβυστία', in *TDNT*, I: 225-26.
Schmithals, W.
    1957   'Die Irrlehrer des Philipperbriefes', *ZTK* 54: 297-341.
    1965a   *Paul and James* (trans. D.M. Barton; London: SCM Press).
    1965b   *Paulus und die Gnostiker* (Hamburg: Herbert Reich Evangelischer Verlag).
    1971a   *Gnosticism in Corinth* (trans. J.E. Steely; Nashville: Abingdon Press).
    1971b   *The Office of Apostle in the Early Church* (trans. J.E. Steely; London: SPCK).
    1973   'Die Korintherbriefe als Briefsammlung', *ZNW* 64: 263-88.
    1975   *Der Römerbrief als historisches Problem* (Gütersloh: Mohn).
Schnackenburg, R.
    1965   *The Church in the New Testament* (trans. W.J. O'Hara; Freiburg: Herder).
    1970   'Apostles before and during Paul's Time', in *Apostolic History and the Gospel* (ed. W.W. Gasque and R.P. Martin; Exeter: Paternoster Press) 287-303.
Schneider, C.
    1939   'καθαίρεσις', in *TDNT*, III: 412-13.
Schneider, G.
    1980, 1982 *Die Apostelgeschichte* (2 vols.; Freiburg: Herder).
Schoeps, H.J.
    1961   *Paul: The Theology of the Apostle in the Light of Jewish Religious History* (trans. H. Knight; London: Lutterworth).
Schulz, F.
    1936   *Principles of Roman Law* (trans. M. Wolff; Oxford: Clarendon Press).
Schulz, S., and G. Quell
    1964   'σπέρμα', in *TDNT*, VI: 536-47.
Schürer, E., *et al.*
    1973, 1979, *The History of the Jewish People in the Age of Jesus Christ* (3 vols.;
    1986   Edinburgh: T. & T. Clark).
Schütz, J.H.
    1975   *Paul and the Anatomy of Apostolic Authority* (Cambridge: Cambridge University Press).
Schweitzer, A.
    1931   *The Mysticism of Paul the Apostle* (trans. W. Montgomery; London: A. & C. Black).
Schweizer, E.
    1959   *Gemeinde und Gemeindeordnung im Neuen Testament* (Zürich: Zwingli-Verlag).
Scobie, C.H.H.
    1964   *John the Baptist* (Philadelphia: Fortress Press).
Scott, J.
    1977   'Patronage or Exploitation?', in *Patrons and Clients* (ed. E. Gellner and J. Waterbury; London: Gerald Duckworth) 21-40.
Scroggs, J.R., and W.G.T. Douglas
    1979   'Issues in the Psychology of Religious Conversion', in *Current*

Perspectives in the Psychology of Religion (ed. H.N. Malony; Grand Rapids: Eerdmans) 254-65.

Scroggs, R.J.
1975   'The Earliest Christian Communities as Sectarian Movement', in *Christianity, Judaism and other Greco-Roman Cults*, II (ed. J. Neusner; Leiden: Brill) 1-23.
1980   'The Sociological Interpretation of the New Testament: The Present State of Research', *NTS* 26: 164-79.

Segal, A.F.
1980   'Heavenly Ascent in Hellenistic Judaism, Early Christianity and their Environment', in *ANRW* 23.2 (ed. W. Haase; Berlin: de Gruyter) 1333-94.
1986   *Rebecca's Children* (Cambridge, MA: Harvard University Press).
1990   *Paul the Convert* (New Haven: Yale University Press).

Sellin, G.
1987   'Hauptprobleme des ersten Korintherbriefes', in *ANRW* 25.4 (ed. W. Haase; Berlin: de Gruyter) 2940-3044.

Sennett, R.
1980   *Authority* (New York: Vintage, 1981).

Service, E.R.
1971   *Primitive Social Organization* (New York: Random House).

Sevenster, G.
1953   'De wijding van Paulus en Barnabas', in *Studia Paulina* (ed. J.N. Sevenster and W.C. van Unnik; Haarlem: Bohn) 188-201.

Shaw, G.
1983   *The Cost of Authority* (London: SCM Press).

Shaw, M.
1975   *Marxism and Social Science: The Roots of Social Knowledge* (London: Pluto).

Sherwin-White, A.N.
1969   *Roman Society and Roman Law in the New Testament* (Oxford: Clarendon Press).

Silverman, S.
1977   'Patronage as Myth', in *Patrons and Clients* (ed. E. Gellner and J. Waterbury; London: Gerald Duckworth) 7-20.

Smallwood, E.M.
1976   *The Jews under Roman Rule* (Leiden: Brill).

Smith, J.Z.
1975   'The Social Description of Early Christianity', *RSRev* 1: 1-5.

Smith, T.V.
1985   *Petrine Controversies in Early Christianity* (Tübingen: Mohr).

Snow, D.A., and R. Machalek
1983   'The Convert as a Social Type', in *Sociological Theory 1983* (ed. R. Collins; San Francisco: Jossey Bass) 261-76.

Sohm, R.
1892   *Kirchenrecht. I. Die geschichtlichen Grundlagen* (Munich: V. Duncker and Humblot).

Spilka, B., R.W. Hood and R.L. Gorsuch
   1985   *The Psychology of Religion* (Englewood Cliffs, NJ: Prentice-Hall).
Stambaugh, J.E., and D.L. Balch
   1986   *The Social World of the First Christians* (London: SPCK).
Starbuck, E.D.
   1914   *The Psychology of Religion* (London: Scott).
Stark, W.
   1967   *The Sociology of Religion. II. Sectarian Religion* (London: Routledge & Kegan Paul).
   1969   *The Sociology of Religion. IV. Types of Religious Man* (London: Routledge & Kegan Paul).
Steck, O.H.
   1976   'Formgeschichtliche Bemerkungen zur Darstellung des Damaskusgeschehens in der Apostelgeschichte', *ZNW* 67: 20-28.
Stendahl, K.O.
   1967   *The School of St Matthew* (Lund: Gleerup).
   1976   *Paul among Jews and Gentiles* (Philadelphia: Fortress Press).
Stephenson, A.M.G.
   1965   'A Defence of the Integrity of 2 Corinthians', in *The Authorship and Integrity of the New Testament* (London: SPCK) 82-97.
Stern, M.
   1974   'The Province of Judaea', in *The Jewish People in the First Century*, I (ed. S. Safrai and M. Stern; Assen: Van Gorcum) 308-76.
Stogdill, R.M.
   1974   *Handbook of Leadership* (New York: Free Press).
Stowers, S.K.
   1985   'The Social Sciences and the Study of Early Christianity', in *Approaches to Ancient Judaism. V. Studies in Judaism and its Greco-Roman Context* (ed. W.S. Green; Atlanta: Scholars Press) 149-82.
Strack, H.L., and P. Billerbeck
   1926   *Kommentar zum Neuen Testament aus Talmud und Midrasch* (Munich: Beck).
Straus, R.A.
   1979   'Religious Conversion as a Personal and Collective Accomplishment', *SocAn* 40: 158-65.
Streeter, B.H.
   1930   *The Four Gospels* (London: Macmillan).
Strobel, A.
   1974   'Das Aposteldekret in Galatien: Zur Situation von Gal I und II', *NTS* 20: 177-89.
Stuhlmacher, P.
   1968   *Das paulinische Evangelium* (Göttingen: Vandenhoeck & Ruprecht).
   1989a   *Der Brief an die Römer* (Göttingen: Vandenhoeck & Ruprecht).
   1989b   'Die Stellung Jesu und des Paulus zu Jerusalem: Versuch einer Erinnerung', *ZTK* 86: 140-56.
Suhl, A.
   1975   *Paulus und seine Briefe* (Gütersloh: Mohn).

258 *Paul, Antioch and Jerusalem*

1987   'Der Galaterbrief—Situation und Argumentation', in *ANRW* 25.4 (ed. W. Haase; Berlin: de Gruyter) 3067-134.

Sumney, J.L.
1990   *Identifying Paul's Opponents* (Sheffield: JSOT Press).

Tabor, J.D.
1986   *Things Unutterable* (Lanham, MD: University Press of America).

Talbert, C.H.
1987   *Reading Corinthians* (New York: Crossroad).

Taubenschlag, R.
1955   *The Law of Greco-Roman Egypt in the Light of the Papyri* (Warsaw: Państwowe Wydawnictwo Naukowe).

Taylor, N.H.
1987   *The Divine Agent in Intertestamental Judaism* (unpublished MA dissertation, University of Cape Town).
1991a   'The Composition and Chronology of 2 Corinthians', *JSNT* 44 (forthcoming).
1991b   'The Conversion and Apostolic Vocation of Paul' (SBL Seminar Paper).
1991c   'Paul's Apostolic Legitimacy: Autobiographical Reconstruction in Galatians 1.11–2.14' (British New Testament Conference Short Paper).

Tcherikover, V.
1961   *Hellenistic Civilization and the Jews* (trans. S. Applebaum; Philadelphia: Jewish Publication Society of America).

Theissen, G.
1978   *The First Followers of Jesus* (trans. J.S. Bowden; London: SCM Press).
1982   *The Social Setting of Pauline Christianity* (trans. J.H. Schütz; Edinburgh: T. & T. Clark).
1987   *Psychological Aspects of Pauline Theology* (trans. J.P. Galvin; Edinburgh: T. & T. Clark).

Thiselton, A.C.
1978   'Realized Eschatology at Corinth', *NTS* 24: 510-26.
1980   *The Two Horizons* (Exeter: Paternoster Press).

Thouless, R.H.
1971   *An Introduction to the Psychology of Religion* (Cambridge: Cambridge University Press).

Thrall, M.E.
1980   'Super-Apostles, Servants of Christ, and Servants of Satan', *JSNT* 6: 42-57.

Trocmé, E.
1981   'Paul-la-Colère: éloge d'un schismatique', *RHPR* 61: 341-50.

Troeltsch, E.
1931   *The Social Teaching of the Christian Churches* (trans. O. Wyon; London: George Allen & Unwin).

Trudinger, L.P.
1975   'ΕΤΕΡΟΝ ΔΕ ΤΩΝ ΑΠΟΣΤΟΛΩΝ ΟΥΚ ΕΙΔΟΝ, ΕΙ ΜΗ ΙΑΚΩΒΟΝ: A Note on Galatians i 19', *NovT* 17: 200-202.

Turner, V.W.
1969   *The Ritual Process* (London: Routledge & Kegan Paul).

Urbach, E.E.
    1981   'Self-Isolation or Self-Affirmation in Judaism in the First Three Centuries: Theory and Practice', in *Jewish and Christian Self-Definition*, II (ed. E.P. Sanders *et al.*; London: SCM Press) 269-98.

Vielhauer, P.
    1966   'On the "Paulinism" of Acts', in *Studies in Luke–Acts* (ed. L.E. Keck and J.L. Martyn; trans. W.C. Robinson and V.P. Furnish; Nashville: Abingdon Press) 33-50.
    1975a   *Geschichte der urchristlichen Literatur* (Berlin: de Gruyter).
    1975b   'Paulus und die Kephaspartei in Korinth', *NTS* 21: 341-52.

Vincent, M.R.
    1897   *A Critical and Exegetical Commentary on the Epistles to the Philippians and to Philemon* (Edinburgh: T. & T. Clark).

Wainwright, A.
    1980   'Where Did Silas Go? And What Was his Connection with *Galatians*?', *JSNT* 8: 66-70.

Wallis, R.
    1982   *Millennialism and Charisma* (Belfast: Queens University Press).

Walster, E.
    1964   'The Temporal Sequence of Post-Decision Processes', in Festinger 1964: 112-28.

Walster, E., and L. Festinger
    1964   'Decisions Among Imperfect Alternatives', in Festinger 1964: 131-44.

Walter, N.
    1989   'Paul and the Early Christian Jesus-Tradition', in *Paul and Jesus* (ed. A.J.M. Wedderburn; Sheffield: JSOT Press) 51-80.

Wanamaker, C.A.
    1990   *The Epistles to the Thessalonians* (Grand Rapids: Eerdmans).

Waterbury, J.
    1977   'An Attempt to Put Patrons and Clients in their Place', in *Patrons and Clients* (ed. E. Gellner and J. Waterbury; London: Gerald Duckworth) 329-42.

Watson, A.
    1965   *The Law of Obligations in the Later Roman Republic* (Oxford: Clarendon Press).

Watson, F.B.
    1984   '2 Cor. X-XIII and Paul's Painful Letter to the Corinthians', *JTS* 35: 324-46.
    1986   *Paul, Judaism and the Gentiles* (Cambridge: Cambridge University Press).
    1987   *A Guide to the New Testament* (London: Batsford).

Weber, M.
    1947   *The Theory of Social and Economic Organization* (ed. T. Parsons; trans. T. Parsons and A.M. Henderson; New York: Oxford University Press).
    1948   *From Max Weber: Essays in Sociology* (trans. H.H. Gerth and C.W. Mills; London: Routledge & Kegan Paul).
    1952   *Ancient Judaism* (ed. and trans. H.H. Gerth and D. Martindale; New York: Free Press).

1964   *The Sociology of Religion* (ed. and trans. E. Fischoff; Boston: Beacon).
Weber, W., *et al.*
1973   *Macht: Dienst: Herrschaft* (ed. W. Weber; Freiburg: Herder).
Wedderburn, A.J.M.
1981   'Keeping up with Recent Studies: Some Recent Pauline Chronologies',
          ExpTim 92: 103-108.
1987   *Baptism and Resurrection* (Tübingen: Mohr).
1988   *The Reasons for Romans* (Edinburgh: T. & T. Clark).
Weingrod, A.
1977   'Patronage and Power', in *Patrons and Clients* (ed. E. Gellner and
          J. Waterbury; London: Gerald Duckworth) 41-52.
Wellmann, B.
1983   'Network Analysis: Some Basic Principles', in *Sociological Theory 1983*
          (ed. R. Collins; San Francisco: Jossey Bass) 157-76.
Wendland, H.-D.
1965   *Die Briefe an die Korinther* (Göttingen: Vandenhoeck & Ruprecht).
Westcott, B.F.
1881   *A General Survey of the History of the Canon of the New Testament*
          (Cambridge: Macmillan).
White, L.M.
1985   'Adolf Harnack and the "Expansion" of Early Christianity: A Reappraisal
          of Social History', *The Second Century* 5: 97-127.
1986   'Sociological Analysis of Early Christian Groups: A Social Historian's
          Response', *SocAn* 47: 249-66.
1987   'Social Authority in the House Church Setting and Ephesians 4.1-16', *RQ*
          29: 209-28.
1988   'Shifting Sectarian Boundaries in Early Christianity', *BJRL* 70: 7-24.
Wilckens, U.
1959   'Die Bekehrung des Paulus als religionsgeschichtliches Problem', *ZTK* 56:
          273-93.
1963   'Der Ursprung der Überlieferung der Erscheinungen des Auferstandenen',
          in *Dogma und Denkstrukturen* (ed. W. Joest & W. Pannenberg; Göttingen:
          Vandenhoeck & Ruprecht) 56-95.
Williams, C.S.C.
1964   *A Commentary on the Acts of the Apostles* (London: A. & C. Black).
Willis, W.L.
1985   *Idol Meat in Corinth* (Chico, CA: Scholars Press).
Wilson, B.R.
1964   'An Analysis of Sect Development', in *Religion, Culture and Society* (ed.
          L. Schneider; New York: John Wiley & Sons) 482-96.
1975   *The Noble Savages* (Berkeley: University of California Press).
1982   *Religion in Sociological Perspective* (Oxford: Oxford University Press).
Wilson, R.McL.
1982   'Gnosis at Corinth', in *Paul and Paulinism* (ed. M.D. Hooker and
          S.G. Wilson; London: SPCK) 102-14.

Wilson, S.G.
  1973   *The Gentiles and the Gentile Mission in Luke–Acts* (Cambridge: Cambridge University Press).
  1983   *Luke and the Law* (Cambridge: Cambridge University Press).
Wittgenstein, L.
  1958   *Philosophical Investigations* (trans. G.E.M. Anscombe; Oxford: Basil Blackwell).
  1961   *Tractatus Logico-Philosophicus* (trans. D.F. Pears and B.F. McGuiness; London: Routledge & Kegan Paul).
  1969   *On Certainty* (ed. G.E.M. Anscombe and G.H. von Wright; Oxford: Basil Blackwell).
  1974   *Philosophical Grammar* (ed. R. Rhees; trans. A.J.P. Kenny; Oxford: Basil Blackwell).
  1981   *Zettel* (ed. G.E.M. Anscombe *et al.*; Oxford: Basil Blackwell).
Wolff, C.
  1982   *Der Erste Brief des Paulus an die Korinther* (Berlin: Evangelische Verlagsanstalt).
Wood, H.G.
  1955   'The Conversion of St Paul: Its Nature, Antecedents and Consequences', *NTS* 1: 276-82.
Worsley, P.
  1968   *The Trumpet Shall Sound* (New York: Schocken Books).
Wrong, D.H.
  1979   *Power* (Oxford: Basil Blackwell).
Wünsche, A. (ed.)
  1881   *Bereschit Rabba* (Leipzig: Schulze).
Yinger, J.M.
  1970   *The Scientific Study of Religion* (London: Macmillan).
Young, F.M., and D.F. Ford
  1987   *Meaning and Truth in 2 Corinthians* (London: SPCK).
Zahn, T.
  1909   *Introduction to the New Testament* (trans. M.W. Jacobs *et al.*; 3 vols.; Edinburgh: T. & T. Clark).
Zerwick, M.
  1983   *Biblical Greek* (trans. J. Smith; Rome: Pontifical Biblical Institute).
Ziesler, J.A.
  1988   *Paul's Letter to the Romans* (London: SCM Press).
Zygmunt, J.F.
  1972   'Movements and Motives', *Human Relations* 25: 449-67.

INDEXES

INDEX OF REFERENCES

BIBLICAL REFERENCES